# The Science of College

# The Science of College

*Navigating the First Year and Beyond*

BY

**PATRICIA S. HERZOG, CASEY T. HARRIS,**

**AND SHAUNA A. MORIMOTO**

**SHANE W. BARKER, JILL G. WHEELER, A. JUSTIN**

**BARNUM, AND TERRANCE L. BOYD**

OXFORD
UNIVERSITY PRESS

# OXFORD
UNIVERSITY PRESS

Oxford University Press is a department of the University of Oxford. It furthers the University's objective of excellence in research, scholarship, and education by publishing worldwide. Oxford is a registered trade mark of Oxford University Press in the UK and certain other countries.

Published in the United States of America by Oxford University Press
198 Madison Avenue, New York, NY 10016, United States of America.

Library of Congress Cataloging-in-Publication Data
Names: Herzog, Patricia Snell, author.
Title: The Science of college : Navigating the First Year and Beyond /
By Patricia S. Herzog, Casey T. Harris, Shauna A. Morimoto, Shane W. Barker,
Jill G. Wheeler, A. Justin Barnum, and Terrance L. Boyd.
Description: New York, NY : Oxford University Press, [2020] |
Includes bibliographical references and index.
Identifiers: LCCN 2019039324 (print) | LCCN 2019039325 (ebook) |
ISBN 9780190934507 (paperback) | ISBN 9780190934514 (updf) |
ISBN 9780190934521 (epub) | ISBN 9780197503478 (online) | ISBN 9780197506424 (online)
Subjects: LCSH: College student orientation. | College freshmen. |
College students—Conduct of life.
Classification: LCC LB2343.3 .H47 2020 (print) | LCC LB2343.3 (ebook) |
DDC 378.1/9—dc23
LC record available at https://lccn.loc.gov/2019039324
LC ebook record available at https://lccn.loc.gov/2019039325

9 8 7 6 5 4 3 2 1

Printed by Marquis, Canada

# CONTENTS

# ACKNOWLEDGMENTS

This book could not have existed without the many students that we each have known and worked with along the way. In particular, we thank Tasmiah Amreen for her contributions to the book. Tasmiah interviewed Shane Barker, Jill Wheeler, Terrance Boyd, and Shauna Morimoto in order to more thoroughly integrate their voices into this book, and it was through Tasmiah's careful questioning that Herzog was able to translate their helpful verbal advice into text. Christina Williams and DeAndre' Beadle participated in independent studies on emerging adulthood scholarship, during which both provided insights about the applicability of these studies for navigating one's own college decisions.

Several additional students assisted with research on young people or regularly talked during office hours in ways that indirectly affected this book, including Tatianna Balis, Sanjana Vengupal, Tiffany Hood, Bryn Smernoff, Alexis Rizzolo, Olivia Tzeng, Nicole Breaux, Jada Holmes, Melissa Conry, Kristen Eldridge, Andrew Garcia, Emily Lau, Catherine Talor, Seth Washishpak, Rhyker Dye, Zina Hardin, Olivia Chambers, Bradley Reed, Caylin Craig, Jacob Fluech, Stephanie Collier, Chao Liu, Ashley Wagner, Elizabeth Word, James Brown, Angela Cox, Carrie Nelms, Randi Combs, Connor Thompson, April Moore, Emma Thompson, Grant King, Camille Wildburger, Zanaib Shipchandler, Mark Trainer, Xiannan Lu, Gabriel David, Angela Wu, Richard Woo, Jessica Technow, Marie Sanchez, Robbee Wedow, Kaitlyn Conway, Molly Kiernan, Scott Mitchell,

Josh Cook, Molly Kring, Chris Gonzales, Scott Hurley, Josh Cook, Caitlin Smith, Janice James, Allison VenderBroek, Jennifer Jesse, Michael Thompson, and Michelle Saucedo.

In the later stages of the book, the following students also contributed insights from navigational discussions: Jamie Goodwin, Julia Kohl, Tiara Dungy, Haley Turisi, Andy Williams, Jin Ai, Dana Doan, and Bryan Fegley. Several unnamed students also helped contribute insights regarding the ways that emerging adults can get lost during the process of college, and the motivation behind needing to articulate in this book how better to navigate crucial decisions and challenging experiences in ways that are authentic and meaningful.

We also are tremendously grateful for the institutional support provided for this book. Most notably, Anna Zajicek and the Department of Sociology and Criminology at the University of Arkansas contributed a substantial portion of the costs to allow this book to be provided as an open resource, which eliminates cost barriers to students who we hope will greatly benefit from its insight and advice. This also allows instructors to be able to adopt the book in college courses, especially first-year seminars and general education courses, without risking adding to potential financial barriers for college during that crucial first year of acclimation.

Additionally, Linda Coon and the Honors College at the University of Arkansas also subsidized the open access costs in order to support high-achieving students in navigating college in ways that support formation and articulation of professional identities, which is a precursor to winning undergraduate research grants and other student awards.

Moreover, the "people power" of the co-authorship team would not have been possible without the support of Todd Shields and Yvette Murphy-Erby in the J. William Fulbright College of Arts and Sciences at the University of Arkansas, in which six of the authors were located. We are also indebted to Ro Di Brezzo and the Office of the Provost at the University of Arkansas for supporting the first-year seminar course that led to this book's creation.

Our own mentors and advisors were instrumental in guiding our earlier college navigations, and we thank the colleagues in each of our academic units for the ongoing support they provide, especially in co-advising the students about which we care so dearly.

Last but not least, we thank the three anonymous reviewers and the Oxford University Press editors for their extensive feedback on the manuscript. Their thoughtful and helpful advice greatly enriched the material and underscored the benefits of a community of scholars. Despite these tremendous contributions to this book, we retain any remaining errors as our own.

It is worth noting that this book is meant to launch many different directions for navigating college, and we hope it opens discussions for how best to do that more than it firmly closes doors or forevermore answers questions. We aim for students to be able to launch from the ideas in this book into face-to-face and online encounters with the many caring faculty and student support staff available on college campuses. On their behalf, we want this book to be a sign of the deep commitment we have to your success. We're here to help navigate.

With gratitude,

*Patricia Herzog, Casey Harris, Shauna Morimoto,*
*Shane Barker, Jill Wheeler, Justin Barnum, and Terrance Boyd*

# AUTHOR BACKGROUNDS

**Patricia Snell Herzog, PhD,** is the Melvin Simon Chair and Associate Professor of Philanthropic Studies in the Lilly Family School of Philanthropy at Indiana University–Purdue University Indianapolis (IUPUI). Prior to joining IUPUI, Herzog was Associate Professor of Sociology and Co-Director of the Center for Social Research at the University of Arkansas. She was a postdoctoral fellow in the Kinder Institute for Urban Research at Rice University after completing her doctoral degree in sociology at the University of Notre Dame, where she was also Assistant Director for the Center for the Study of Religion and Society. Herzog's co-authored books include *American Generosity: Who Gives and Why* (Herzog & Price, Oxford University Press 2015), *Souls in Transition: The Religious Lives of Emerging Adults in America* (Smith & Snell, Oxford University Press 2009), *Lost in Transition: The Dark Side of Emerging Adulthood* (Smith et al., Oxford University Press 2010), and *Passing the Plate: Why American Christians Don't Give Away More Money* (Smith, Emerson, & Snell, Oxford University Press 2008). Herzog has also published on youth and emerging adults in publications such as the *Journal of Adolescent Research, Youth & Society,* and *Journal for the Scientific Study of Religion.*

**Casey T. Harris, PhD,** is Associate Professor in the Department of Sociology and Criminology and Co-Director of the Center for Social Research at the University of Arkansas. Harris completed his doctoral degree at The Pennsylvania State University in 2011 where he served as a research associate for both a National Science Foundation project and the state court system. His primary research interests center on stratification and crime, emphasizing communities and urban sociology, race/ethnicity, immigration, religion, and media. Harris has published extensively in top sociology and criminology journals, including *Criminology, The Sociological Quarterly, Journal of Quantitative Criminology*, and *Social Science Research*, and has taught over a dozen distinct courses while being recognized for his mentorship and teaching with the prestigious Nolan Award at the University of Arkansas.

**Shauna A. Morimoto, PhD,** is Associate Professor, Director of Graduate Studies, and Vice Chair in the Department of Sociology and Criminology, and a faculty affiliate of the Center for Social Research at the University of Arkansas. Prior to this, Morimoto completed her doctoral degree in sociology at the University of Wisconsin-Madison and was as a Visiting Scholar at Texas A&M University. In 2015–2016, Morimoto received a Fulbright Cambridge Visiting Faculty Fellowship to spend a year in residence at the Lucy Cavendish College at the University of Cambridge. Morimoto's primary research interests include civic engagement, political sociology, institutional equity, youth, gender, and social inequalities. Currently, Morimoto is working on a book manuscript on millennials and social media use and doing research on US and UK policies for gender and racial equity in higher education.

## STUDENT DEVELOPMENT AND STUDENT SUPPORT PRACTITIONERS

**Shane W. Barker, EdD,** is Assistant Dean for Advising and Student Development in the J. William Fulbright College of Arts and Sciences at the University of Arkansas. Barker has been an academic advisor since 2006 and received both his bachelor of arts in history and master of science in community economic development from the University of Central Arkansas, and a doctor of education in higher education from the University of Arkansas. In 2011, Barker was awarded the NACADA Research Support Grant to fund his examination of student experiences within shared models of academic advising, the findings of which were presented at the Conference for the Association for the Study of Higher Education and published in the *Journal of Student Affairs Research and Practice*. Barker has also presented multiple times at the state, regional, and national level on topics related to academic advising and undergraduate student development. Barker is a recognized leader within professional organizations for academic advisors at both the regional and national levels, having served as president of his state organization in 2013 and 2014, chair of a regional conference in 2012, and national chair of a pre-law interest group in 2014.

**Jill Geisler Wheeler, MEd, MS,** is Associate Director of Honors Studies in the J. William Fulbright College of Arts and Sciences at the University of Arkansas. Wheeler has been an academic advisor since 2006. She completed her undergraduate degree in marketing and both master's degrees in higher education as well as counseling through the University of Arkansas, Fayetteville. Wheeler has served on the Arkansas Academic Advising Network's (ArkAAN) Executive Board, including the Office of Vice President of Membership in 2013–2015 and President Elect 2018 to 2019. Wheeler was appointed chair of the Webinar Advisory Board (2017–2019) for the Global Community for Academic Advising (NACADA). Wheeler has presented at the state, regional, and national level through these two associations. Wheeler was named Outstanding Advisor by ArkAAN in 2010 and, in that same year, her co-presentation on student veterans won Best of Region for NACADA's Region 7 annual conference. Wheeler is a Provost guest lecture and has instructed hundreds of students through first-year success courses in her more than 12 years in advising.

**Anthony Justin Barnum, PhD,** is Visiting Assistant Professor in the Department of Sociology and Criminology at the University of Arkansas. Barnum completed his bachelor of arts degree in International Relations and Global Studies at Hendrix College in 2003, after which he completed a master of arts in sociology in 2005 and a master of arts in French language and literature in 2007, both at the University of Arkansas. Subsequently, Barnum earned his doctoral degree in sociology at Howard University in 2014. Barnum's teaching experience includes spending two years living in Cape Verde, West Africa, teaching English at the Universidade de Cabo Verde and the Instituto Superior de Educação while serving in the Peace Corps as a teacher trainer, as well as having taught at the University of Central Arkansas, Trinity Washington University, Dickinson College, and Arkansas State University-Beebe. Currently, Barnum teaches courses on Race, Class, and Gender, Social Theory, and Senior Seminar, and he has previously taught a large section of an Introduction to Sociology course. Barnum has conducted research for the US–Brazil Race, Development, and Social Inequality Program at the Universidade Federal da Bahia in Salvador, Bahia, and Brazil, and he served as Principal Investigator for the auto-ethnographies included in this book.

**Terrance L. Boyd, MS,** is the former director of recruitment and the Honors College Path Program, a mentoring initiative geared toward increasing diversity in honors education and graduation. Boyd is an advocate of education and equity, especially for individuals from underrepresented communities. He focuses on the professional, diversity, and leadership development of rising talent. Boyd earned his bachelor of science degree in business administration (cum laude) in 2013 and completed his master of science in operations management in 2014. Immediately after graduating, he joined the University of Arkansas Honors College staff, tasked with creating and developing the Path Program, now a Walton Family Foundation and National Science Foundation funded program. Boyd has direct experiences with how student organizations, campus citizenry, and peer-to-peer interactions aid students in navigating college successfully.

Hashtag Keyword List, and Summaries of Student Stories

| Chapter | Name | Hashtags | Summary | Topic Themes |
|---|---|---|---|---|
| 1 | Devon | #adulting #20something #transition | I'm learning how to take care of myself and think about my future for the first time. | Emerging into adulthood; transitioning to college; shifting social contexts; and changing expectations. |
| | Brittany | #onmyown | Being responsible means something totally different now that I live without my parents and have the freedom to choose what to do. | |
| | Charlie | #wherestheparty #yolo | Balancing school and a social life is much harder than it was in high school. | |
| 2 | Sanjana | #movingagain | All of the different places I've lived have made me the person I am today. | Moves, identity and social changes; resocialization; romantic partnerships and tough breakups. |
| | Troy | #changingidentity | I sometimes feel I'm two different people: one from home and one from my new college life. | |
| | Derrick | #brokenhearted | My breakup has made me feel stuck, distracted, and wondering how to make sense of my life. | |

| Chapter | Name | Hashtags | Summary | Topic Themes |
|---|---|---|---|---|
| 3 | Cooper | #bornlucky #welleducated | I worked hard to get into college, but I realize that my family background matters. | Money, working, social class backgrounds, and what they mean for how easy or hard college can be; the value of a college degree for building credentials and for acquiring cultural and social capital; the hidden rules of college; and the importance of letting college change you. |
| | Regan | #livingthedream #flagshipU | I always planned to go to college and I feel lucky my family can afford the extra things, too. | |
| | Riberto | #strappedforcash #dutycalls #distracted | I have to juggle school and taking care of family, and money is in short supply. | |
| | Gabby | #needtowinthelottery #lemonstolemonaid | I never realized my own social class until I came to college, and now I notice it all of the time. | |
| | Julius | #broke #workingtwojobs | Working while in college is a challenge, and I wish I could focus more on school. | |
| | Leolia | #lifeisrough #dead-beatparents #wantabetterlife | Growing up, my family hid our money struggles, and I don't have the resources for college. | |

| | Name | Hashtags | Quote | Description |
|---|---|---|---|---|
| | Bryce | pressuretosucceed #fearoffailure | Although I know I come from privilege, I am afraid of failing or that I won't measure up. | |
| 4 | Abby | #greeklife #IAmASororityWoman | Being part of my sorority is central to my friend group and forms much of my identity. | Developing identity in college; finding friends and groups that offer belonging; carving a path; trying out different options and sorting which identities will stick; taking ownership of learning; deciding whether to switch majors and careers; identifying personal values; and understanding how values connect to college choices. |
| | Austin | #notgoinggreek #onbeingme | I chose not to join a fraternity so I could be the only one in control of my college experience. | |
| | Kyndal | #collegeainthighschool #findingyourself | In high school, the groups were so set that it was easy to know who I was, but now with all the options in college, I have to work to find myself. | |
| | Emma | #findingnewfriends #nomorecliques | Friend groups and what they mean for my identity are very different than in high school. | |
| | Melissa | #whatamidoingwithmylife #stilldreaming | My heart is torn between my passion and what everyone tells me is a practical future. | |

| Chapter | Name | Hashtags | Summary | Topic Themes |
| --- | --- | --- | --- | --- |
| | Chikako | #wrongmajor #wronglife | I think I may want to change my career goals, but switching majors may disappoint my parents. | |
| | Camille | #toomanychoices #howdoidecide | I have a lot of different skills, but I can't decide what to do with so many options. | |
| | Mateo | #toomanychoices #howdoidecide | Maybe I'm in the wrong major and I wish I could be sure I am making the right choice. | |
| 5 | Aaron | #outsider #identitycrisis | I feel like an outsider when I think about how my family and background shaped my identity. | Encountering some setbacks; building personal resiliency within families, cultures, groups, and organizations; challenging a sense of academic entitlement with grit and a growth mindset. |
| | Alexa | #recentering #notbrandname | Since my parents divorced, I struggle with how I present myself to others, even now in college. | |
| | Chen | #shy #followingtherules | My strict upbringing makes it a struggle for me to figure out how to make friends and be me. | |
| | Michalyn | #movingon #emotionalabuse | A bad relationship and past emotional abuse hurts my ability to relate with others in college. | |

| | | | |
|---|---|---|---|
| Connor | #notgettingit #saywhat | I'm working hard in my classes, but somehow seem to be falling behind everyone else. | |
| Jacob | #fishoutofwater #sodifferent #diversity | I grew up in a community with little diversity, but everyone is different from each other here. | Experiencing diversity in college: for some students college is more diverse than prior experiences, while for other students prior experiences were more diverse than college; being and discovering diverse students; reflecting on inclusion and belonging; learning how uniqueness can be a strength; building a personal and professional story; sharing that story; balancing perceived uniqueness with recognizing fun commonalities and differences in friend groups; finding where you belong. |
| Andrea | #fishoutofwater #sodifferent #diversity | My hometown was diverse, but now I rarely see anyone like me and have encountered racism. | |
| Cody | #fishoutofwater #sodifferent #diversity | My high school was diverse, but now my college classes are full of people mostly like me. | |

6

| Chapter | Name | Hashtags | Summary | Topic Themes |
|---|---|---|---|---|
| | Cameron | #diversity #racism | I've changed schools enough times to experience different attitudes about race, but I'm still learning what's acceptable in each type of place. | |
| | Eduardo | #frommexico #opportunity | As an immigrant, I had to first learn English before I could show my full academic potential. | |
| | Marco | #frommexico #opportunity | In some ways I live two lives: one in the culture of my family and the other of my home country. | |
| | Linda | #interracialdating #interracialfamily | Being in an inter-racial relationship makes me question what diversity means for my family. | |
| | Nikolaus | #adopted #becomingwhite | As an adopted Asian from Russia, my experiences with race are complicated. | |
| | William | #whitemale #pressure | With my privileges, I face lots of pressure to succeed and failure would carry a heavy cost. | |
| | Hayden | #bipride #notjustaphase | Bi-sexuality allows me to blend in, but I'm also never fully accepted in any one sexual identity. | |
| | Erin | #notcatholic #agnostic | My faith was challenged in high school and now I no longer believe as my family does. | |

| Name | Hashtags | Statement | |
|---|---|---|---|
| Braden | #christian | My religion gives me a connection to others around me and provides support in college. | Becoming a leader; being purposful online and in-person; identifying the wide variety of ways that students can engage in college campuses; figuring out what experiences animate involvement; building future citizenship. |
| Landon | #islamaphobia | I have a passion for religious diversity, but my family is not enthusiastic about this passion. | |
| Shawn | #ihatetechnology #isolation | Technology increases isolation in families and among individuals across campus. | |
| Felicia | #ilovetechnology #connection | Technology allows me to manage my identity and be involved at anytime and from anywhere. | |
| Norah | #marchingband #ilovemusic | The marching band provides me with a social life and a connection to a diverse group of peers. | |
| Omar | #collegesports #studentathletes | Student-athletes like me have very structured lives, but we do it together as a team. | |
| Desiree | #sistersforlife #volunteering | Joining a sorority allowed me to continue my love for philanthropy, a big part of Greek life. | |
| Phillip | #friendgroups #campusministry #theatre | I have two distinct friend groups, with each involving different types of interactions. | |

7

| Chapter | Name | Hashtags | Summary | Topic Themes |
|---|---|---|---|---|
| 8 | Ellie | #drivingwithoutdirection #whyamihere | College seems just as alienating as high school; I'm not really a part of the campus community. | Switching majors; exploring career options during college; learning to expect the unexpected; recalibrating; sorting vocation and careers; engaging personal and professional identities. |
| | Tyronne | #tooeasy #notchallenged | This seems too easy, and I wonder if I'd be better off going somewhere more challenging. | |
| | Kiersten | #parallelplan #changingmajors | I'm changing my career plans to better fit with what I've decided I want to be and do. | |
| | Isabella | #americandream #proudimmigrant | My family's immigrant success story leads me to want to achieve security for myself. | |
| | Abram | #vocation #publichealth | My faith leads me to help others, and my career choice reflects that desire to help. | |
| | Sierra | #genderinstem #findingyourownway | I won't let gender stereotypes curtail my aspirations to be a scientist or an engineer. | |

# The Changing College Student

## *Why First-Year Students Today Are Different*

The first chapter explains why and how social science can help students navigate college. The introductory chapter begins with student case studies and then describes how a number of social changes over the last several decades resulted in the relatively new life stage called "emerging adulthood." Emerging adults today are different from the entering college students of the past, which means that the parents and grandparents of young students may have had different experiences in college than most young people do today. This chapter explains these differences across generations of entering college students, as well as the implications of these changes for understanding entering college students today. This introductory chapter also introduces and summarizes the content of the other book chapters.

*The Science of College*. Patricia S. Herzog, Casey T. Harris, Shauna A. Morimoto, Shane W. Barker, Jill G. Wheeler, A. Justin Barnum, and Terrance L. Boyd, Oxford University Press (2020) © Oxford University Press.
DOI: 10.1093/oso/9780190934507.001.0001

This book aids entering college students—and the people who support college students—in navigating college successfully. In an environment of information overload, where bad advice abounds, this book offers practical tips and guidance. Unlike some of the more widely available advice that is based on outdated, misinformed, or uninformed ideas about what college students need to know, the advice in this book is based upon real students and sound social science research. The wide range of college pathways available to students presents challenges for understanding what information is applicable to their individual path. What students and their parents and mentors need is a book that provides clear guidance on how to navigate different pathways with their own preferences in mind. This guide provides tips that assist readers along well-traveled (and less traveled) pathways through and out of college.

The central thesis of the book is that the transition to adulthood is a complex process, and college is pivotal to this experience. This book seeks to help young people navigate that process. For many, college represents the culmination of ambition, independence, and individualism, and each of these themes is represented in this book, especially through the student stories. Challenges vary depending on a student's demographics and social background. Getting invested in the community is critical to college success, no matter what the point of entry. Universities have many resources, but students have to realize when they need them and figure out how to connect with them. There is no single template for student success, whether considering how to navigate through college or how to find gainful employment afterward. Each student needs to balance their evolving life in their own way. Nevertheless, this book highlights some common issues that many college students face and provides science-based advice for how to navigate college.

Every chapter of this book begins with stories from real college students and then summarizes research that is relevant to their stories. The third section of each chapter turns insights from both sources of information into advice for students. The author team of faculty, instructors, advisors, and other campus support staff provide students with tips on how to understand their circumstances, process various situations, and find their way around academic and social life on campus. The final chapters of the book offer interactions among student stories and tips to give students an overall sense of how to forge their own path through college.

With each chapter we paint an increasingly complex picture of the challenges and opportunities college students encounter. One way of characterizing this progression is that this chapter focuses on individuals in a developmental stage during which self-focus is normal. Chapter 2 contextualizes the changing life course within larger economic, social, and cultural trends, and discusses the role of contemporary higher education in understanding those changes. Social class, economic resources, and how family backgrounds condition students' college experiences are addressed in chapter 3. Chapter 4 integrates these topics by advising students to consider the ways that they exercise personal agency in making key decisions during college, while warning students to appreciate the difficulty of these choices and pay attention to the realities of the options they have available to them. Resiliency, or how students can bounce back from personal and structural challenges to build a successful college career, is the focus of chapter 5. Chapter 6 addresses race, ethnicity, gender, sexuality, religion, and other aspects of diversity that shape individual students' expectations and experiences of college life. Chapter 7 examines how learning from personal experiences and structural challenges can put students on a path to leadership. The final chapter attends to the exploration of college life, and how switching and recalibrating allows students to realize their professional and career identities and goals.

## THIS BOOK'S GOALS

Our goal in writing this book is to convey the contemporary experiences for emerging adult college students in a meaningful way. We identify a number of social issues; describe how these present challenges to students; place students' personal experiences within a broader social context; and offer research-based tips for young people—and the people who support them—in navigating college. Our objectives are as follows:

- Respond to the changing needs of incoming college students;
- Synthesize social science research into practical tools;
- Challenge preconceived and outmoded understandings of career pursuits;
- Discuss socioeconomic status, race, gender, and other identities in college experiences;
- Identify multiple segments of students, and describe both the differences and the commonalities in their needs;
- Develop useful skills for navigating college;
- Empower students to access campus resources and discern which individuals on campus can assist them in specific situations;
- Reveal the unwritten rules of college;
- Build competencies that transfer to careers and life after college.

In sum, our goal is to empathize with the often-challenging experiences of emerging adults as they explore individual and social identities, encounter rifts in their sense of self or conflict between their various social roles, and then work to achieve balance. We view students to be in the midst of an exciting and demanding life stage that requires they take increasing ownership of who they are and what they want to do, and we want to help them acquire the skills they need to set out on their own particular pathway.

## WHY THIS BOOK IS NEEDED

The typical first-year student entering college today differs from the average first-year student of just a few decades ago. To meet the changing needs of incoming students, many universities now have first-year seminar courses. These courses often draw upon texts that were not designed for first-year seminars, and which may give practical tips that are not based on scientific evidence or may summarize academic research while failing to provide useful advice. This book combines the strengths of these approaches by offering science-based advice to students on how to navigate college. This book engages the real issues that entering college students face, contextualizes individual experiences of these issues, and offers advice. While (often misguided) advice abounds in the broader public, the advice of this book targets specific kinds of student situations drawn from the lives of real students.

This book sees students as situated within the changes of recent decades, which explains why parents and other well-meaning adults in students' lives may not know about the contemporary college experience, as it could be quite different from their own. For example, many technological and social media changes have occurred since late 2006 and early 2007, which may seem like ages ago to many of our student readers but seems recent to many of their professors. These changes include the invention of the iPhone, with more processing power RAM and gigabits of flash memory than had ever been held in a palm-size device up until that moment. Additionally, Facebook was released to the general public, formerly being confined only to college users; Twitter launched on its own platform and went global; Google bought YouTube and launched Android; Amazon launched Kindle; Airbnb was conceived; and Change.org became an important social mobilization website.[1] To understand this broader social context of today's college students, it is important to summarize several changes surrounding higher education.

These include economic, technological, social, cultural, familial, generational, and educational changes. For example, today's entering college students are accepting and supportive of monumental changes in gender norms, such as expecting women to be regularly engaged in long-term labor and thus also establishing meaningful careers during college, as well as accepting and participating in same-sex relationships at a greater rate than previous generations, which means that same-sex partnerships are equally included within an understanding of how romantic partnerships affect college and career pursuits.[2] All of these changes, and more, have shaped the experiences of American young people, or "emerging adults," as scholars of life course development call them. First, we will explain what emerging adulthood is.

*Becoming an Adult Takes Longer.* Emerging adulthood is an exploratory age during which young people make decisions that have long-lasting effects on their life chances.[3] Major social and economic restructuring over the last several decades[4] contributes to the precariousness of long-term employment,[5] a collective sense of insecurity in social positions,[6] and greater economic churning (or turnover) in adult transitions.[7] To put those trends in more concrete terms: First, prior generations were able to earn more money at earlier ages, relative to inflated costs. Second, those generations were better able to keep the same job and work their way up within a company. Now young people change jobs more frequently. Third, only a small minority of emerging adults view their current job as a viable, long-term career—meaning it takes longer now to secure positions that reliably pay the rent or a mortgage.[8] Fourth, the skills required for top positions in an increasingly technological society require greater levels of cognitive capacities, which have continually increased the demands for higher education. College degrees, and often advanced degrees, are required more often for entry-level positions now than for previous generations.[9]

*College Has Unequal Risks and Rewards.* While enrollment in higher education institutions is increasing, the return on a bachelor's degree is declining. This means that going to college is becoming more of a requirement to get a desired position, but the additional income people are likely to earn with that degree (relatively speaking) is smaller now than it was for previous generations, especially for particular student subgroups.[10] At the same time, the intersection of parental income level with race and ethnicity has never mattered more. For example, research finds that students from poor families are less likely to go to college at all, and especially unlikely to be able to attend Ivy League schools, just as black and Latino students are less likely than white students to attend Ivy League schools. Yet students who are both poor and black or Latino are especially less likely to attend those schools than are wealthier white students.[11] All of which is why public universities are key to expanding equal opportunities. Parental income level affects the financial burden of college too. Research finds that students from the highest *and lowest* income levels are the least likely to acquire student loan debt—the former because they have less need for loans and the latter because they have less chance of enrolling—while students from middle-income families are the most likely to risk high student loan debt without gaining the same returns as more advantaged peers.[12,13] Beyond the debt incurred, parental income can also impact the earnings of their children, meaning the impact of student debt can be experienced in different ways depending on one's family background.

*Within College Inequalities.* Partially due to rising participation in college, "within-college differences," or differences between groups of students who are attending the same college, are increasingly important in predicting life outcomes.[14] This finding contradicts the popular perception that people can choose any which way they want to navigate college. The impression of young people that "anything goes" in becoming an adult may partly be due to the attention that scholars of emerging adulthood devote to individual experiences, such as describing young adults as "self-focused." This focus, while helpful, can hide some of the broader social patterns from view. In actuality, the ways that young people take on adult roles can lead to better or worse social and economic outcomes.[15]

In addition, emerging adults rely on different kinds of "cultural capital" as they go through college.[16] Cultural capital refers to the stock of knowledge that people have about how to fit in across different kinds of social contexts. For example, what it takes to fit in with a group of engineering students is different from what it takes to fit in among art majors. While it is not always obvious, college is a new cultural context and has different norms for fitting in and succeeding than high school. Some entering college students have been more exposed to college norms than others because of their family members' college experiences or the kinds of class norms their high school had. Different cultural resources offer various pros and cons in distinct contexts, but the point is that getting used to college takes more adjustment for some students than for others. Taken together, these trends indicate the need for emerging adults to have "extra-familial support" (caring adults beyond parents and extended family members) in navigating college. Because this book addresses these issues, all incoming college students (and their more advanced peers) can benefit from reading it, and many universities creating first-seminar courses will find this book is helpful as assigned reading.

*College Success.* To help all students succeed in college, this book makes visible some facts about college that can be hidden in plain sight. For example, researchers find that prior aptitude does not adequately predict the skills necessary to succeed in college.[17] This means that doing well in high school does not guarantee success in college, a counterintuitive idea that many formerly high-achieving students experience as a shock when they earn their first C in college. Similarly, recent research has expanded the notion of college readiness to include "extra-cognitive" factors, such as *ownership of learning* (understanding that ultimately one is responsible for whether and what one learns in college), *perseverance* (sticking it out even when it is rough or boring), and *self-efficacy* (believing that one can learn what is needed to succeed in different college situations).[18] In short, students can learn skills and capacities that drive their success during college. When we examine what separates students who do well in college from students who struggle or drop out, these factors turn out to be important. Applying social cognitive theories on college readiness and perseverance,[19] we focus in this book on the role of college social self-efficacy in academic success.[20] This is because prior studies indicate that this is a central factor in college success. It helps to clarify why students who leave college explain their periods of "stopping out" of college by citing experiences that students who remain in college also experience, but while staying enrolled.[21]

*Overcoming Obstacles.* Relatedly, one of the central goals of this book is to help students build perseverance and learn how to overcome obstacles that they may experience in college. Indeed, scholars find that emerging adulthood is a key life-course development stage during which the brain matures in important ways, allowing young people to engage in more concerted regulation of themselves and their actions than was present at earlier life stages.[22] Notably, we approach this subject in a unique manner because many of us authors are sociologists. This means that, counter to the individual focus of popular American culture, we emphasize the social aspects of college. For example, we understand the ability to overcome college hurdles not as an individual quality alone, but as a trait resulting from interwoven social and personal processes over time.[23] In short, students' belief that they can succeed in college may reflect how much their prior experiences have prepared them for it. Social experiences take place within more or less advantaged contexts,[24] and feeling that one has control over one's life is a combination of belief and social experiences.[25] In essence, people who have greater control over their life circumstances wind up feeling more in control of their life. This is what sociologists refer to as "invisible identities": the way that people make decisions is patterned by what feels comfortable based on the ways their identities have been shaped in relation to their social contexts.[26] With this in mind, we think the key to helping students succeed in college is in teaching them how to "weather the storm" by addressing obstacles with the support of campus resources.

## THE BOOK'S AUDIENCE

This book is primarily intended for undergraduate students, especially incoming first-year students. A secondary audience includes parents, academics, and other higher education professionals. Our goals for each group are as follows.

*Students*: We aim for this book to aid incoming and current students in finding a viable path through the many facets of college life, both academic and social, and later in transitioning into adult roles. Our goal is to make the hidden rules of college visible to all, and thus to level the playing field for all students, regardless of background and exposure to formal and academic settings. To ensure the book reflects the experiences of contemporary college students, we begin every chapter with stories from real students and refer back to these as we provide advice. Appendix A also offers students a variety of activities that can be completed alone or in groups to engage the concepts in this book through reflective and engaging exercises.

*Parents*: Secondarily, we intend for this book to equip parents to support their children during the college years and acknowledge the valuable resource that parents can be for college campuses. While the main text is written for students, parents can learn a great deal about their emerging adult college students from this book. In addition, we include advice specifically for parents of emerging adult college students in appendix B. This advice ties the student stories, relevant science, and advice into practical tips for supporting college students.

*Academics and Professionals*: We aim for this book to also help academics and professionals (including faculty, instructors, administrators, advisors, and staff) in understanding the social scientific research relevant to emerging adulthood, higher education, and the transition into college. This book could serve as the primary text for first-year experience courses, and we have included ideas for classroom activities within the academic appendix that correspond to each chapter. Appendix C, our academic appendix, also provides further details on the methods employed and offers implications of the summarized research and case studies for faculty, instructors, administrators, advisors, and other staff who work with college students. Additionally, we provide an online supplement for instructors with classroom activities.

## CHAPTER SECTIONS

Each chapter has the following three sections: (1) student stories; (2) scientific research summaries; (3) advice on accessing campus resources to gain support from advisors, faculty, and other mentors on campus. The final chapters of the book have two additional sections: (a) social interactions among students; and (b) overarching tips for navigating college to launch successful and satisfying careers. The scientific research summaries were primarily written by the first three authors of this book, all of whom are faculty members, specifically associate professors with primary disciplinary training in sociology, along with psychology, social work, and criminology. The advice sections were primarily written by the remainder of the authorship team, who are student development and student support practitioners, mostly staff and also an instructor.

It is worth noting that the tone varies across these sections in ways that reflect the diversity of approaches that college students encounter on campuses. For example, the tone of the student stories and togetherness sections best reflect the voices of students who are conversing with each other. The scientific research summaries best reflect discussions with faculty whose scholarship aligns with college and emerging adult related topics; these are the voices that students are most likely to hear when seeking assistance from professors in office hours. In yet another set of voices, the advice sections best represent those of student support and development practitioners. These are the kind of responses that students are most likely to hear during new student orientations, academic advisor meetings, and in other staff office discussions. Rather than reconcile this rich diversity into a single author voice, this book provides readers with the wide variety of approaches and tones that students actually experience on the college campus. From informal talk among friends to formal interaction with professors, college provides experiences with multiple, even conflicting, voices.

Stories: What We Experience

Each chapter begins with multiple stories that illustrate different types of college students. The majority of these are direct quotes from students who wrote *autoethnographies*, a form of qualitative research which involves self-reflection and an interpretation of one's personal biography within the broader social, cultural, and political context (Ellis, Adams, & Bocher 2011; see appendix C, note 1). Supplementing these, we also include scenarios that combine aspects of the many students whom we have taught or assisted. All student names are changed to protect confidentiality.

These stories help to show what it is like for students to find their way through college. On the one hand, these stories underline that there is no one-size-fits-all approach, as there are many distinct kinds of students and backgrounds that affect how college feels, especially during the first year. On the other hand, few student experiences are entirely unique. Every student reading this book is likely to identify with at least one of these stories.

Many first-year seminar books and courses seem to assume all college students are essentially the same, but we form every chapter around the diverse perspectives that real college students bring to campus. We also tailor our interpretations and advice toward scenarios like the ones these students confronted, which should teach students what they could do if they find themselves in a similar situation.

Through the narratives, we describe the complex issues that many students face during college. Scholars call this time in life "demographically dense," because it involves so many major life changes and fluctuations: young people are establishing career choices, often forming longer-term romantic partnerships, gaining career experiences, accruing (or not) financial credit, and sometimes breaking up, temporarily dropping out, or moving back home. It is no wonder that many students feel lost at some point. In the course of tackling these issues, we address how race, ethnicity, gender, socioeconomic status, and other background characteristics condition college experiences, basing our analyses not on stereotypes but on lived realities. Drawing from the experiences of our students, including many navigating their first year, we tell the stories of college students who we think will resonate with our readers.

## Science: What We Know

Building on these stories, the second section of each chapter summarizes scientific research. We describe our approach as "the science of college," because we are drawing on social science theories and data to provide interpretations, advice, and tips. Social sciences engage similar tools to those used in the natural sciences: in both sets of disciplines, researchers often form a hypothesis based on a theory and then test the theory with data, as well as collecting data to detect patterns and develop theories.

Additionally, social scientific knowledge is also advanced as a collective enterprise that is based heavily on peer-review processes to accumulate more valid and careful information over time. This peer-review process is crucial for distinguishing legitimate forms of knowledge from common sense and culturally biased notions about how the (social) world works. Yet as an art, the social sciences also involve imagining reality, accepting the unknown, theorizing based on logical reasoning, and relying on a collective imagination. In this way, the social sciences can serve as a bridge between the natural sciences (such as biology and chemistry), on the one hand, and the arts and humanities (such as philosophy and history), on the other. Examples of social science disciplines include sociology, psychology, social psychology, communications, political science, and economics.

Perhaps more importantly, at least for entering college students, social science can help young people make sense of their experiences in college. To succeed in college, it helps to understand the context of higher education and changes in the economy and career availability. There can be something empowering about viewing personal experiences within life course development, and in students gaining perspective on how they are not alone in encountering some issues and confusions in college. Seeing broader social patterns is a key insight of sociology, and this aspect of the book helps to set it apart from many self-help books that tend to highlight the individual uniqueness of a person and their personal ability to create any change desired. Yet, thinking about people as embedded within larger social contexts can perhaps feel alienating, or in some ways de-emphasizing of the personal experiences that can feel so intense and powerful at the individual level. Beyond naming the challenges that social and cultural inequalities present to students (which, unfortunately, is often where introductory textbooks on these topics end), we connect these findings to research on identity formation, career development, social self-efficacy, and ownership of learning. Armed with this knowledge, students can better manage the choices they make during college to smooth their path into successful adult roles later in life. Relying on a research-informed perspective for guidance rather than outdated, confusing messages is like having a GPS with turn-by-turn options instead of ambiguous "word of mouth" directions.

In providing advice for students, we merge three broad perspectives:

a. A sociological framework, illustrating how some students encounter more or less hardship than their average classmates;
b. A psychological and counseling framework, empathizing with the existential crisis and tasks confronting young people during their college experiences;
c. A higher educational framework, underlining the need for diversified social supports within university ecosystems.

See appendix C for more information on this social science approach. More broadly, most of navigating college in the way we advise students to do is about learning to employ research-based thinking to solve, or at least respond to, real-world issues. The book also provides examples of making science-informed decisions, beginning first with college.

## Advice: What We Provide

The third section of each chapter offers responses and support from campus resources. There are literally hundreds (on smaller campuses) or thousands (on larger campuses) of people whose full-time job is to assist students at a given college. Some of these people are faculty and instructors, whose classroom instruction provides a knowledge resource and whose one-on-one time in office hours provides a mentoring resource. Other resources come in the form of professional staff and administrators. Many staff members serve students in various advising roles, depending on the programs that employ them.

One aspect of the college campus that is "hidden in plain view" is that students can turn to any number of people for help on a daily basis. Many students form lasting relationships with faculty and staff during their time in college, which serves both their short-term needs and provides long-term support via recommendation letters and career networking. Thus, one of our goals in this section of each chapter is to spread the word about the tremendous amount of support students have available and make them more comfortable accessing these resources for a wide array of needs.

We do not provide a list of the offices on college campuses that can be resources to students. Based on conversations with our students, we think the obstacle is not that students do not know of their existence, but rather that they do not view these resources as necessary or useful to *them*, in particular. Thus, our case studies illustrate how these offices can tailor the kind of support they provide to fit the needs of individual students.

## Togetherness: What We Share

In the later chapters, we describe social interactions among students and in groups. Because we view students not merely as individuals but also as friends, peers, classmates, roommates, and participants in other groups, we recognize them as a primary campus resource for one another. Many books on higher education pay considerable attention to official campus resources. Conversely, many sociological, anthropological, and ethnographic investigations into college campuses indicate the importance of peer-to-peer networks and friendships as a primary mechanism through which college "works."[27] However, these approaches are rarely combined.

We offer a text that covers both formal and informal college processes, allowing students and their social supports to understand the breadth of people and relationships available to them on campus. This bolsters college students' understanding of who to turn to for what form of assistance, and of the tradeoffs between available resources. It also provides students and their supports the opportunity to learn from the social interactions that some students have with each other, and—in the process—acquire tips for how friends, roommates, and student organization peers can help one another navigate college successfully, and enjoyably!

Tips: What We Can Do

The final chapters of the book also bring together the insights laid out in each chapter in the form of specific tips for each of our audiences. These takeaways aid young people in making informed decisions during college that set them up for successful life outcomes, while also providing them with practice in consuming research-based information to guide life decisions now and in the future. In addition, we teach the adults who support young people in transitioning to adulthood—faculty, instructors, staff, administrators, scholars, parents, practitioners, and other interested readers—how to respond to the personal troubles encountered by college students, in ways that both value the intensity of their individual experiences and normalize their experiences within their broader social context.

## ADDITIONAL UNIQUE FEATURES

Two other unique features of this book are (1) voices drawn from a representative university context, and (2) hyperlinked keywords that are denoted as hashtags.

### Representative University Context

We draw upon a representative university context: public universities that are research-intensive, which have large student populations with a high degree of socioeconomic diversity (ranging from low to high income), and that enroll many students who are the first in their family to attend college. Many of the books available on higher education and emerging adults draw on small, private, liberal arts universities, often in the Ivy League. Yet navigating those contexts is quite different from navigating the universities that most average American young people attend. Recognizing that students in the latter setting also need resources, we focus here on large, public universities, summarize research findings, and offer responses that are reasonable for faculty, instructors, staff, and administrators, given the opportunities and constraints of their institutions.

## Hyperlinked Keywords as Hashtags

Another unique contribution that our text offers is a hyperlinked keyword system. We think it is important that a book of this kind be written in the "native language" of young readers. Thus, we borrow inspiration from the popularity of hashtags—as used on Twitter and Instagram—to convey meaningful information concisely over social media. By providing this text in electronic format, we are able to hyperlink student stories throughout the book, allowing readers the opportunity to read the book in order, or alternatively to click hyperlinks to read all the content on one student story within each of its different chapters. In other words, the book can be read sequentially, as a traditional text, or it can be read nonsequentially, in a way that is more akin to browsing social media.

## STUDENT STORIES: WHAT WE EXPERIENCE

To introduce the rest of the book, we present the first three student stories and our analysis in the same structure that later chapters follow. In the stories, the gray highlighted text should be read as a tweet or status update from these students sharing a bit of their story on social media. Some of these stories were written by real students who took one of our sociology classes and completed an autoethnography, in which cases their quoted text is a portion of what they wrote about themselves. In other cases, we drafted stories that combine elements from several of the students we have met over the years. The hashtags that begin the student status updates can be read as keywords for the tweet and for their fuller story that follows, and they can be clicked on to bring up all the sections in the book that are part of the same story.

**#adulting #20something**: I just bought all my own books and school supplies, and paid all my own bills. Now I'm broke and eating cereal for dinner, probably will show up to class tomorrow in my pajamas.

**Devon** had this to say in writing an autoethnography about the transition to college:

> Even with all the preparation in high school, I was overwhelmed with the things that college life brought me. As my parents hugged me goodbye and left me in my tiny shoe box, I realized that not only was I alone, I was about to begin the true journey into adulthood . . . I had to learn how to take care of myself, without the help of my parents, including doing my own laundry and dishes, and getting my own food. My mind was no longer focused on just being successful in school. Now I had to do that and figure out everyday living. Along with new studies, I had to start thinking about my future after college. My dad continued to pressure me about preparing for the real world, even though I had just started classes. He stressed to me the importance of appearance and preparation for the future workforce.

**#onmyown**: I just realized that I do not have any soap, and I will have to go to the grocery store for the first time without my parents to buy my own soap.

Like Devon, **Brittany** found that starting college entailed many changes:

> Before I came to college I had my values and the way I did things, but that changed dramatically when I came to school last year. I have always been responsible, but in the past I was under my parents' roof and had to do whatever they told me to do. I could not do whatever I wanted or go wherever I wanted without having their permission. But when I got to college I was now on my own, in charge of myself but able to do whatever I wanted. I had to change how I lived completely since I was on my own time and

literally everything was up to me, and I did not need parental approval for anything.

**#wherestheparty #yolo**: I'm flunking bio! Every time I talk with my professors, they give me advice on classes, and I just keep thinking, "does my breath smell like alcohol?"

**Charlie** has always been a social butterfly. High school was pretty stress-free, allowing her to do her fair share of partying while still making good enough grades to go to college. Things are different now. In college, there's a party every night, but there's also a huge amount of schoolwork. Everything seems to be snowballing out of her control. Maintaining her new friendships is very important to her, but she tends to overdo it when they go out. Then she feels sluggish the next day, skips class, and gets a late start on studying. Today she had a paper due and three tests to take, but after finishing the paper last night, she chose to go out and celebrate before studying for her tests. Deep down she knows that it was the stress of being so unprepared for an exam that caused her to go out. She wonders how worried she should be about this. Her friends party just as much. She wonders, "Are they stressed like me? What's more important: studying or taking advantage of the college experience? Should I ask my friends?"

## SCIENCE: WHAT WE KNOW

According to Jeffrey Arnett in *Emerging Adulthood: The Winding Road from the Late Teens Through the Twenties*,[28] the life stage that most college students are in is called "emerging adulthood." Emerging adulthood describes the experience of having one foot in adulthood and the other in adolescence, in limbo between the younger years under the protection and social control of parents and the completed launch into adulthood.

Popularly some aspects of this are known as "adulting." The life stage of emerging adulthood is characterized by being self-focused, exploring self-identity, experiencing instability, and feeling in-between. It is the age of possibilities. This is a new stage in life course development that resulted from several converging trends: people are devoting more years to college and pursuing advanced degrees; they are getting married and becoming parents at older ages; and they are switching jobs more frequently than their predecessors did at their age. While most emerging adults feel like their life is disjointed, since they do not know what will come next, it is also a tremendously exciting period—partly because of that uncertainty, and because emerging adults have not had to pay the price for their choices.

Although emerging adults (and their parents) have a wide variety of opinions on what it takes to be considered an adult, there are three criteria that are regularly identified. The first is accepting responsibility for yourself. The second is making independent decisions, perhaps with the input of family and friends, but still making final calls for yourself. The third is becoming financially independent. This last milestone is perhaps the hardest to achieve and is the aspect of transitioning into adulthood that emerging adults have the least control over. Accomplishing these aspects of adulthood is typically a gradual, incremental process. Many young people in the United States spend a decade or more in limbo, feeling ambiguous about whether or not they are adults.

For many emerging adults, college is a period of "resocialization," when they unlearn some of their prior ways of being and doing and acquire new norms regarding how to act and what to value. In the student stories, **Devon** and **Brittany** referenced something they read on this subject in their sociology class.[29] The excerpt, by Gwynne Dyer, is from a chapter called "Anybody's Son Will Do," which appeared in his book *War: Past, Present, and Future*. In this book, Dyer describes the resocialization process of military training, and how young men and women in the military eventually acquire the norm of killing during combat and accept this as part of their everyday business. Interestingly, these students (along with several other students who appear in later chapters, such as **Gabby** in chapter 3, **Kyndal** of chapter 4, and **Marco** of chapter 6) compare the process that Dyer describes to their experience of entering college. For example, **Marco** says, "Socialization is the lifelong process through which an individual is incorporated into a social group by learning that group's norms, social roles, and values (Kane 2013; see chapter 5, note 7). Resocialization, by contrast, is the sacrifice of the set of values acquired through socialization for the adoption of another set (Dyer 2013)." Likewise, **Kyndal** says, "As I look at the 'culture' of college, it is clear that it is an entirely new atmosphere and basically makes you forget everything you had ever known as 'normal' and makes a complete 180 shift; college resocialized me. Resocialization occurs when an old identity is taken away and adaptation to a new identity happens (Dyer 2013: 158)."

Similarly, **Devon** described this experience of resocialization in college by saying, "I had to undergo a process of resocialization, completely changing my values and ideals to fit my current situation (Dyer 2013)." **Brittany** mentioned "how I experienced resocialization when coming to college." She explained, "This is when you learn new norms and values when joining a new group or when your life circumstances change dramatically, like going to college (Dyer 2013: 158)." Brittany continued with the following:

> Some of the new norms and values I learned were things like going out and drinking every weekend is the cool thing to do, or if you did not find a person of the opposite sex to go home with after a party you are considered lame. These have really clashed with the values and norms my parents taught me growing up because they never allowed me to drink and they definitely were not supporting random hook-ups like everyone does here. This has really helped me grow as an individual and given me insight on what the rest of my life will entail [being in situations where my values clash with group values].

Two students we will introduce in a later chapter, **Abby** of chapter 4 and **Desiree** of chapter 7, liken their sororities to the "total institution" of the military and relay, affectionately, how well their sororities absorbed members into a community. New members proudly adorn themselves in Greek letters and feel an instant bond with people wearing those same letters. Abby said, "A total institution is a setting where a group of people is isolated from the rest of society and made to act a certain manner (Dyer 2013). My sorority became a total institution [to me] . . . Similar to how proud a marine is to be a marine after boot camp, I am proud to be a member of my sorority." While students find their social groups in different places on campus, college itself can serve as a total institution. Many students come to associate the school mascot with their identity and feel an instant bond with people anywhere in the world wearing their university's clothing.

**Devon** also references a reading by Robert Granfield on socialization, one entitled "Making It by Faking It: Working-Class Students in an Elite Academic Environment":

> As a young adult, I took golf lessons. My dad believed the benefits of knowing things like how to play golf could help me better associate myself with future employers. Learning sports such as golf are a form of cultural capital, which are social assets of a person that promote one's cultural competence, and thus social standing in society (Granfield 2013).[30] Being able to golf with a future employer, as well as dressing appropriately and having the 'look' of a successful young adult, are things that I keep in the back of my mind as I navigate college.

Drawing on the theories of Erving Goffman,[31] Granfield describes how students undergo a process of socialization during college that not only teaches them the norms and expectations of their future profession, but that also teaches them new ways of being and interacting with others while in college. Granfield applies Goffman's idea of stigma management to the law school scene, explaining that while American culture generally promotes individual uniqueness, people do not want to have "undesirable differentness." That is, few people want to stick out in noticeably negative ways. **Austin**, a student we introduce in chapter 4, describes this by saying, "Social stigmas can limit the opportunities and level of success of

23

an individual (Granfield 2013: 150). To compensate, people use stigma management to conceal their financial status to increase the opportunities afforded to them (Granfield 2013: 150)." Another student, **Aaron** of chapter 5, explained how he used stigma management himself: "Although I was a capable student, I lacked 'manners of speech, attire, values and experiences' that my other classmates had already acquired (Granfield 2013) . . . As the years of high school went on, I began to identify more with the upper-class than the lower class, especially as I hid the fact that my family was middle-class,* just as the students in Granfield's study did (2013). I began to wear as much designer clothes as my parents could afford because it was a part of the upper-class 'dress-code' (Granfield 2013)."

Part of what college is about, then, is learning the rules of the game, how to fit into a new social scene, acquiring "cultural competence." The college socialization process is even more intense for students who grew up with very different sets of norms than the middle-class college scene. Granfield describes students from working-class backgrounds attempting to avoid class stigma, struggling to show they belong rather than risk being marginal: "While most students experience some degree of uncertainty and competency crisis during their first year, working-class students face the additional pressure of being cultural outsiders (Granfield 2013: 149)." **Alexa**, a student introduced in chapter 5, recalls, "This was another part of socialization in my life, when I had to learn how to fit into the social norms and behaviors of my surrounding community so [that] I would not look like an outsider. Many people in these social class type of situations, use a sort of stigma management to ensure that even though they are of a lower class, they are going to mask this fact and try to transform so that people think they are part of the upper class (Granfield 2013: 145)." We

* "Middle-class" here is Aaron's description; we are directly quoting from his autoethnography. Based on Aaron's description of his living conditions and his parents' educational background, we would characterize him as a member of the working class (a lower socioeconomic status than middle class). To the extent that he is "middle class," he is on the margins of this status.

will return to Granfield's ideas again in chapter 3, as they clearly resonate with many contemporary college students.

## ADVICE: WHAT WE (CAN) PROVIDE

Based on research on emerging adults, we would offer the following advice to Devon, Brittany, Charlie, and students with similar stories.

**#adulting #20something #onmyown** In many ways, **Devon** and **Brittany** are typical emerging adults. Being self-focused during emerging adulthood is normal and part of learning to stand on one's own feet. Knowing this information, emerging adults can explain to professors, parents, and other supportive adults that they are not "off track" but going through a common experience for young people in the United States.

**#adulting #20something** Though Devon is not struggling with a particular issue, it would still be helpful for him to talk to an advisor to gain some general advice about college. Though many students are focused on studies when they begin college, they soon realize that studies are only one part of the equation; they must also get used to dealing with laundry, food, and such matters. Then they feel pressure (from parents or others) to further expand their focus and think about long-term career stuff. That is a common college transition.

Even though Devon is doing well in general, he should be careful not to put too much emphasis on mastering the social norms he mentions (for example, learning golfing to enhance his long-term career goals). At least as important as learning social norms during college is working on forming an authentic self, connecting with people in a genuine way, not merely as a means to an end (such as getting a job later). Students need to truly experience college, and learn from the new people and situations they encounter.

Students who relate to Devon need to focus on the big picture. Form a steady plan. It is important to have a life plan in college, especially during the first year. This includes something as small as doing laundry all the way up through making time for quality studying. The plan will help ensure that it is all integrated. The second piece of advice is to learn from Devon's story that it is important to form authentic connections with people. Meeting people strategically for job opportunities is fine, but it is important first to connect genuinely with people who are similar and different, and to allow oneself to be changed in positive ways by these interactions.

**#onmyown** Students that resonate with **Brittany** should remember that it is common to arrive in college and be surprised by all the out-of-classroom adjustments that have to be made. College is different than past experiences, and this is good. It can cause some stress, however, because students are trying to decide where they fit in. When encountering new values and norms, many wonder whether to reject what they once took for granted, and to question which of the norms from childhood still matter. But students need to embrace this process by remembering who they are at root. Our advice for students like Brittany is to embrace that they are in control of what changes they will make. We advise students to question their assumptions about campus life. It may seem that everyone is drinking and hooking up, but that actually happens less than students think. Although one group of students does that, another group is completely different, and there are at least ten different groups of students in between those opposite ends of the spectrum. We thus advise students to be careful not to overgeneralize. The other point is to form personal values by being focused on the broader picture of where individual decisions are leading, and in what direction a student is heading.

Changing as an individual is an important part of emerging adulthood and college life. Amid these changes, however, people are not abandoning their true selves. People do not simply become somebody completely different, or wind up as someone that they do not want to be, especially if they reflect on what they value and who they want to become. We advise students to remember that there are people on campus that can help in their journey, such as advisors and professors, when they are outside the classroom. Professors or advisors can be a bridge of sorts between what life was like growing up and what it is like now. They can stand between those two cultural scenes and assist students in navigating new terrain. A key piece of advice: do not be afraid to ask for help.

**#wheretheparty #yolo** In **Charlie's** story it is clear how different daily life can be in college. Students can do what they want—when they want. It truly is a great time in life, but it comes with a lot of new decisions. Many students plunge in head first, and some crash hard. That is especially common when people have in mind the "movie version" of college, envisioning that it is all about having fun. It is easy to get caught up in that. Most college students struggle at first with their newfound freedom. It may take a while to decide how much time in the day should be devoted to academics, how much should go to extracurricular activities, and how much should go to "fun." All three of these are important! However students choose to spend leisure time, they can benefit from meeting new people, trying new things, and discussing ideas learned in class with friends.

One of our biggest pieces of advice for students is to reflect on what they truly want out of college. During college, students are discovering who they are, where they are going, and, most importantly, what they want out of college. Everybody approaches college in their own way, but there are also some shared experiences. It comes down to finding balance. College is different than high school, not just in the classroom but in campus life as well. Explore a variety of activities, both social and academic. Decide what is right, and then spend time accordingly. Everyone else is exploring their goals, desires, and even their party habits too. Do not be afraid when it gets difficult to juggle all these new choices, and do not worry about setbacks. Choose activities that are meaningful and that help to explore what college life has to offer. It is all fine!

That said, it is also normal to get stressed during college, and colleges have counseling centers where students can get support when feeling anxious. Just talking through the stress with a counselor can help. As intimidating as it may be to sit down with professors and advisors, it is also important that students talk to people on campus and contextualize their advice by role.

Another piece of advice that we have for students like Charlie is to reflect on their assumptions. Charlie mentions seeing students that are partying just as much as she is and still making good grades. That could be the case, but maybe they are doing some things that Charlie is not. She could connect with those people outside of parties and see if she can study with them, or at least ask them how it is going, how they do it. A lot of times, a situation like Charlie's is based on assumptions that are false. Maybe her peers are studying way more than she realizes, or maybe they are partying less than she thinks. The people she sees at a party may have been there only twenty minutes while she was there for three hours. We have to question our assumptions and connect with the people who seem to have it all together, to see if that's true.

A further tip to consider: step outside the situation and talk to someone. Start with an advisor, a faculty mentor, a peer mentor, or the counseling center. A trip to a health clinic or counseling center doesn't require a life-threatening situation. There are always multiple people that can be approached. Start by talking about studying. Then casually mention not having enough time for studying, and then mention social life, without having to be specific. There are many ways to handle that. Just talking out the issue with someone not in the situation helps.

Our final piece of advice to students like Charlie is to embrace the change while remembering who they are, how they grew up, and what they liked about themselves going into college. Connect on campus with what you like, and seek challenges to grow in positive ways. Be okay with change, with evolving and learning and a whole new way of doing things. Also students need to know that they are in charge of that process. When it seems like things are spinning out of control, talk to people, remember to be intentional, and reflect on what you want out of college. Connect with people; seek advice; and then make decisions.

We also offer a few general pieces of advice. Our author team consists of faculty, instructors, advisors, and higher education staff. Each voice represents the kinds of responses that students can receive from people in different roles across campus. Most students are at least mildly confused by whom to go to for what, and we often experience (and have committed ourselves!) blunders in approaching people in certain roles with questions that are better suited for other roles. Students would benefit from knowing that, for example, faculty office hours are helpful for certain kinds of sup-port, while meeting with advisors is helpful for others.

Gaining clarity on who can provide what kinds of support not only reduces the chances of awkward blunders in going to the wrong person, it also ensures that students gain the best social resources when expend-ing their time and avoid frustration (or even apathy) in taking ownership of their own learning. Most people choose to work on college campuses because they truly enjoy supporting young people, but many are also incredibly busy and can sometimes seem off-putting to students who approach them with questions that are mismatched to their roles. For example, it is unlikely a faculty member will know how many more cred-its are needed to complete a dual degree across colleges, and they could seem bothered by the question. That question would be better suited for an advisor who serves students across campus. Likewise, it is not ter-ribly helpful to ask during an advising appointment designed to select courses for the coming semester how best to find an internship within a particular field that could lead to a paid position. This is better-suited for a faculty member, who has a deeper knowledge of and connection to that field.

Nobody expects incoming college students to have all this figured out. But some students do know more about this than others, and they can "hit the ground running" by engaging with the appropriate campus resources. This cuts down on the amount of time spent running around, feeling like each person recommends asking someone else. This is why seven different authors, from the perspective of four different campus roles, can provide valuable direction. It is also worth saying that we do not assume that dis-connect between campus resources and students is only a student issue. Parents can play a role in helping advise their children, and academics and professionals can do a better job communicating this. And through our diverse author team, we provide academic and professional readers with a model for how to build a more cohesive, relevant, and tailored set of responses to students' issues.

## The Chapters Ahead

The second chapter explains further how the life stage of emerging adult-hood, and the changes that created it, help to make sense of modern col-lege students. Students will learn how experiences with moving, changing identities, romantic partnering, and breakups all fit within the life stage tasks of establishing identity while forming intimate romantic relation-ships and friendships. Achieving a better grasp of how transitioning into adulthood looks for young people today makes it easier for students to explain themselves to others.

Chapter 3 covers the value of college: why it is important to earn a degree for specific skills (or "human capital") and credentials, and how doing well in college is largely about acquiring "cultural capital," aka learn-ing the rules of the game. This third chapter also addresses how students' social class backgrounds affect how easy, hard, or different college can be.

The fourth chapter explains how exploring and forming a personal and social identity is key to learning to navigate college well. In chapter 4, students will learn that one key to college success is taking ownership of learning and exposing themselves to a variety of classes and majors in order to decide what is the best fit for them.

Chapter 5 teaches students about the importance of having resiliency amid challenging experiences during college. College also presents the opportunity to reflect on childhood experiences in families, cultures, groups, and within organizations. For students, reflecting on how their backgrounds affect current choices is crucial for shaping a personal and professional story that can guide choices in college, frame personal state-ments, and point toward potential career paths after college.

The sixth chapter introduces several students who are struggling with identity as they navigate diversity at a large public university. Some find the university to have a greater degree of diversity than their smaller hometowns, while others came from urban settings more diverse than their campus. Many of the students share stories of struggling to understand how they fit in, as well as how to make sense of others' attitudes about diversity in terms of race and ethnicity, biculturalism, and immigration, along with gender, sexuality, and religion. In chapter 6, students reflect on experiences with inclusion and exclusion during college, and many come to understand these experiences as part of larger social structures. Students will also learn how to harness their identities as a personal strength, while also finding others who are similar enough to understand and support their perspective, values, or interests.

Chapter 7 shows students that another important aspect of college is figuring out how to become a leader. Being a leader requires recognizing one's personal strengths and learning how to engage those strengths on campus, which builds skills and experiences for later civic engagement. The goal in this chapter is to enable students to use college in a way that helps them find their way through future life changes and carve their own paths in future endeavors. Moreover, this seventh chapter presents several student stories that suggest the wide array of options for finding a niche group or activity on campus, which makes students feel integrated on campus and gives them valuable leadership skills.

The eighth chapter, which concludes the book, describes why college provides a safe place to explore different career options. In chapter 8, students will learn how switching majors, interning, working as a research assistant, and talking with professors are all excellent ways to test out their major, to see whether a career in that field is a good fit. This chapter addresses tips for major changes, talking with parents about desired careers, finding a vocation or career path, and shaping professional identity. The book culminates with a section about how to navigate college, and life generally, with research-based decisions.

## FURTHER READING ONLINE

- Here is a post about what "adulting" means: Steinmetz, Katy, June 8, 2016, "This Is What 'Adulting' Means," *Time*, retrieved from http://time.com/4361866/adulting-definition-meaning/.

- Our favorite GIF of adulting depicts a man tumbling backward on an escalator while the escalator keeps carrying him up, posted here: http://www.psherzog.org/single-post/2017/06/09/The-Perfect-GIF-of-Adulting.

- As described in the blog, this GIF implies that growing up can be hard: Kelner, Simon, September 3, 2015, "For the Twenty-Somethings of Today, Growing Up Is Hard to Do," *Independent*, retrieved from http://www.independent.co.uk/voices/comment/for-the-twenty-somethings-of-today-growing-up-is-hard-to-do-10485276.html.

- This TED Talk covers what people think they need to be happy and successful, as compared to what research shows is needed to experience feelings of success and happiness: Waldinger, Robert, November 2015, "What Makes a Good Life? Lessons from the Longest Study on Happiness," TedTalk, retrieved from https://www.ted.com/talks/robert_waldinger_what_makes_a_good_life_lessons_from_the_longest_study_on_happiness?language=en.

- Finally, it is important to know that parts of college, and of growing up generally, can be tough: Grossman, Nick, December 10, 2014, "Everyone Is Broken and Life Is Hard" [Blog post], retrieved from http://www.nickgrossman.is/2014/everyone-is-broken-and-life-is-hard/.

- It is important for students to give themselves, and each other, a break. There is a great deal happening in the midst of the fun time that college can be, and students need to rest too. These years in college are important, and life-shaping, but they are not the end of the story. Do not be like Bryan Adams, saying that these years were the best of his life (https://www.youtube.com/watch?v=9f06QZCVUHg). Instead, build a life that keeps getting better, and see college as a key that will open doors that you want to walk through.

## NOTES

1.  Friedman, Thomas. 2016. *Thank You for Being Late: An Optimist's Guide to Thriving in the Age of Accelerations*. New York: Macmillan.
2.  Giordano, Peggy C., Monica A. Longmore, and Wendy D. Manning. 2006. "Gender and the Meanings of Adolescent Romantic Relationships: A Focus on Boys." *American Sociological Review* 71(2): 260–287.

    Hart-Brinson, Peter. 2014. "Discourse of Generations: The Influence of Cohort, Period, and Ideology in Americans' Talk about Same-Sex Marriage." *American Journal of Cultural Sociology* 2(2): 221–252.

    Lueptow, Lloyd B. 1980. "Social Change and Sex-Role Change in Adolescent Orientations toward Life, Work, and Achievement: 1964–1975." *Social Psychology Quarterly* 43(1): 48–59.
3.  Arnett, Jeffrey Jensen. 2015. *Emerging Adulthood: The Winding Road from the Late Teens Through the Twenties* (2nd ed.). New York: Oxford University Press.

    Arnett, Jeffrey Jensen. 2007. "Emerging Adulthood: What Is It, and What Is It Good For?" *Child Development Perspectives* 1(2): 68–73.

    Arnett, Jeffrey Jensen. 2000. "Emerging Adulthood: A Theory of Development from the Late Teens through the Twenties." *American Psychologist* 55(5): 469–480.

    Arum, Richard, and Josipa Roksa. 2014. *Aspiring Adults Adrift: Tentative Transitions of College Graduates*. Chicago: University of Chicago Press.

    Arum, Richard, and Josipa Roksa. 2010. *Academically Adrift: Limited Learning on College Campuses*. Chicago: University of Chicago Press.

    Berzin, Stephanie Cosner, and Allison C. De Marco. 2010. "Understanding the Impact of Poverty on Critical Events in Emerging Adulthood." *Youth & Society* 42(2): 278–300.

    Settersten, Richard, and Barbara E. Ray. 2010. *Not Quite Adults: Why 20-Somethings Are Choosing a Slower Path to Adulthood, and Why It's Good for Everyone*. New York: Bantam.
4.  Browne, Irene. 1995. "The Baby Boom and Trends in Poverty, 1967–1987." *Social Forces* 73(3): 1071–1095.
5.  Mendenhall, Ruby, Ariel Kalil, Laurel J. Spindel, and Cassandra M. D. Hart. 2008. "Job Loss at Mid-Life: Managers and Executives Face the 'New Risk Economy.'" *Social Forces* 87(1):185–209.
6.  Cooper, Marianne. 2014. *Cut Adrift: Families in Insecure Times*. Berkeley: University of California Press.
7.  Krahn, Harvey J., Andrea L. Howard, and Nancy L. Galambos. 2014. "Exploring or Floundering? The Meaning of Employment and Educational Fluctuations in Emerging Adulthood." *Youth & Society* 47(2): 245–266.
8.  Carnevale, Anthony P., Andrew R. Hanson, and Artem Gulish. 2013. *Failure to Launch: Structural Shift and the New Lost Generation*. Washington, DC: Georgetown Public Policy Institute, Georgetown University.

9.  Settersten, Richard, and Barbara E. Ray. 2010. *Not Quite Adults: Why 20-Somethings Are Choosing a Slower Path to Adulthood, and Why It's Good for Everyone.* New York: Bantam.

10. Mettler, Suzanne. 2014. *Degrees of Inequality: How the Politics of Higher Education Sabotaged the American Dream.* New York: Basic Books.

Mullen, Ann L. 2010. *Degrees of Inequality.* Baltimore, MD: Johns Hopkins University Press.

National Center for Education Statistics. 2008. *Ten Years After College: Comparing the Employment Experiences of 1992–93 Bachelor's Degree Recipients with Academic and Career-Oriented Majors* (NCES 2008-155). U.S. Department of Education. Retrieved from http://nces.ed.gov/pubsearch/pubsinfo.asp?pubid=2008155.

National Center for Education Statistics. 2011. *2008–09 Baccalaureate and Beyond Longitudinal Study: A First Look at Recent College Graduates* (NCES 2011-236), Table 3: "Time to Degree." U.S. Department of Education. Retrieved from http://nces.ed.gov/fastfacts/display.asp?id=569.

National Center for Education Statistics. 2015. *The Condition of Education 2015* (NCES 2015-144), Annual Earnings of Young Adults. U.S. Department of Education.

Torche, Florencia. 2011. "Is a College Degree Still the Great Equalizer? Intergenerational Mobility across Levels of Schooling in the United States." *American Journal of Sociology* 117(3):763–807.

11. Reardon, S. F., R. Baker, and D. Klasik. 2012. "Race, Income, and Enrollment Patterns in Highly Selective Colleges, 1982–2004." Retrieved from http://cepa.stanford.edu/content/race-income-and-enrollment-patterns-highly-selective-colleges-1982-2004.

12. Houle, Jason N. 2013. "Disparities in Debt: Parents' Socioeconomic Resources and Young Adult Student Loan Debt." *Sociology of Education* 87(1): 53–69.

13. Porter, Katherine (ed.). 2012. *Broke: How Debt Bankrupts the Middle Class.* Palo Alto, CA: Stanford University Press.

14. Armstrong, Elizabeth A., and Laura T. Hamilton. 2013. *Paying for the Party: How College Maintains Inequality.* Cambridge, MA: Harvard University Press.

Arum, Richard, and Josipa Roksa. 2014. *Aspiring Adults Adrift: Tentative Transitions of College Graduates.* Chicago: University of Chicago Press.

Bozick, Robert, Karl Alexander, Doris Entwisle, Susan Dauber, and Kerri Kerr. 2010. "Framing the Future: Revisiting the Place of Educational Expectations in Status Attainment." *Social Forces* 88(5): 2027–2052.

Hällsten, Martin. 2010. "The Structure of Educational Decision Making and Consequences for Inequality: A Swedish Test Case." *American Journal of Sociology* 116(3):806–854.

Hamilton, Laura T. 2013. "More Is More or More Is Less? Parental Financial Investments during College." *American Sociological Review* 78(1):70–95.

15. Osgood, D. Wayne, E. Michael Foster, Constance Flanagan, and Gretchen R. Ruth (eds.). 2005. *On Your Own without a Net: The Transition to Adulthood for Vulnerable Populations.* Berkeley: University of Chicago Press.

Radmacher, Kimberley, and Margarita Azmitia. 2013. "Unmasking Class: How Upwardly Mobile Poor and Working-Class Emerging Adults Negotiate an 'Invisible' Identity." *Emerging Adulthood* 1(4): 314–329.

Silva, Jennifer M. 2012. "Constructing Adulthood in an Age of Uncertainty." *American Sociological Review* 77(4): 505–522.

Silva, Jennifer M. 2013. *Coming Up Short: Working-Class Adulthood in an Age of Uncertainty.* New York: Oxford University Press.

16. Lareau, Annette. 2011. "Class Differences in Parents' Information and Intervention in the Lives of Young Adults," In Annette Lareau, *Unequal Childhoods: Class, Race, and Family Life* (2nd ed., pp. 305–311). Berkeley: University of California Press.

Lareau, Annette. 2015. "Cultural Knowledge and Social Inequality." *American Sociological Review* 80(1): 1–27.

17. Strayhorn, Terrell L. 2013. "Modeling the Determinants of College Readiness for Historically Underrepresented Students at 4-Year Colleges and Universities: A National Investigation." *American Behavioral Scientist* 58(8): 972–993.

18. Conley, David T., and Elizabeth M. French. 2014. "Student Ownership of Learning as a Key Component of College Readiness." *American Behavioral Scientist* 58(8): 1018–1034.

19. Bandura, Albert. 2006. "Guide for Constructing Self-Efficacy Scales." In F. Pajares and T. Urdan (Eds.), *Self-Efficacy Beliefs of Adolescents* (Vol. 5, pp. 307–337). Greenwich, CT: Information Age Publishing.

Choi, Bo Y., Heerak Park, Eunjoo Yang, Seul K. Lee, Yedana Lee, and Sang M. Lee. 2012. "Understanding Career Decision Self-Efficacy: A Meta-Analytic Approach." *Journal of Career Development* 39(5): 443–460.

Hoover, Kathleen. 2003. "The Relationship of Locus of Control and Self-Efficacy to Academic Achievement of First-Year Students." *Journal of the First-Year Experience & Students in Transition* 15(2): 103–123.

Komarraju, Meera, Alex Ramsey, and Virginia Rinella. 2013. "Cognitive and Non-Cognitive Predictors of College Readiness and Performance: Role of Academic Discipline." *Learning and Individual Differences* 24: 103–109.

Krumrei-Mancuso, Elizabeth J., Fred B. Newton, Eunhee Kim, and Dan Wilcox. 2013. "Psychosocial Factors Predicting First-Year College Student Success." *Journal of College Student Development* 54(3): 247–266.

Olson, Joann S. 2014. "Opportunities, Obstacles, and Options: First-Generation College Graduates and Social Cognitive Career Theory." *Journal of Career Development* 41(3): 199–217.

Wright, Stephen L., Michael A. Jenkins-Guarnieri, and Jennifer L. Murdock. 2013. "Career Development among First-Year College Students: College Self-Efficacy, Student Persistence, and Academic Success." *Journal of Career Development* 40(4): 292–310.

20. Betz, Nancy E., and Fred H. Borgen. 2009. "Comparative Effectiveness of CAPA and FOCUS Online Career Assessment Systems with Undecided College Students." *Journal of Career Assessment* 17(4): 351–366.

Chung, Y. Barry. 2002. "Career Decision-Making Self-Efficacy and Career Commitment: Gender and Ethnic Differences among College Students." *Journal of Career Development* 28(4): 277–284.

Grabowski, Stanislaw, and Valerie Sessa. 2014. "Academic Engagement among First-Year College Students: Precollege Antecedents." *Journal of the First-Year Experience & Students in Transition* 26(1): 37–61.

Hansen, Michele J., and Joan S. Pedersen. 2012. "An Examination of the Effects of Career Development Courses on Career Decision-Making Self-Efficacy, Adjustment to College, Learning Integration, and Academic Success." *Journal of the First-Year Experience & Students in Transition* 24(2): 33–61.

Olson, Joann S. 2014. "Opportunities, Obstacles, and Options: First-Generation College Graduates and Social Cognitive Career Theory." *Journal of Career Development* 41(3): 199–217.

21. Terriquez, Veronica, and Oded Gurantz. 2015. "Financial Challenges in Emerging Adulthood and Students' Decisions to Stop Out of College." *Emerging Adulthood* 3(3): 204–214.

22. Caulum, Melissa S. 2007. "Postadolescent Brain Development: A Disconnect between Neuroscience, Emerging Adults, and the Corrections System." *Wisconsin Law Review* 2007(3): 730–758.

Luecken, Linda J., and Jenna L. Gress. 2010. "Early Adversity and Resilience in Emerging Adulthood." In John W. Reich, Alex J. Zautra, and John Stuart Hall (Eds.), *Handbook of Adult Resilience* (pp. 238–257). New York: Guilford Press.

Pharo, Henry, Clark Sim, Mikala Graham, Julien Gross, and Harlene Hayne. 2011. "Risky Business: Executive Function, Personality, and Reckless Behavior during Adolescence and Emerging Adulthood." *Behavioral Neuroscience* 125(6): 970–978.

Taber-Thomas, Bradley, and Koraly Perez-Edgar. 2016. "Emerging Adulthood Brain Development." In Jeffrey Jensen Arnett (Ed.), *Oxford Handbook of Emerging Adulthood*. New York: Oxford University Press.

23. Crosnoe, Robert, and Monica Kirkpatrick Johnson. 2011. "Research on Adolescence in the Twenty-First Century." *Annual Review of Sociology* 37(1):439–460.

Schlosser, Lewis, and William Sedlacek. 2001. "The Relationship between Undergraduate Students' Perceived Past Academic Success and Perceived Academic Self-Concept." *Journal of the First-Year Experience & Students in Transition* 13(2): 95–105.

24. Giudici, Francesco, and Aaron M. Pallas. 2014. "Social Origins and Post-High School Institutional Pathways: A Cumulative Dis/advantage Approach." *Social Science Research* 44: 103–113.

25. Mirowsky, John, and Catherine E. Ross. 2007. "Life Course Trajectories of Perceived Control and Their Relationship to Education." *American Journal of Sociology* 112(5): 1339–1382.

26. Radmacher, Kimberley and Margarita Azmitia. 2013. "Unmasking Class How Upwardly Mobile Poor and Working-Class Emerging Adults Negotiate an 'Invisible' Identity." *Emerging Adulthood* 1(4):314–329.

27. Chambliss, Daniel F., and Christopher G. Takacs. 2014. *How College Works*. Cambridge, MA: Harvard University Press.

28. Arnett, Jeffrey Jensen. 2015. *Emerging Adulthood: The Winding Road from the Late Teens Through the Twenties* (2nd ed.). New York: Oxford University Press.

29. Dyer, Gwynne. 2013. "Anybody's Son Will Do." In Susan J. Ferguson (Ed.), *Mapping the Social Landscape: Readings in Sociology* (7th ed., pp. 158–168). New York: McGraw-Hill Education.

30. Granfield, Robert. 2013. "Making It by Faking It: Working-Class Students in an Elite Academic Environment." In Susan J. Ferguson (Ed.), *Mapping the Social Landscape: Readings in Sociology* (7th ed., pp. 145–157). New York: McGraw-Hill Education.

31. Goffman, Erving. 1986. *Stigma: Notes on the Management of Spoiled Identity*. Parsippany, NJ: Simon & Schuster.

# How to Understand
# Emerging Adulthood

Chapter 2 contextualizes the changing life course within larger economic, social, and cultural trends, and discusses the role of contemporary higher education in understanding those changes. The second chapter helps to make sense of modern college students by explaining the life stage of emerging adulthood, along with the changes that have created an elongation of life course development, including longer periods of transition into adulthood. In chapter 2, students learn how experiences with moving, changing identities, and romantic partnering and breakups all fit within the life stage tasks of establishing identity while forming intimate romantic relationships and friendships. Achieving a better grasp of how transitioning into adulthood looks for young people today makes it easier for students to understand themselves and explain themselves to others.

*The Science of College*. Patricia S. Herzog, Casey T. Harris, Shauna A. Morimoto, Shane W. Barker, Jill G. Wheeler, A. Justin Barnum, and Terrance L. Boyd, Oxford University Press (2020) © Oxford University Press.
DOI: 10.1093/oso/9780190934507.001.0001

This chapter explains in more detail how contemporary college students are different from students who enrolled a generation ago. First, we introduce more stories from students who describe in their own words what it is like to begin college today. Next, we summarize research on the changing economy, workforce opportunities, and an increasing number of moves as people relocate for jobs. We also talk about changes to marriage and families, discussing what some scholars call the "marriage-go-round." All of this affects what it means to grow up, and cause delays in the forms of "settling down" that most people consider signs of adulthood. Plus, we discuss changes surrounding higher education, including rising costs and questions about whether the financial investment in college will pay off. These trends and questions underline the need for critical thinking skills, which this chapter's advice will help students develop.

## STUDENT STORIES: WHAT WE EXPERIENCE

We begin with stories of three students—**Sanjana**, **Troy**, and **Derrick**—who explain several of the experiences that are common for incoming college students and that are often experienced by emerging adults in general.

---

**#movingagain**: I'm moving again, caught up in a whirlwind of always changing situations, wondering if I am—or how I could possibly be—the same person I was two years ago.
**Sanjana** explained this in her own words with the following:

> I still remember the uneasiness I felt in my stomach as I boarded a plane for the first time, leaving my hometown of twelve years and starting a new life in California. Flash forward 8 years, two more moves, far too many flights, and I am preparing to move all over again. However, I can't help but notice how different I have become within those 8 years. Moving to different states has been the single biggest influence of who I am today. Each state had

---

its own unique culture, people, and life experiences that have permanently changed me as a person.

**#changingidentity**: Wow, high school seems like ancient history! Hard to believe that just four months ago I was in homeroom wondering when the bell would ring. Now I can go to class when I want to, have a totally new group of friends, and can barely remember my home address.

**Troy** explained the dramatic shift that most students feel from their high school identity to the new version being shaped in college: "In the past year, a lot has changed in my life as I have made the transition from high school to college. Since I moved out of state, I have two completely different lives in two entirely different social environments. As a result of this, I sometimes feel caught between two places."

**#brokenhearted**: Anybody else having trouble concentrating? I'm still not over her, and I just can't focus. But I have a test tomorrow. Help!

**Derrick** and Serena split up. He had followed her to college because they dated throughout senior year and talked about their future together. Within the first six weeks of their first semester though, she said they each needed space to become who they are meant to be but that they would always be an important part of one another's lives. Derrick was more reserved, while outgoing Serena made friends easily, and he didn't realize how much he depended on her personality to meet new people. He has not only lost his girlfriend, but much of his circle of friends too. He had only chosen to go to this school because she wanted to, and now he is stuck. Derrick recognizes the tremendous opportunity a college education affords him, and he does not want to take that for granted. But he can't help being distracted. Every time he tries to write a paper, his mind wanders to Serena, and where he went wrong. How did it all just evaporate? This all comes to a head when he forgets to submit an assignment and finds himself in his professor's office trying to explain how he is still the A student he has always been, despite having an F.

## SCIENCE: WHAT WE KNOW

These students provide a glimpse into common difficulties among young adults, including moving, changing romantic partnerships, and grappling with identity as their lives are splintered across multiple locations and significant others. In a book called *Our Kids: The American Dream in Crisis*, Robert Putnam[1] summarizes the broader context to which these students refer. People are getting married and having kids later in life, so romantic partnerships change—often multiple times—throughout emerging adulthood and beyond. College-educated women delay childbearing more than less educated women, while Americans in the lowest third of the income distribution are more likely to have children outside of marriage than within it. Moreover, blended families and "multi-partner fertility" scenarios, in which children in the same household were born of different parents, are more common today. In *Labor's Love Lost: The Rise and Fall of the Working-Class Family in America*, Andrew Cherlin refers to marital turnover as the "marriage-go-round."[2] People are increasingly getting on and off the carousel of marriage, or choosing to cohabit with romantic partners instead of marrying at all. Some scholars refer to this as relationship "churning," to reflect the degree of mix-up and stirring that occurs as people sort their relationships.[3] But these trends are not merely the result of people deliberately choosing to marry and have kids later; they are likely also the outcome of economic changes.

Emerging adults are experiencing these changes to romantic partnerships and family life in the midst of a changing economic context. The US economy has undergone a "structural shift" in which the available jobs and skills needed for most jobs have changed markedly in the past decade.[4] In a report on the economy called *Failure to Launch*, Anthony Carnevale and colleagues state the following:

> The model of the labor market that presumed entry at age 18 and exit at age 65 is obsolete, and instead, young people often start their careers later, after developing more human capital from postsecondary education and training, and work experience from internships,

work-study, mentorships, fellowships, job shadowing, and part-time work. Young people today change jobs more frequently between the ages of 18 and 25 and only one out of 10 describes his or her current job as a career (Carnevale et al. 2013: 4).

These delays in establishing career paths mean that the significant adult developmental markers happen less in the early 20s today than they do in the 30s, and often after multiple moves.

Taking these trends together, the ways that people transition into adulthood are more variable: there are multiple options for when, how, and in what order to take on adult roles, such as completing education, establishing careers, forming long-term romantic partnerships, and having children. In fact, one study found that there are more than 60 possible sequences in the timing and order of acquiring adult roles.[5] Sociologists view all these options as a combination of personal choices and available opportunities shaped through a process of personal agency (individual choices) within larger social forces (such as family background, economic changes, culture of origin, global and national political policies).[6] Many young people may prefer to have children later in life than their parents did, but it is unlikely that they prefer to put off earning a stable income. Plus having kids later may be a choice made in response to difficulties establishing economic stability. In essence, it takes young people longer to become adults not only because they want to spend a long time developing themselves but also because of limited and changing economic options, shifts in cultural values regarding the centrality of work and family, and a rising need for advanced education.[7] Coupling this with Maslow's hierarchy of needs, the longer time spent with unsettled belongingness, love, and esteem needs can delay a focus on self-actualization: fulfilling one's potential, in college and in life after college.[8]

For individual students in the midst of chasing these markers of adulthood, the process can feel disorienting. Students are juggling multiple senses of self in that the different social groups with which they interact can bring out one kind of personal identity or another, not always feeling like these different identities fit together into a coherent whole. Identities are also renegotiated as new friend groups and romantic partners[9] emerge, or as old friend groups or previous romantic partnerships dissolve. In the midst of these changes, emerging adults are attempting to form their college-enabled professional identities, all while also forming intimate connections, in friendships and with potential long-term romantic partners.[10] Many studies find that the academic and career goals of romantic partners and friend groups are strong predictors of an individual's school and career goals.[11] Some of this may be because people tend to hang out with others who are similar to them, including finding friends and romantic partners who have similar levels of academic achievement and career identity. But it is also likely that this is due to causal relationships, meaning that people are influenced by the people they hang out with, and the choices for leisure with friends and romantic partners can directly impact the amount of time people invest in school work, as well as the extent to which students form particular career paths.

Thus, dismantling an emerging professional identity may spill over into pressure to dissolve a new romantic relationship, or a split with a romantic partner may result in a move, a change of friends, or a new job, or, in the most impactful of circumstances, a change in all of these simultaneously. Such turmoil in work and personal life can lead to emerging adults experiencing "existential crises"—the psychological distress of having to reconsider foundational senses of meaning. "Meaning frameworks" guide people's ability to make sense of new situations, but collisions in ways of making meaning can cause disorienting confusion and take considerable effort to resolve. The many changes of emerging adulthood can cause people—like Sanjana, Troy, and Derrick—to reevaluate all that they once took for granted, questioning what they thought they knew, what they want to believe, and who they want to help them make sense of it all.[12] Broadly, this means emerging adults are learning how to balance their ability to personally choose their own paths while building awareness of all the different social influences that surround their individual choices, including social media interactions. In this way, navigating college, and life generally, is a *social construction*. We return to this issue more in chapter 5.

Amid these struggles to establish themselves, young people are also confronting a changing array of available careers. The kinds of jobs available to most current college students are fairly different from those available to their parents, and the skills that most contemporary employers desire are also distinct. Most important is establishing transferable skills: talents built in college and other experiences that can later be transferred to career skill sets. In an article called "Voices of Employers," Varda Konstam[13] reports that many employers, often from the Baby Boom generation, view emerging adults (who are from the millennial and younger generations) as "intelligent and flexible," but found that they "did not bring valued skill sets to the work place." Konstam explains:

> Employers are increasingly privileging the learning ability of their employees, that is their "ability to put together disparate bits of information" on demand, as the need emerges (Friedman 2014, para. 3). They are interested in employees' capacity to solve problems, using their leadership skills when appropriate, and having sufficient humility to know when to take a back seat and relinquish power if a fellow employee has a better solution to the presenting problem. Employers are looking beyond traditional metrics such as GPA, and are devising metrics that will predict on-the-job skills such as flexibility, humility, leadership, and know-how within a context of a team of fellow employees (Konstam 2015: 163–164).

Echoing this, Richard Arum and Josipa Roksa, in their book *Aspiring Adults Adrift: Tentative Transitions of College Graduates*,[14] discuss how many disgruntled employers are critical of college graduates for not having the skills they desire. Employers place emphasis on needing a generic set of skills produced by higher education. Rather than emphasizing job-specific training, which is likely to be outdated within a few years, employers say they want recent hires to have the ability to learn, ensuring they will acquire the knowledge they need on the job over time. They want college graduates with evident critical thinking abilities:

> Recent surveys of employers have highlighted dissatisfaction with the preparation of college graduates, noting that only approximately a

quarter of college graduates entering the labor market have excellent skills in critical thinking and problem solving, and only 16 percent have excellent written communication . . . "Woefully unprepared" is how one employer described college graduates . . . employers tended to ding bachelor's-degree holders for lacking basic workplace proficiencies, like adaptability, communication skills, and the ability to solve complex problems (Arum & Roksa 2014, pp. 19–20).

The majority of young people in the United States show up for a college education, but many of these students begin college thinking their primary task is just to be there. Since the prior generation was more likely to go to college than the generation before it, many entering students expect to go to college merely because their parents did[15] (see the student story about **Ellie** in chapter 8 for more on this). But this is not enough.

Succeeding in college is about acquiring the skills needed to establish stable careers. Showing up and doing just enough to wind up with a degree is not sufficient. Students need to develop lifelong critical thinking skills. Achieving this, however, is difficult during the highly volatile stage of emerging adulthood, during which students experience tremendous fluctuations in identity and intimacy, especially within the context of engagement on social media. This is why George Kuh (2008)[16] recommends "high-impact educational practices" for incoming college students (see further reading section), all of which share an approach to helping incoming first-year students adjust to the hidden curriculum of college. Also key is Bloom's taxonomy of critical thinking skills. (e.g., Anderson et al. 2000).[17] For example, in high school teachers often give review sessions for exams, and these reviews often reveal many of the answers for the exam. In college, however, many instructors do not provide review sessions at all, and when they do, they are often more focused on reviewing the key topics, less close to answers on exams, and instead expect students to fill in the topics through studying outside of class time. Similarly, on the job a boss often expects an employee to meet a deadline with little to no guidance.

While there is a progression in both the freedom and responsibility expected of emerging adults, many incoming first-year students (and later, upper-level students ) struggle to make the adjustments needed as they advance to higher levels. These students, like those in the stories at the start of this chapter, are beginning to socially construct their own identities. Identity construction is done within a new recognition that emerging adults have freedom to choose their path. At the same time, past experiences and backgrounds shape opportunities to some degree. Notably, digital footprints are a relatively new aspect to self-and-social identity construction, which like other aspects of identity formation also deserve conscious thought and attention. As with other social representations, reputations online can leave positive footprints that help to support a strong academic and professional identity, or alternatively can cause damage.[18] Thus, emerging adults can be empowered to shape society as they develop into adults while, at the same time, they leave behind any naivety that everything is within their power and controlled by them alone. Society shapes what it means to be a person of different ages, and wise emerging adults consider these social influences even while they navigate their choices through college.

## ADVICE: WHAT WE PROVIDE

The advice sections of each chapter are intended to help students develop needed critical thinking skills, in this case about themselves and their college pathways. Based on research about employers and changing labor markets, we—in particular the portion of our authorship team that are student development and student support practitioners—advise students to treat college as an opportunity to explore how different majors can lead to various careers after graduating. While college is not about vocational training specifically—since its purpose is to facilitate the development of well-rounded people who can work in a variety of careers in their lifetimes—it is important to talk in the classroom and outside of class about how majors serve careers and aid transitions to work. Through a somewhat hidden curriculum, college teaches students how to put up with doing things that others tell them they have to accomplish. In the course of studying for an exam or writing a paper by a certain date, students are learning much more than the content for the exam or paper. They are also building "soft skills" that employers value: the ability to fight boredom, to put up with mundane tasks, to cope with aspects of working and learning that are not fun, and to work with people from a range of backgrounds.

We—in particular the portion of our authorship team that are faculty members who teach many students in class and visit with many students in office hours—advise students to think of college as practice in per- severance. Especially in the early years, college helps students acquire tenacity, the ability to stick it out stubbornly to achieve the desired end result. Rather than pressuring professors for rubrics and step-by-step instructions on how to get an A, we encourage students to view con- fusing assignments or classes as opportunities to learn how to navigate through vague work assignments. Future employers are unlikely to give rubrics, and "get it done by Friday" may be the extent of the instruc- tions from a boss. Knowing how to write the best report, even without specific instructions, is an important tool for college-educated workers. This is part of developing the general critical thinking skills that employ- ers want, and successful students rise to the occasion. That said, college students do encounter many difficult situations that we do not mean to write off. In what follows, we offer some specific advice related to each of the classic emerging adult experiences our students described at the beginning of this chapter.

**#movingagain** Students who find themselves in a similar situation to **Sanjana** should know they are in good company. It is normal to be impacted and changed in various ways by passing through diverse social environments and encountering new situations. We commend students like Sanjana for their awareness of this process. It is a wonderful thing to be able to understand how social environments actually affect a person— who they become, how they interact with others, and their future. Our first piece of advice, then, is to understand such an experience as normal, even desirable.

We advise other students to learn from Sanjana by recognizing that different social environments affect people in unique ways; the new social environment of college is going to affect everyone.

At the same time, one must recall that the places that students have already been impact them now as well. Sanjana is aware of the change in her life, but she also needs to be aware of the stability. College may be new and exciting, but all of the old influences from previous places are still part of who people are and continue to affect them during college. Emerging into adulthood is a socially constructed process that involves the freedom to choose one's own path, while also recognizing that one's path is affected by social forces that are not fully controlled or chosen by any one person. Our third piece of advice, then, is to reflect on how previous experiences still play a role in students' new and evolving selves. Engage self-awareness to assess feasible choices within real social constraints and opportunities. Do not pretend to have full power, nor to be powerless.

**#changingidentity** Students who resonate with **Troy** should also understand their experiences as normal aspects of college. When students come to college, they begin to adapt to the new environment, the new social settings. We advise students to understand that this comes from a feeling of wanting to belong, to fit in, and to make new friends. It is also common for students to recognize that having new experiences on campus means they are not sharing those experiences with people in their hometown. Many students feel, to a certain extent, that they have left their old friends behind, or that they no longer have much common ground with them. After people have been away from a place for a while and go back, the conversation with old friends can revert to the last set of shared experiences, which could have been two, three, however many years ago. There is so much of life that happened in between that it can highlight what is no longer shared in common. There is nothing wrong with this feeling of separation, of having two different identities—the feeling of fragmentation that Troy describes.

Though to some extent this can be a sad realization, we urge students to understand it as a normal part of college and of life afterward as well. That does not mean that we suggest dismissing the experience. Instead, students should reflect upon the different social contexts that they are part of and consider what that means for the life they are shaping during college. There is no rule that says people have to act a certain way in college, or that people can only be friends with a certain kind of people. We therefore advise students to notice the relationship (both similarities and differences) between experiences in their hometowns and in college. It is also understandable to view different places as separate pieces of a self, so long as students know their task is to work on integrating them.

Troy and students like him would benefit from talking with a caring instructor with whom they feel a sense of connection. Talking in person would help an instructor get a sense for Troy's perspective on the situation. It could also lead to inviting a faculty mentorship. When students view such an experience negatively, we would encourage them to spend some time thinking about the significance of different relationships in their life, to consider where they get emotional stability or emotional fulfillment. We advise students to evaluate the value of these relationships, what they bring to their life, and how important they are to them. Based on that evaluation, we advise students to decide how much energy they want to devote to maintaining these older relationships and how much to growing new relationships.

Most importantly, all students, especially in their first year, must recognize that they need a strong support network, which has to be actively created. Whether that means maintaining ties with friends from home or developing new friends in college, or both, finding emotional stability and enjoying support from one's friends will be crucial in navigating college. Having a good support network enables students to do many things that they would struggle to do without it. A second key takeaway for students who resonate with Troy is that—even while feeling like they are being two different people—they may benefit from reflecting on the ways they are the same person in both places. Identifying one's core self provides a sense of continuity across geographic lines.

**#brokenhearted** For students like Derrick, it is vital to speak with a supportive adult on campus regarding what is getting in the way of academics. If Derrick showed up to one of our offices to talk about his poor performance in class amid the relational challenges he is facing, we would focus on conveying three points to him. First, we would recognize and offer an empathetic understanding of the intense experience he is now immersed in. Specifically, we would acknowledge the pain that Derrick is feeling as he works to dismantle the dreams he had established in his relationship with Serena. In a way, Derrick and Serena shared a marriage-like experience, beginning to form their lives together and envision a shared future. Yet, they had not made a mutual commitment to be married, or participated in a ceremony to demarcate their lives in a shared direction. This can make Derrick's loss more challenging to understand, as some could view him as going through just another breakup. But to Derrick, more was lost than that. The first step then to helping Derrick regain focus on his academic dreams is to acknowledge that he lost something more than a simple romantic relationship; he lost a potential life partner.

Second, we would want to normalize Derrick's experience for him. Drawing on research on emerging adulthood, we would share that one reason that this life stage is both so fantastic and so troubling is that identity and intimacy formation overlap. For prior generations following the normative life course development process, identity construction reached near completion during adolescence, and intimacy formation followed in young adulthood. But now identity formation and intimacy occur in the same period. Throughout life, people have to make decisions based on a particular set of circumstances, but those circumstances can change. When that happens, people need to sit down and reevaluate their lives, goals, objectives, and their sense of self. We advise students in similar circumstances to Derrick to view this challenge as an opportunity to rethink who they are and figure out what they want, or at least to spend some time thinking about these questions. Once people figure out what they want out of life, it is easier to remain focused in the face of adversity. Of course, most of who Derrick is and will be is still the same. Experiencing unsettling experiences present an opportunity to reshape one's identity, but people are also fairly stable underneath. Much like the turbulence of the sea that can be found on the surface, as compared to the calmer waters beneath, people can experience life storms without total devastation to their calmer undercurrents. Yet, a small thunderstorm is different than a hurricane. To the extent that a romantic relationship took on characteristics of a long-term partnership, it can be a hurricane-level devastation. Important here is to understand that this long-term romantic identity is not necessarily represented in the actual duration of the relationship, which may have been quite short, but in the intimate identity the person imagined for the future.

For a student like Derrick, who had plans to build a life with Serena, this breakup is not only emotional, it also disrupts his identity: who he thinks he is and why he is here. Derrick is in the midst of adult-like life experiences (such as excelling in college, working toward graduating, and getting committed to a career), but now he feels he has had the roots he was growing chopped out from under him. No longer on solid ground, he wonders how he can keep growing and moving forward. We encourage students in Derrick's shoes to go to counseling services, as a way to gain a new perspective from an outside observer. Such counseling services are often readily available on college campuses. In these counseling sessions, students can learn good coping strategies for how to maintain focus when they are working on a paper and find their mind wandering and beginning to relive the breakup. It is worth acknowledging that relationship turmoil and low coping skills can interfere with academic progression. Yet, it is also the case that academic support is not meant to offer primary responses to relationship and coping issues. Rather, it is appropriate to share with a professor or academic advisor that this romantic relationship disturbance occurred, and to ask for help in navigating the pain. However, it is not appropriate to treat the professor or academic advisor as the counselor. Rather, academic support can be helpful for referrals to counseling services. Understanding this difference is key for empowering students with knowing what to ask, and what not to ask, when sharing this devastation with academic support. In addition to seeking counseling services to work through the personal issues surrounding relationships, we also encourage students to do some self-evaluation, by considering how to make the best of the situation, to grow and learn from the experience, and to become a better person as a result. This kind of thinking, not just following breakups but about any experience encountered during college, helps set students up for a better future. It also gains students power over what can seem to be a powerless situation.

Third, returning to the academic issues that he is facing, Derrick and similar students should try to think strategically about how to (a) access campus resources and other social supports to attend to the emotional issues involved in this identity-intimacy resorting, and (b) work with professors and campus support staff to get caught up on schoolwork and maintain a successful academic record while sorting through next steps. Students should know that their heart sometimes needs mending in the midst of all their new experiences. Also, when life circumstances change abruptly and disrupt academic focus, it remains important to ask how to meet obligations to ourselves, to others, and to society. The world does not stop turning for one's personal loss, and academic expectations must continue. In this regard, students need to acknowledge the ways that their personal experience does not globalize to a collective experience. In life after college, people still need to show up for work, or they will not get paid. Sustained lack of participation in work can result in loss of a job. In this respect, college is no different. Dropping out of class participation entirely is likely to result in a low grade. Professors cannot, and should not be expected to, completely alter the course design because of one person's tragedy. Yet, just as people can take a personal day at work, there can be some short-term accommodations made to provide students the opportunity to work through their loss and remobilize themselves back to the academic tasks at hand. Key to sorting this out well is to understand the distinction between these two points: (a) students can access campus counseling resources to work on their coping skills and recover from their personal loss, and (b) students can talk with professors and academic advisors to arrange short-term academic accommodations.

## ACTIVITIES: WHAT WE (CAN) LEARN

To help students work through developmental tasks of emerging adult-hood, while challenging them to break down preconceived notions regarding college, we recommend the following kinds of activities. In the first set, we recommend that students discuss with each other the trends identified in the science section of this chapter, regarding increased churning in jobs, locations, families, and romantic partnerships. The key here is to normalize experiences as emerging adults and give each other permission to talk about these issues. One option is for students to read the student stories at the beginning of the chapter and then ask each other with which of these students they most identify. This could be done as an icebreaker for student groups or at orientation, and could be adapted for classroom use as well. (See appendix C for more instructions on implementing such an activity in class.)

Second, we recommend that students orient themselves to the higher education system. They can do so through a number of approaches. One is to find the organizational charts of the university (typically available by searching the university website), and to discuss with professors and others on campus the various roles, including chancellors or presidents, deans, and department chairs. Another activity is to review academic and university terms, since many students—especially those unfamiliar with universities—are taken aback by the sheer number of acronyms and confused by the whole vocabulary. Sometimes universities compile their own lists of vocabulary and acronyms, and there are also several general lists available. (See appendix C for class activities to orient students to higher education.)

Another way to orient students to campus is to invite them to review university identity on the web, reading about and discussing the history of the mascot or other important campus traditions. As some of the students throughout this book report, fraternities and sororities are often effective in building strong groups because of the ways they join students to each other through their connection to campus. Other student groups can also engender similar kinds of campus identity through exploring campus together (see appendix C for a class activity involving a campus scavenger hunt). The key is to investigate higher education and to connect with other students.

In a third set of activities, we recommend spending some time improving skills for studying, taking notes, reading comprehension, and testing. Based on the science section, which describes the value of a college education (beyond income earned) and the kinds of skills that employers desire, we invite students to take ownership of their learning by employing strategies that work. Building from the student story regarding what a big switch college can be from high school, we urge students to realize that university study habits need to be more elaborate than the approaches employed in high school. Keywords to investigate on the Web include the forgetting curve, Cornell note taking, and study skills for college. There are many different approaches to improving study skills that are readily available on the Web and that professors may engage in class. Most important is recognizing that nearly all students need to upgrade their skills for receiving, interpreting, synthesizing, and reporting back information. This skill set is not only crucial for surviving and excelling in college, it is also a key tool kit that employers expect college graduates to have. Begin making changes now.

A fourth kind of activity is to engage with professors outside of class, both by talking with them briefly before or after class, and by making at least one visit to a professor during office hours. Rather than approaching professors to ask, "What do I need to do to get an A?" or "What are the steps for getting into medical school?", students should try to engage professors as a resource for developing their own plan. Succeeding in college, and in life afterwards, is not like following the step-by-step directions of a recipe. The ingredients and the mixing process need to be created by students themselves. Professors and other professionals on campus are available to facilitate that process, but they should act more like coaches than cookbooks. Instead of looking for a cookie-mold process, ask instead how to embody the college experience.

## FURTHER READING ONLINE

- On greater flexibility in work options: Annese, Lisa, September 19, 2016, "Life Is Messy. If We Want the Brightest Workforce, We Need More Flexible Work," *Guardian*, retrieved from https://www.theguardian.com/sustainable-business/2016/sep/20/the-future-is-flexible-why-companies-must-rethink-work-arrangements.
- On reasons to get a college degree: Lucier, Kelci Lynn, April 23, 2018, "Reasons to Get a College Degree," ThoughtCo., retrieved from https://www.thoughtco.com/reasons-to-get-a-college-degree-793187.
- On financial benefits of a college degree: Lucier, Kelci Lynn, March 21, 2019, "6 Financial Benefits of a College Degree," ThoughtCo., retrieved from https://www.thoughtco.com/financial-benefits-of-a-college-degree-793189.
- On challenges facing American higher education today, especially how students can ensure that they are getting out of their college education what they need to in order to develop employable skills: Ebersole, John, January 13, 2014, "Top Issues Facing Higher Education in 2014," Forbes, retrieved from https://www.forbes.com/sites/johnebersole/2014/01/13/top-issues-facing-higher-education-in-2014/#67b327767489.

**For specific college tips, see the following:**

- "Keys to College Success," Student Learning Assistance Center, Texas State University, retrieved from http://gato-docs.its.txstate.edu/jcr:2c1040cd-a05f-422b-b7c2-c5874f950feb/Keys%20to%20College%20Success.pdf.
- "SQ3R—A Reading and Study Skill System," Simpson University, retrieved from https://simpsonu.edu/assets/doc/ASC/ASC-SQ3R.pdf.

- On explanations for and advice on taking quality notes on class lectures: http://thetgi.sae.net/TheTruegentlemaninitiativelibrary/82/Module?module=taking_lecture_notes.
- On tips for improving test taking: "General Test-Taking Strategies," Lone Star College, retrieved from http://www.lonestar.edu/departments/learningcenter/General_Test_Taking_Strategies.pdf.
- "Conquering Finals: A 10-Point Plan," Central Carolina Community College, retrieved from http://www.cccc.edu/csc/resources/files/Study_Skills/Conquering_Finals.pdf.
- "High-Impact Educational Practices," Association of American Colleges and Universities, retrieved from https://www.aacu.org/sites/default/files/files/LEAP/HIP_tables.pdf.

## NOTES

1. Putnam, Robert D. 2015. *Our Kids: The American Dream in Crisis*. New York: Simon & Schuster.
2. Cherlin, Andrew J. 2014. *Labor's Love Lost: The Rise and Fall of the Working-Class Family in America*. New York: Russell Sage Foundation.
3. Halpern-Meekin, Sarah, Wendy D. Manning, Peggy C. Giordano, and Monica A. Longmore. 2013. "Relationship Churning in Emerging Adulthood On/Off Relationships and Sex with an Ex." *Journal of Adolescent Research* 28(2): 166–188.
4. Carnevale, Anthony P., Andrew R. Hanson, and Artem Gulish. 2013. "Failure to Launch: Structural Shift and the New Lost Generation." Center on Education and the Workforce. Washington, DC: Georgetown University. Retrieved from https://cew.georgetown.edu/cew-reports/failure-to-launch/.
5. Mouw, Ted. 2005. "Sequences of Early Adult Transitions: A Look at Variability and Consequences." In Richard A. Settersten, Frank F. Furstenberg, and Rubén G. Rumbaut (Eds.), *On the Frontier of Adulthood: Theory, Research, and Public Policy* (pp. 256–291). University of Chicago Press.
6. Mayer, Karl Ulrich. 2009. "New Directions in Life Course Research." *Annual Review of Sociology* 35(1): 413–433.
7. Aronson, Pamela. 2008. "The Markers and Meanings of Growing Up: Contemporary Young Women's Transition from Adolescence to Adulthood." *Gender & Society: Official Publication of Sociologists for Women in Society* 22: 56–82.
8. Maslow, Abraham. 1987. *Motivation and Personality* (3rd ed). London: Longman.

9. Throughout this book, we engage romantic partnerships to be inclusive of opposite-sex and same-sex partnerships. As discussed in chapter 1, today's emerging adults are more likely to be accepting of same-sex partnerships and less likely to view this subset of romantic partnerships as notably distinct from opposite-sex forms of romantic partnerships (see for example, Hart-Brinson 2014; Lueptow 1980, references that follow). Because same-sex long-term partnerships and marriage are increasingly common and accepted among today's emerging adults, the implications of romantic partnerships on academic and career pursuits are treated similarly under the broader banner of romantic partnerships discussed here and throughout the book.

Hart-Brinson, Peter. 2014. "Discourse of Generations: The Influence of Cohort, Period, and Ideology in Americans' Talk about Same-Sex Marriage." *American Journal of Cultural Sociology* 2(2): 221–252.

Lueptow, Lloyd B. 1980. "Social Change and Sex-Role Change in Adolescent Orientations toward Life, Work, and Achievement: 1964–1975." *Social Psychology Quarterly* 43(1): 48–59.

10. Arnett, Jeffrey Jensen. 2015. *Emerging Adulthood: The Winding Road from the Late Teens through the Twenties* (2nd ed). New York: Oxford University Press.

Erikson, Erik H. 1950. *Childhood and Society*. New York: W. W. Norton.

Erikson, Erik Homburger. 1968. *Identity: Youth and Crisis*. London: Faber & Faber.

11. Barry, Carolyn McNamara, Stephanie D. Madsen, Larry J. Nelson, Jason S. Carroll, and Sarah Badger. 2009. "Friendship and Romantic Relationship Qualities in Emerging Adulthood: Differential Associations with Identity Development and Achieved Adulthood Criteria." *Journal of Adult Development* 16(4): 209–222.

Branje, Susan, Lydia Laninga-Wijnen, Rongqin Yu, and Wim Meeus. 2014. "Associations among School and Friendship Identity in Adolescence and Romantic Relationships and Work in Emerging Adulthood." *Emerging Adulthood* 2(1): 6–16.

Giordano, Peggy C., Kenyatta D. Phelps, Wendy D. Manning, and Monica A. Longmore. 2008. "Adolescent Academic Achievement and Romantic Relationships." *Social Science Research* 37(1): 37–54.

Halpern-Meekin, Sarah. 2012. "Unlikely Optimists, Skeptics, and Believers Understanding Adolescents' Prospective Relationship Views." *Journal of Adolescent Research* 27(5): 606–631.

Halpern-Meekin, Sarah, Wendy D. Manning, Peggy C. Giordano, and Monica A. Longmore. 2013. "Relationship Churning in Emerging Adulthood On/Off Relationships and Sex With an Ex." *Journal of Adolescent Research* 28(2): 166–188.

Kopala-Sibley, Daniel C., David C. Zuroff, Nicola Hermanto, and Keven Joyal-Desmarais. 2016. "The Development of Self-Definition and Relatedness in Emerging Adulthood and Their Role in the Development of Depressive Symptoms." *International Journal of Behavioral Development* 40(4): 302–312.

Manning, Wendy D., Jessica A. Cohen, and Pamela J. Smock. 2011. "The Role of Romantic Partners, Family, and Peer Networks in Dating Couples' Views about Cohabitation." *Journal of Adolescent Research* 26(1): 115–149.

Mazur, Elizabeth, and Lauri Kozarian. 2010. "Self-Presentation and Interaction in Blogs of Adolescents and Young Emerging Adults." *Journal of Adolescent Research* 25(1): 124–144.

Raley, R. Kelly, and M. Kate Sullivan. 2009. "Social-Contextual Influences on Adolescent Romantic Involvement: The Constraints of Being a Numerical Minority." *Sociological Spectrum* 30(1): 65–89.

Ranta, Mette, Julia Dietrich, and Katariina Salmela-Aro. 2014. "Career and Romantic Relationship Goals and Concerns during Emerging Adulthood." *Emerging Adulthood* 2(1): 17–26.

Roberson, Patricia N. E., Jessica N. Fish, Spencer B. Olmstead, and Frank D. Fincham. 2015. "College Adjustment, Relationship Satisfaction, and Conflict Management: A Cross-Lag Assessment of Developmental 'Spillover.'" *Emerging Adulthood,* 3(4): 244–254.

Rosenfeld, Michael J., and Reuben J. Thomas. 2012. "Searching for a Mate: The Rise of the Internet as a Social Intermediary." *American Sociological Review* 77(4): 523–547.

Sassler, Sharon, and Kara Joyner. 2011. "Social Exchange and the Progression of Sexual Relationships in Emerging Adulthood." *Social Forces* 90(1): 223–245.

Seiffge-Krenke, Inge, and Koen Luyckx. 2014. "Competent in Work and Love? Emerging Adults' Trajectories in Dealing with Work–Partnership Conflicts and Links to Health Functioning." *Emerging Adulthood* 2(1): 48–58.

Shulman, Shmuel, and Jennifer Connolly. 2013. "The Challenge of Romantic Relationships in Emerging Adulthood Reconceptualization of the Field." *Emerging Adulthood* 1(1): 27–39.

Towner, Senna L., M. Margaret Dolcini, and Gary W. Harper. 2015. "Romantic Relationship Dynamics of Urban African American Adolescents: Patterns of Monogamy, Commitment, and Trust." *Youth & Society* 47(3): 343–373.

Warner, Tara D., Wendy D. Manning, Peggy C. Giordano, and Monica A. Longmore. 2011. "Relationship Formation and Stability in Emerging Adulthood: Do Sex Ratios Matter?" *Social Forces* 90(1): 269–295.

12. Dezutter, Jessie, Alan S. Waterman, Seth J. Schwartz, Koen Luyckx, Wim Beyers, Alan Meca . . . S. Jean Caraway. 2014. "Meaning in Life in Emerging Adulthood: A Person-Oriented Approach." *Journal of Personality* 82(1): 57–68.

13. Konstam, Varda. 2015. "Voices of Employers: Overlapping and Disparate Views." In *Emerging and Young Adulthood: Advancing Responsible Adolescent Development* (pp.161–182). Cham, Switzerland: Springer International. Retrieved from http://link.springer.com/chapter/10.1007/978-3-319-11301-2_10.

14. Arum, Richard, and Josipa Roksa. 2014. *Aspiring Adults Adrift: Tentative Transitions of College Graduates*. Chicago: University Of Chicago Press.

15. Crosnoe, Robert, and Monica Kirkpatrick Johnson. 2011. "Research on Adolescence in the Twenty-First Century." *Annual Review of Sociology* 37(1): 439–460.

16. Kuh, George D. 2008. "High-Impact Educational Practices: What They Are, Who Has Access to Them, and Why They Matter." *Making Excellence Inclusive* series, Association of American Colleges and Universities. Retrieved from https://secure.aacu.org/imis/ItemDetail?iProductCode=E-HIGHIMP&Category=.

17. Anderson, Lorin W., David R. Krathwohl, Peter W. Airasian, Kathleen A. Cruikshank, Richard E. Mayer, Paul R. Pintrick . . . and Merlin C. Wittrock. 2000. *A Taxonomy for Learning, Teaching, and Assessing: A Revision of Bloom's Taxonomy of Educational Objectives.* London: Pearson.

18. Costa, Cristina, and Ricardo Torres. 2011. "To Be or Not to Be, the Importance of Digital Identity in the Networked Society." *Educação, Formação & Tecnologias*, April: 47–53.

Croce, Nicholas. 2012. *Enhancing Your Academic Digital Footprint.* Rosen Publishing Group.

Fish, Tony. 2009. *My Digital Footprint: A Two-Sided Digital Business Model Where Your Privacy Will Be Someone Else's Business!* London: FutureText.

Hengstler, Julia. n.d. "Managing Your Digital Footprint: Ostriches v. Eagles." *Education for a Digital World* 1: 51.

Kuehn, Larry. 2012. "Manage Your Digital Footprint." *Our Schools / Our Selves* 21(2): 67–70.

Oliver, John Jason, and Steve North. 2014. "A Strategic Look at How to Extend Your Digital Footprint." *Strategic Direction* 30(7): 1–3.

Philbrick, Jodi L., and Ana D. Cleveland. 2015. "Personal Branding: Building Your Pathway to Professional Success." *Medical Reference Services Quarterly* 34(2): 181–189.

Williams, Shirley Ann, Sarah Christine Fleming, Karsten Oster Lundqvist, and Patrick Neil Parslow. 2010. "Understanding Your Digital Identity." *Learning Exchange* 1.

# Why College Is Worth It

> The third chapter addresses the ways that social class, economic resources, and family backgrounds condition students' experiences of college. Students learn about the value of college: why it is important to earn a degree for specific skills and credentials, and how doing well in college is largely about acquiring "cultural capital," also commonly referred to as learning the rules of the game. The third chapter also addresses how students' social class backgrounds affect how easy, hard, or different they find the college experience to be, and how these experiences can shape the kinds of skills and talents students shape in college.

This chapter ventures further into the subject of money, which is an important and often under-discussed aspect of college. Navigating college requires reflection on the resources one has available. The student stories in this chapter highlight just how wide the spectrum of economic and social resources is among college students. Our students describe in their

*The Science of College*. Patricia S. Herzog, Casey T. Harris, Shauna A. Morimoto, Shane W. Barker, Jill G. Wheeler, A. Justin Barnum, and Terrance L. Boyd, Oxford University Press (2020) © Oxford University Press.
DOI: 10.1093/oso/9780190934507.001.0001

own words what it is like to struggle to make ends meet, or to be born relatively lucky, and to try to meet the pressures that can come with both scenarios. We then situate these stories within studies about social class and pay attention to both the *human capital* and *cultural capital* aspects of college. Human capital refers to the knowledge or skills gained, while cultural capital refers to styles of interacting with particular social groups. Successful students acquire both types of resources along with an academic degree.

## STUDENT STORIES: WHAT WE EXPERIENCE

We begin this chapter by sharing student stories, this time from **Cooper**, **Regan**, **Riberto**, **Gabby**, **Julius**, **Leolia**, and **Bryce**, all of whom talk about the ways their class background shaped their childhood and continues to affect them in college.

---

**#bornlucky #welleducated**: A big shout-out to my parents today! Read something in sociology that rocked my world and realized how lucky I am that my parents went to college too.

**Cooper** explains his experience growing up in a middle-class, educated family in this way:

> I attend a state school in the SEC. My whole school career growing up was aimed toward getting into college, and now I am here. My mother attended a private university where she obtained a degree in psychology and criminology. My father attended another state school in Missouri, but did not graduate . . . My life chances were in favor of me attending the university of my choice, but I always strove for a good education because I was under the impression that my merit would get me into college. I also made sure to try to build up my resume with credentials. I always volunteered; I was involved in sports; I was (and still am) an honors student; I was on

student government; I was in almost every club at my high school; I worked a part-time job.

**#livingthedream #flagshipU**: I am realizing how much of a blessing it is to be able to attend this flagship university, and to be able to be in clubs, and go to dances like the one our sorority house hosted last week. We are living the dream (:

Similarly, **Regan** reports that her affluent background is the reason she is able to attend a flagship university and participate heavily in campus activities:

> I never questioned whether or not I would be able to further my education; I have always had the understanding that college just simply follows high school . . . Although most of my schooling is paid for through scholarships, there are many other costs associated with going to college. One extra cost [that] I have the privilege of having is my sorority . . . Along with my sorority, I am involved in many other clubs, activities, and organizations in college. I have always been very involved with school and community activities; even when I was in middle school, I was always trying to get more involved. Having a busy schedule full of organized events is natural and expected for me.

**#strappedforcash #dutycalls #distracted**: I'm packing a bag and heading home for the weekend. Have to go help take care of my mom. Can I borrow someone's notes from biology class next Monday? I don't think I'll make it back by then.

**Riberto** explains that college life, including involvement in the types of activities Cooper and Regan mention, comes less easily for him, despite having grown up in a middle-class family:

> My father is a lawyer and my mother was a teacher up until a couple of years ago. While my dad makes a decent amount of money, we never had as much as those around us. My little brother was born

with a rare syndrome that requires a lot of medicine and doctors, and recently, my mother fell ill putting her on a lot of medication that she will be on for the rest of her life. Because of the medical expenses that my family faces, we tend to have less money than most of the families in our private school community.

We have met in our offices with students like Riberto, and we know that situations like this can distract students from schoolwork, especially as family members become more ill. If Riberto is similar to the students we have talked with, he probably started his first semester excited about his schedule, and feeling he couldn't wait for a college social life. High school was fine, but he was eager to have more independence and meet like-minded people who shared his interests. A few short weeks into the term, he had already established friendships and was enjoying his classes, motivating him to study and learn. But right before midterms, he received some unsettling news. His mother was diagnosed with cancer and would begin treatment immediately. The prognosis was not good. Suddenly, Riberto found himself pulled apart, wanting to be with his family amid the pain they were experiencing, but also knowing that his mother would want him to complete the term. Weekend trips home gradually stretched into weekdays, and when he was on campus, he could not force himself to go to classes. Deep into the semester, Riberto has not attended class in weeks and has not spoken to his instructors or advisor about the personal problems associated with his absence and his lack of desire to focus on classes. He has not told his parents either, as he does not want to disappoint more people or add to their worries.

#needtowinthelottery #lemonstolemonade: Does anyone know how to fix a scooter? Mine broke, and it's the only way I can get to class. Plus I need to go get some groceries. I'm starving!

**Gabby** shares how college life is more challenging for her:

Transitioning to college life is particularly difficult if you are from a much lower social class than [the] majority of the people that you meet. In high school, I never felt like I was a part of a lower social class than my peers, but that changed once I came to college. When meeting new people, it was obvious that they were from a much higher social class than myself. They dressed in nicer clothes, and walked around with their noses in the air. I eventually made friends with a group of people that seemed very down to earth and a lot like myself, but once getting to know them, I could see that they too were from a higher class. My friends would often talk about all the expensive trips they have gone on for family vacations, or for spring breaks with their friends. They would also talk about all the nice things their family owned or how they can ask their parents for money whenever they needed it. I, on the other hand, have never asked my parents for money and have certainly never left the east coast before coming to this middle state.

**#broke #workingtwojobs**: Just catching up after working back-to-back killer shifts all weekend. I'm going to have to pull an all-nighter now to study for chem. Does anyone have a book I can borrow? I'm so screwed:/

**Julius** describes attending a university that is not his first choice because of money concerns:

Though I am not going to Harvard, I am receiving a higher education with students that are of higher social status. Some of these students do not have two jobs. Some of them have free time. Since I have two jobs to be able to support myself and pay for my tuition, I do not have much free time to focus on school. I cannot afford my own place, parking, or books. I have two jobs for which I am very grateful but they are a burden because I am not able to focus on school [as much as I would like].

**#lifeisrough #deadbeatparents #wantabetterlife:** Anyone want to trade lives? I'm ready to switch this one out, get some new parents, and you know, just start over.

**Leolia** says in her own words:

I was born . . . to my unmarried, fifteen-year-old mother . . . I was constantly reminded that I was not supposed to exist. My mother was abandoned on the doorstep of her aunt and uncle's house when she was a baby. Her biological parents are addicts who are now serving time in prison. A clear distinction was made from my mom and the children of her aunt and uncle. This distinction translated to me since I was being raised by my disappointed "grandparents." Their children were closer to my age, and so we were more like siblings . . . My older cousins, or siblings, would tell the younger siblings that if they were friends with me [then] they would get pregnant, or that I would give them drugs . . . I worked really hard to "be good" so that I would be accepted. Ironically, education was not valued. Besides a few Christian workbooks, I had no formal education until high school. I was only homeschooled for a few years; however my schooling was sporadic and became nonexistent throughout my childhood . . . I was so afraid of not being included and essentially becoming like my parents and my biological grandparents, that I initially followed all the rules out of panic . . . The amount of income that they brought in as minimum wage employees was not enough to meet the demands of a family. Debt was steadily building, as the family acquired more loans to keep up the facade. They were attempting to establish an air of similarity with the rest of our upper middle class family; however, we were lucky to be considered working class. Instead of paying bills, we would pawn gaming systems or tools to eat at *fancy* restaurants in an attempt to maintain a certain prestige. My family avoided the stigmas associated with being a low income, working class family by concealing that fact.

**#pressuretosucceed #fearoffailure**: Whose in for getting together tonight? Let's make it a study session, combined with drinks after. We're going for it all ☺

**Bryce** expresses issues on the opposite end of the socioeconomic spectrum from Leolia:

> With its picture-perfect setting that mirrors one of an ABC Family television series, Prairie Village, Kansas, is often referred to as "Perfect Village." The tree lined streets home to historic mansions, six country clubs located within a five-mile radius of my house, and nearly non-existent crime rate made my hometown seem too good to be true, and over time I was proven right. The seeming flawlessness, due to the high academic, social, and professional standards set by the community's elite, placed immense pressure on me to be perfect in order to prep myself for a successful future . . . Although I understand how extremely fortunate I am to have been raised in a safe community and attend a school that challenged me to reach my full potential, I felt that I never measured up to the greatness I was constantly surrounded by. Because of this, I am forever comparing myself to others and plagued by a fear of failure.

## SCIENCE: WHAT WE KNOW

One theme that resonates through all these varied stories is how students' financial situations growing up and their social classes have shaped their college trajectories. Expectations for lifelong learning, including advanced degrees that are increasingly necessary to obtain even entry-level positions, drive up the costs of education. Though tuition and other costs at four-year public universities vary tremendously across states, the average cost is somewhere around $20,000 per year. This cost is often assumed to be paid off through hard work (either through the parents or by the students themselves), but the rising costs of college are a particularly hard burden for those who do not enter with as many financial resources. This is part of why there is debate about whether college truly facilitates social mobility (i.e., enabling students from lower-income backgrounds to improve their financial circumstances). Summarizing decades of social science studies on higher education, Mitchell Stevens[1] reviews theories regarding whether college degrees mostly reproduce the existing social class structure, by passing on affluence across generations, or whether—as would be the case in a meritocracy—college equalizes the playing field by rewarding those who work hard and flunking out those who squander the opportunities provided by higher education.

Drawing upon the characterization of college offered by Randall Collins, Stevens explains: "The pursuit of college credentials is the widest and most dependable path to the good life that American society currently provides, and the terms of college admission have become the instructions families use when figuring out how to ensure their own children's future prosperity" (Stevens 2013: 570). Stevens then describes how compiling a strong admissions packet is crucial for demonstrating "measurable accomplishment," but highlights that the ability to compile such a packet, and the resources needed to actualize the credentials listed on applications, are not equally distributed. Some families can pay for every advantage and enroll their children in music lessons, pay for sports camps, and hire private tutors. Others cannot. For example, a student in chapter 7, **Desiree**, describes her parents' investment in her application packet by saying: "They [her parents] wanted me to apply to a number of prestigious colleges, so they '[did] everything in their power to make [me] into [an] ideal applicant' (Stevens 2013: 571)." In contrast, **Jacob** of chapter 6 relays how the parents of his classmates had an easier time investing in their children's college applications than did his:

> In schools like the ones I attended, parents of the children in them
> wanted to use education as a means to hand down their privilege
> to the next generation. Mostly everyone was in search of valuable
> undergraduate degrees, so college was an assumed track to be taken

by most students. This makes sense, because in the upper middle class schools I attended, parents' socioeconomic backgrounds are correlated with educational attainment of their children. College is such a dependable path to a stable future, and most everyone was taught to seek a good education. It was easier for kids in my schools to get this good education, since their parents had the means to develop them into an ideal applicant for college. What Stevens says, "affluent families fashion an entire way of life organized around the production of measurable virtue in children," lines up perfectly with the way of life in the place I was raised (Stevens 2013).

Certainly, the students whose stories begin this chapter each recognize how their own family's social class impacts their participation in different activities on campus, and, more broadly, the resources (time, money, experiences) they bring with them to college. For example, **Cooper** notes the following: "There were so many things I did that I thought would be determining factors later on in my life. Reading this article by Stevens makes me rethink everything I ever did. There is nothing I regret doing, but I understand now that more than anything, I lucked out." Likewise, **Regan** notes that "the fact that I am able to attend this university says something about my privilege." Just as Stevens summarizes, Regan's family's relative financial security allowed her to take part in extracurricular activities without having to juggle work and schoolwork. She recalls: "I am able to attend and focus solely on college because I have a mother who financially supports me. She was able to earn enough money through her 'privileged position in the hierarchy of stratification' to pay for my education (Davis, Moore, and Tumin 2013: 248)."

One way that young people experience the effects of social class prior to college is through the formation of cliques, in which privileged people associate with each other in high-status groups while excluding others. This can also occur through spending time in social media platforms that are based upon group membership. Sociologists refer to these processes as *in-group and out-group dynamics*.[2] **Emma**, a student from the next chapter, says: "Primary groups are these small, intimate groups of people like friendship groups . . . Cliques have always been a part of growing up for me, whether in middle school, high school, or even college; having a friend group defined who you are and played a huge part in your social life." She also noted that cliques can involve moments of feeling close and being accepted by groups, as well as moments of exclusion, or what Patricia Adler and Peter Adler[3] refer to as "out-group subjugation." Likewise, **Kyndal** (also of chapter 4) says that "cliques are basically 'friendship circles, whose members tend to identify each other as mutually connected . . . [The popular kids] definitely had the 'most exciting social lives' and they had the 'most interest and attention from classmates' (Adler & Adler 2013: 179). High school was definitely a social hierarchy, unlike college."

Several students reflected on what it takes to be accepted in different social groups. For example, **Norah** of chapter 7 quotes and summarizes some research on joining a clique: "'Individuals gain initial membership into a clique through their actively seeking entry' for that group, also known as an application (Adler & Adler 2013: 181)." And some students recall being excluded. Leolia, whose story began earlier in this chapter, says, "I was excluded based on the stigmas associated with my mom . . . The other children used techniques of exclusion to make sure that I stayed in the outgroup." Similarly, **Phillip** of chapter 7 says, "These talks [about group belonging] serve both as a technique of inclusion and exclusion depending on where you fall on the group's radar. This would be best described as out-group subjugation; which serves to exclude certain people through mockery while also cementing what is acceptable behavior from people within the group." **Aaron**, a student in chapter 5, states, "I managed my identity because I had seen other deviants be stigmatized as a technique of exclusion from the upper-class." Finally, **Chen** from chapter 5 says, "Unlike most others who were excluded by those who were a part of school cliques, I excluded myself because I was uninterested in taking part in large social groups in which I would be scrutinized by others."

G. William Domhoff[4] continues this critical take on the role of schools, clubs, and volunteering in transmitting class structure, often through forming cliques. Indeed, one of our students, **Regan**, describes her own feelings of being in a sorority as one in which "my [social] class gives me the privilege of having an exclusive in-group feeling within a social club." Likewise, **Desiree** of chapter 7 reflects on having participated in volunteering programs and relays: "These women [of the volunteering program] modeled the ideal woman of the upper class by being 'both powerful and subservient, playing decision-making roles in numerous cultural and civic organizations but also accepting traditional roles at home vis-à-vis their husbands and children' (Domhoff 2013: 261). They were intended to serve as role models." She continues: "My mother put me in these programs because being a 'community volunteer is a central preoccupation of upper-class women' (Domhoff 2013: 261). I was put in these programs early in order to instill a love of volunteering . . . another step in my socialization into the upper-class culture aiming to shape me to be a woman 'fulfill[ing] [my] obligation to the community' (Domhoff 2013: 261)."

*Social stratification* (inequalities in wealth, status, and power) exists in every society. Karl Marx and others[5] describe how inequalities bundle into *social classes*: groups of people who share economic and political interests. While scholars disagree over how to define social classes, or exactly how many there are, most agree that there is a group of people in the United States who are commonly referred to as *working-class*. Typically, members of the working class do not have much control over their schedule or work tasks, are paid hourly, and hold jobs that require a high degree of physical labor. In a famous experiment, reporter Barbara Ehrenreich attempted to live as a working-class laborer, living off only what she could make from typical working-class jobs. After trying to do so, she said, "All I know is that I couldn't hold two jobs and I couldn't make enough money to live on with one. And I had advantages unthinkable to many of the long-term poor—health, stamina, a working car, and no children to care for and support" (Ehrenreich 2013: 290).[6] Kathryn Edin and Maria Kefalas describe how social class (which is reproduced through education) can affect everything from wealth accumulation to marriage and family life. **Leolia** cited their work with regard to her own story: "My mother did not marry my father because they were both very poor. When choosing a spouse, many impoverished women will not marry someone who is just as well-off as they are (Edin & Kefalas 2013)."[7]

These themes of stratification and social class emerged when several students documented their efforts to juggle the academic, extracurricular, and financial responsibilities of college, efforts that contrast with the experiences of **Cooper** and **Regan** mentioned earlier. For instance, **Julius's** reading of Ehrenreich's (2013) experiment leads him to state, "it [the college juggle] is [about] social stratification because in order to simply be able to go to school, I must risk not having enough time to complete homework assignments and be well studied . . . I am currently living the life described in *Nickeled and Dimed* by Barbara Ehrenreich (2013)." Similarly, **Riberto's** family deals with chronic medical issues that bring long-term financial strains that, in turn, limit his time and energy to pursue the different opportunities that campus life presents. **Leolia**, too, struggles to make ends meet, distracting her from college life.

Part of why we in the United States are enamored with college, then, is because it symbolizes the hopes of being able to pass on a better way of life, or a similar way of life, to one's children. Sociologists and other social scientists often criticize this understanding of college, since statistically the best way to predict whether a person will enroll in college, and whether they will graduate, is to examine the class and cultures of their parents. That may sound cynical, but it is true. However, it is also the case that every year people born with tremendous privilege flunk out of college after partying too hard, and every year there are students who graduate whose parents never went to college, who had to work multiple jobs to pay their way through, and who embody the merit-pay system that we hope college can be. How do we reconcile these seemingly conflictual facts? The answer lies in better understanding the complexities involved in students' choices: how their decision-making reflects their cultures.[8]

Most of our understanding of the complicated relationship between social class, culture, and individual choices stems from the theories of Pierre Bourdieu.[9] Bourdieu viewed social interactions as deeply patterned by inequalities, but—rather than stressing the domination of the affluent over everyone else—he saw people as partaking in recreating their own unequal status through the choices they make. His term for this, *habitus*, refers to the habits of our daily life, the things that operate in the background, what we take for granted about why things are the way they are and what we want to do. Connecting these ideas to college and career aspirations, Johnson describes Bourdieu's relevant theories by stating the following:

> Bourdieu suggests that goals are formed and modified in an experiential fashion based on individuals' perceptions of the probability of achieving a given goal. Both consciously and unconsciously individuals draw conclusions from the world around them about the chances of reaching a goal, and their hopes tend to reflect those conclusions (Johnson 2002: 1312).

In this sense, what we desire and aspire to be and do reflects who we are as individuals while also, often unintentionally and without our conscious awareness, reproduces the lifestyles in which we were raised, the ways we were socialized, and our social class backgrounds.

Drawing on Bourdieu's insights, Annette Lareau[10] sheds light on how parenting strategies reflect and reinforce social class through the ways kids are taught to interact with organizations, such as colleges. She found that, while most parents want the best for their children, parents operate with different understandings of what their children need from them, and these understandings have lasting effects on young people's expectations of adults even into college. Lareau used a gardening metaphor to describe the two distinct styles of *parent socialization* techniques she observed. *Concerted cultivation* is the name she gave to the style of parenting most often employed by middle-class families. In this approach, children are viewed as needing continual investment; parents must pluck and prune them as they grow to help them flourish. Parents involve children in formal activities—such as after-school programs, sports teams, music classes—and most of the children's social interactions involve talking with adults, either parents or those in charge of their various activities (coaches, music teachers). **Regan** recognized this style of parenting in her own background. She observed that her participation in activities and groups from early in her childhood "is actually a reflection of my family's social class. My parent's childrearing strategies could be characterized as 'concerted cultivation,' which includes enrolling children in activities deemed developmentally important due to their ability to 'transmit important life skills to children' (Lareau 2013: 607)."

On the other hand, *accomplishment of natural growth* is the style of parenting that Lareau found most often among the working-class families. By this way of thinking, children need to grow strong roots by learning to fight their way through adversities and figure things out mostly for themselves. Children spend most of their time interacting with peers—playing in the neighborhood with cousins or neighbors—within the bounds of strict guidelines for when to arrive back home. Parents are not discussion partners but authority figures to be obeyed and respected.

Most importantly for our purposes, Lareau found these two parenting styles affected how children later interacted with formal organizations, such as universities. She found that children from the middle-class families she observed often felt a sense of entitlement, so they were comfortable asking for attention and intervention from authority figures, such as professors. Children from the working-class families instead often felt a sense of constraint, finding formal institutions (such as universities) to be foreign and having confusing expectations regarding how students are to succeed. Children from these families were less inclined to seek help from professors and were often frustrated by college bureaucracy.

In another example of research on how social class background shapes young people's chances of enrolling and succeeding in college, Susan Auerbach[11] studied parents' roles in preparing their high-school students for college among working-class parents of color who did not attend college. She identified three styles of parental involvement: parents were moral supporters, ambivalent companions, or struggling advocates. *Moral supporters* mostly did not participate directly in their children's schooling, though they supported students from home by indirectly guiding them. *Ambivalent companions* were supportive of students, but had ambivalent feelings resulting from concern over losing their closeness with their children as they entered college, which was an unfamiliar world to the parents. *Struggling advocates* attempted to be more directly involved in their children's schooling; however, they encountered setbacks due to the insensitivities of educational bureaucracy. In these ways, parents' form of involvement reflected their own educational experiences in an intersection of what Auerbach calls "a mediated system of structure, culture, and agency"—referring to parent roles in education as "(a) socially structured by class and race but also (b) culturally mediated by particular cultural schemas and scripts as well as (c) psychosocially enacted according to individual psychosocial resources and relationships within families" (Auerbach 2007: 254).

Bringing all this back to life as a college student, in a book called *Inside the College Gates: How Class and Culture Matter in Higher Education*, Jenny M. Stuber[12] finds that the cultural backgrounds and socialization of students at earlier stages affects their university experiences. Especially important, she says, is that class shapes the ways that students integrate themselves into the college setting. Even choices about who to be friends with, and which extracurricular activities to partake in, reflect their social backgrounds. This is not to say that class completely determines all these social interactions, but it tends to do so when we are not paying attention.

In a vivid example of how class affects social interactions at college, a student named **Gabby** recalls her initial experiences making friends in college while recognizing her social class background for the first time. She states the following:

> Being from a lower class may not seem like a big deal to some people, but when starting out in a new place, the last thing I wanted was to have this social stigma. Stigma can limit one's social opportunities; however, people with class stigmas can often conceal their identity to fit in with the higher class . . . To conceal my identity as a lower-class student, I had to quickly go through resocialization. Resocialization is the act of unlearning the culture you have been taught throughout a lifetime, and adopting a new culture . . . For me that meant not talking about my background, and simply keeping to myself as much

as I possibly could. Even though keeping to myself seems like an extreme act, it was a lot easier than listening to my friends say how they would never put their kid in a daycare because it was "too gross" or that they want an on-campus meal plan sophomore year so that their parents would pay for it. From my first year as a college student, I learned that I should not be embarrassed about coming from a lower-class family because it has taught me many valuable lessons in life. It has taught me the value of money and what it means to work hard for what you want. It has also taught me that class does not define a person, and instead it is what someone makes of their class.

Echoing this feeling, **Leolia** focuses on the stigma of her lower–social-class upbringing and how she works to overcome it in her daily (and often unconscious) interactions with her peers.

As a student at this university, I lack a reasonable income, and I have acquired a great deal of debt in student loans. My parents are not funding my education as many of my peer's parents are. However, I still dress like others of the middle class; wearing brands that maintain status. I have obtained cultural capital by pursuing a higher education in medicine, by quieting my southern accent while speaking more eloquently, and by enjoying activities that those of my desired class enjoy (volunteering, hiking, sporting events, theater, etc.). Cultural capital refers to the process of acquiring properties that assist in upward mobility in society . . . This is the process of identity management. Identity management is a technique to cover stigmas associated with a position in a society . . . Through my efforts, I have been mostly successful at concealing the stigmas associated with my working class past.

Now, we return to the question we posed earlier: How can it be that, during college, success mostly reflects students' backgrounds, and, at the same time, college also indicates that merit pays off? Taking insights from Stuber and others summarized in this section, students must understand education as both a possession and a process. As a possession, a college diploma is a "piece of paper." It is something one owns upon graduating and a credential necessary for applying for many jobs. But importantly, college is also a process: a series of social interactions that change the ways people interact. To make the most out of college, then, regardless of their background, students need to allow college to happen to them, to shape who they are becoming, and to contextualize who they have been and where they are headed. Plus, students need to graduate to get the paper. In the end, college is about owning human capital, which opens doors, and about acquiring cultural capital, knowledge of how to interact with people on the other side of those doors once they are opened.

## ADVICE: WHAT WE (CAN) PROVIDE

In this section, we now switch from the primary voices of faculty members, in the previous section, to the primary voices of student development and student support practitioners. What follows is the kind of advice that students would be most likely to receive if they visited with an academic advisor to discuss the student experiences described at the beginning of this chapter, or previous chapters.

**#adulting #20something #transition #onmyown** Returning to the student stories in chapter 1, since they relate to the content of this chapter, **Devon** and **Brittany** may not yet realize or care that average student debt after college has been rising. College remains a great time in life to have fun, explore life choices, and construct adulthood identities. In the process, however, students should seek input from family, friends, and university support staff (especially helpful people in the office of financial aid). Those from financially supportive family backgrounds may not need to be too worried about their spending habits in college. But many college students come from modest family backgrounds and could benefit from guidance about how to enjoy college while also protecting their future financial well-being. There are many people on college campuses who can help students with this, especially if their own family and friends did not attend college, had more affordable costs during college, or otherwise lack up-to-date financial information.

**#wherestheparty #yolo** Drawing from another story in chapter 1, a student like **Charlie** may feel like she is the only one who cannot handle the pace of college. The reality, however, is that everyone comes from a specific social and cultural background and, as Stuber (2011) points out, each will experience college in a distinct way. A great example of this is the possibility that some of Charlie's partying peers may be struggling as much as she is, but they were taught early on by family and friends about how much their outward perception matters, so they know to at least pretend that they can easily keep up with both the academic and the party scene. Or perhaps some of her friends were raised around large, public social gatherings and know how to "have a good time" without overdoing it.

Most importantly, odds are that many of Charlie's friends, behind the scenes, know who and how to ask for help because they have done so in the past. For Charlie, this experience may be a brand new one. She would probably benefit most from acknowledging that people are traversing different paths through college, and that being honest with herself about what she does and does not know is the first step to getting the support she needs. Focusing on that insight instead of comparing herself to others will help her turn things around.

**#bornlucky #welleducated** We encourage **Cooper** to stop by his sociology professor's office to express how the class was helping him make sense of his life. He described the exact kind of moment that professors get excited about: when the light bulb turns on and students have that " 'aha' moment." A sociology professor would commend Cooper for beginning to recognize patterns of social reproduction, inequalities, and the ways that social forces structure experiences. In addition to commending Cooper for these skills, we would also want to make sure that they develop a balanced perspective: realizing that personal choices do make a difference, so that they do not feel like life is all just luck. There is also agency involved in the process. Students still have power to create their life stories.

In addition to thinking about specific objectives, such as getting a job, students have the opportunity in college to think about what success looks like to them as they imagine where they see themselves in the longer term. One task right now, as an emerging adult college student, is to consider not only the hoops that have to be jumped through in order to attain that next goal, but also the meaning behind those goals and how those meanings combine with personal identity and ideas about the future. Being aware of parents' experiences in navigating college is important. Also important is to focus on how to balance academics and other activities. Parents who did not attend college sometimes do not know much about student debt or do not know how to discuss it adequately with their college students. To ensure students have access to adequate information and opportunities, we recommend students stop by the financial aid office to learn about scholarships for which they may be eligible. When things are going well on other fronts, students should take a moment to remember and address the financial element of college.

**#livingthedream #flagshipU** Similarly, we encourage students like **Regan** to stop by a professor's office hours, particularly to reflect on her social identity. We would be likely to commend students like her on their general energy and excitement, as it is contagious! At the same time, we caution such students to make sure they are not spreading themselves too thin. They need to reflect on how to focus their energy, especially when they desire to be part of so many different organizations. In addition, we would point out to Regan that she describes this sorority as an exclusive organization (which many would consider to be a negative thing), yet she also says that it plays a significant role in her social identity (which implies it has a positive impact on her). That tension in Regan's understanding of the pros and cons of her sorority participation presents an excellent opportunity to consider how both these aspects are reconciled and what this means for the kind of person she will be as she moves forward in college and life. Students in exclusive organizations should think about why they joined that organization, what the organization does, what its objectives are, and how students are part of fulfilling those objectives. By pondering these subjects and the in-group and out-group dynamics of their organization, students can take a reflective role that makes them more of an active participant within the larger structure. Our main advice for

Regan is to be mindful of becoming over-involved and to make deliberate choices about involvement.

**#strappedforcash #dutycalls #distracted** One of the aspects of sociology that we think is most helpful to understand at a time like this in **Riberto's** life is what C. Wright Mills calls the "sociological imagination."[13] This has to do with understanding one's own life experiences in the context of broader social and public issues. Riberto is confronting what we call a "structural pinch," meaning a personal pain or struggle that is related to a position within social and institutional structures. Despite being well-prepared for the academic and social aspects of college, Riberto lacks the social and cultural resources to help him successfully weather this difficult period. He grapples with how to talk to friends, professors, or other people who can support him, especially about such personal and emotional matters. It hurts to talk about his family's health struggles, and he doesn't really see how talking to anyone could help. After all, what can others do to make the situation better for his mom or their family? The grades on his transcript are black and white and do not tell the complete story. In situations like Riberto's, it is important for him to advocate for himself, to request that faculty and staff take a deeper look at his situation, and it will ultimately be crucial for him to have strong letters of support from people who can describe the aspects of Riberto's story that extend beyond the grades.

We advise students like Riberto to recognize that they need to talk to people and seek support groups and other options for helpful conversations. There is nothing wrong with asking for help, even when our gender and cultural identities may tell us we should go it alone. It is important not to let personal and academic issues compound until they are unmanageable; instead, students need to find help and address problems one step at a time. Being concerned about taking care of family brings an emotional and social burden. Thus, we advise students to think about what coping strategies they have and what else they need. They do not have to go it alone. Also, understand that all is not lost in the classroom, despite struggles to complete exams and assignments. Talking with professors can teach students about what options are available in the case of such contingencies arising, and many available services, people, and resources can help students in difficult situations to cope and find ways to catch up.

**#needtowinthelottery #lemonstolemonade Gabby** sees this time in her life as one which is full of potential, a period when she can focus on herself and the person she wants to become. As discussed in the first two chapters, Arnett and other developmental scholars call emerging adulthood the self-focused age,[14] but Gabby did not really like that term when a professor mentioned it, since "self-focused" sounded too much like being selfish. While that's an understandable interpretation, that is not what Arnett and others mean. What Gabby needs is someone who is familiar with this research to help her sort it out in a different way. One of the many caring adults on campus, or Gabby's parents, could explain that, in devoting time to themselves, emerging adults develop skills for daily living and gain a better understanding of who they are and what they want from life, which allows them to build a foundation for their adult life.[15] Yet many emerging adults simultaneously begin to realize that what they can become is not unlimited. This life stage is often marked by "high hopes and great expectations" for the future, but emerging adults are also functioning "in between" the clearer life stages of earlier adolescence and later adulthood.

Most importantly, we advise students like Gabby to learn to accept responsibility for college and life goals and to practice making independent decisions, with the help of friends, family, and people on campus. Even if her path is not typical or as straightforward as that of her peers, it can still lead her to a successful and happy life. Perhaps once Gabby emerges into adulthood, she may feel greater ownership over her career path and life experiences than some of her more-resourced peers, considering success is something she has to work hard for.

The college experience extends beyond what happens in the classroom and includes outside activities and social interactions. As Stuber says, "because students spend only about fifteen hours each week within formal academic environments, most of this cultivation takes place outside of the classroom." Gabby is discovering that college does not furnish a level playing field, that she must work harder than some to obtain a college degree.

Though not necessarily working-class, she comes from a background that does not afford her the freedom or the money to participate in activities like Greek life and study abroad, or even trips to the mall. The lack of time and resources means that Gabby is not connecting with her peers as much through organizations on her campus, which inhibits her from establishing peer and friendship groups and thus acquiring a social network that could boost her social, marital, and employment status in the future.

We also advise Gabby to meet with a sociology professor, who can be sensitive to her social class background. Such a professor could encourage Gabby not to let her social class background define her, while also recognizing that not everybody in college is wealthy. There are more people with situations similar to Gabby's than she may recognize. We encourage students like Gabby to recognize that inequalities affect people differently. Trying hard is going to look different depending on people's socioeconomic circumstances. Also be sure to take advantage of the opportunity to learn how to get along with people who have different experiences, and be careful not to dismiss people who do not have the same success.

**#broke #workingtwojobs** During this time of identity exploration, **Julius** is at a crossroads. There is no one-size-fits-all approach to what he should do. Some on campus may advise Julius to stick it out and find ways to engage with his current university and student community. Others back home may advise him to come back to his home community while he decides what to do, or may recommend that he transfer universities. In fact, receiving mixed messages from people on campus and back home can intensify Julius's confusion and disconnection. Researchers describe emerging adults as transient, and that applies to Julius's feeling about making a decision that will shape his future. But there is an added element to Julius's story that is "off the beaten path" from the mainstream trends of emerging adulthood. What Julius is experiencing is best understood as an instance of what can be called the "come on back home" tendency for families of students who have less experience with college, or who are unfamiliar with a particular university.

Well-meaning adults faced with an unfamiliar situation may want to urge Julius to return to familiar territory (i.e., retracing your steps to get home rather than finding a new route to your destination). That may be best for Julius, or it may not be, depending on how "best" is defined and to what extent that is based on Julius's financial prospects. Julius has had his eyes set on his dream school for years, but that plan was derailed. Like other emerging adults, he has the freedom to explore different options, namely reapplying to his top school. He is also likely to be self-focused, turning inward to search for the right answer as he sorts through his evolving identity. But at the same time, it is important to recognize that for some emerging adults, the messages across social groups do not all converge and thus he receives conflicting advice.

Julius is experiencing an added level of confusion, in the midst of his identity exploration, that has to do with the mismatch between his aspirations for himself and the reality of his current situation. He does not feel any obligation or desire to invest in his current institution. Sure, doing so may make his day-to-day experiences easier, but at this point he is still preparing for leaving to be easy, as the alternative is something he is not ready to accept. One of the markers of emerging adulthood is becoming independent of one's parents, including financially. Julius began that journey early on as he worked to earn money for his college education. Some researchers refer to this as "accelerated adulthood," describing how Julius did not have the luxury of slowly contemplating his next steps. He had to move rather quickly into adult roles. While he knows that college can put his eventual goals within reach, he can't help but think about what he is forfeiting because of his lack of funds. Julius is experiencing what emerging adults see as the age of possibility, considering the what-ifs and could-bes, but he also demonstrates how resources condition aspirations. Wondering what is possible is fairly constant across emerging adults, but believing that all is possible may not be.

We encourage Julius to find a professor or advisor on campus who can relate to his story. When he hears someone talk about holding two jobs when they were in college, he could ask them to say more about what they learned from this, and he might receive the following advice: Navigating college with just one job is hard enough. With two jobs, it is really difficult. Thinking practically about this challenge, we encourage students like

Julius to explore whether there is a way to get a job that is related more to school, such as a research assistant, tutor, or working in a resident hall. It is worth it to check whether there are opportunities on campus that would alleviate the financial burden, while also respecting one's obligations as a student.

We also encourage students to find out what loans, scholarships, and other financial options are open to them. Go to the appropriate people and offices to consider all the options, as it may be there is another way than working two jobs. There are scholarships for people who need books, and scholarships for people who are first-year college students, both locally and nationally. There are people on campus who can help connect students with these resources. While some economic circumstances may be unchangeable, more people on campus face precarious circumstances than Julius and many other students realize. College can be a stratifying agent as much as one of social mobility. This knowledge can empower students to investigate their circumstances and seek out campus resources. Ensuring that students are integrated and connected on campus can help them focus on college now so they can build the kind of life they want later.

**#lifeisrough #deadbeatparents #wantabetterlife** We encourage **Leolia,** too, to reach out to a professor, especially one who conveys that he or she came from or understands the kind of family experiences that she describes. Students like Leolia should recognize their strength in overcoming formidable obstacles. We also encourage students to see college not just as a means to achieving social mobility but as a valuable aid to thinking critically about the world around them. Leolia's story sounds incredibly difficult, but it is also a great story of perseverance and self-reflection.

While we would commend Leolia for persevering to this point, we also would draw her attention to some alarms that we hear in her story. One is about the debt that she is acquiring by herself. We want to make sure that she is aware of the dangers of debt. Although there is no way to prevent all the possible hazards of taking out loans, we encourage her to be aware of what debt means and the impact that it can have on her future. Of course, she should continue pursuing her education, but at this relatively early point she may be able to find other options—such as scholarships or low-interest loans—to help keep the costs down.

A further piece of advice for students like Leolia is to ask themselves whether they are concealing too much in the effort to enter a new social class. Is Leolia putting on an act in college and not letting others see behind the scenes enough? She is such a powerful agent in her story, but we advise her to recognize that she is moving against the grain in significant ways. She may be carrying too much on her own shoulders and could stumble at some point as a result. We encourage her to reflect on how to integrate more of her past with her present. Instead of simply trying to change her cultural and social position, she should think about how her past can inform her present and future self. We would advise her to develop a more integrated, holistic identity that is rooted in her past but is also reshaped in a way that can help her thrive in her future. While it may be painful to think about the disadvantages of the past, moving forward entails recognizing that they are part of her experiences and influence the ways she interacts with others.

Taking this into account, we encourage students like Leolia to devote extra thought to finding the best path forward. For example, does Leolia truly feel a passion for studying medicine, or is she more interested in the social status that doctors enjoy? There are many career options that offer a way to prosper, and students need not fixate on only one option. We advise students to consider a number of paths in order to ensure they find a career that is interesting and fulfilling to them.

**#pressuretosucceed #fearoffailure** We have spent much of this chapter focusing on the difficulties of students at the lower end of the socioeconomic spectrum. **Bryce**, by contrast, talks about struggles that students from affluent backgrounds are more likely to confront. The fear of failure he describes is something that John Reynolds and Chardie Baird[16] and others address. They study the ways that high expectations can exert pressure and unrealistic expectations can result in disappointment. This kind of pressure can cause real struggles for college students, and its occurrence highlights that challenges in college (and life after college) arise for students from every background. Each group of students faces a particular set of opportunities to learn during college, sometimes as a result of confronting frustrations. The threatening and sometimes saddening sense that "bad things could happen" can actually be greater for people who have more to lose. In fact, exposure to the fact that others are less well off, even homeless, can cause wealthier individuals to feel more fear and resistance than compassion or empathy.[17] Some struggle to gain. Others struggle not to lose, or not to disappoint. Both situations are challenging.

We encourage students like Bryce to visit with a professor during office hours. One major tip we would give to Bryce is to stop comparing himself to other people. As someone coming from a position of privilege, he needs to take care to avoid mindlessly doing what others expect him to do. Instead, he should think about college as an opportunity to consider what kind of life is meaningful for him as he decides what his major is, what his career goals are, and what he wants other aspects of his life to look like. When students use the word "should," such as "I should be . . ." or mention feeling that they are not meeting others' expectations, it makes us want to drill down and stir some critical reflection. Who holds these expectations, and how easy or hard are they to change? Does the pressure on Bryce come from parents, family, neighborhood, church, or community? Do they expect him to be a straight-A student with the "white picket fence"? How realistic is this? Adults with high expectations might mean well, but we encourage students like Bryce to question whether they truly know what a successful life will look like for them. Students may need to carve out something different to find fulfillment.

We advise students to think about what avenues their campus has to offer that can help them grow and experience new things during college. Experimenting with different career possibilities and identities are part of becoming an adult and taking responsibility for oneself. Though students like Bryce are lucky that they do not have to be concerned with finances, that does not mean they do not have any issues to face during college. Their challenges are just as real. These students need to figure out how they can be satisfied with their situation, with themselves, and with the choices they make. It is empowering to become conscious of implicitly expected lifestyle choices, to question social pressures, and to chart out a personal path of one's own to build a life that brings meaning beyond filling others' expectations.

## FURTHER READING ONLINE

- One of the most well-known facts about Americans is that, on the whole, we are not very financially literate—though we can be, if we focus for a little while on the uncomfortable topic of money: Farber, Madeline, July 12, 2016, "Nearly Two-Thirds of Americans Can't Pass a Basic Test of Financial Literacy," retrieved from http://fortune.com/2016/07/12/financial-literacy/
.

- We recommend that students peruse a loan debt clock, such as this one: "Student Loan Debt Clock," FinAid, retrieved from http://www.finaid.org/loans/studentloandebtclock.phtml.
- The figure is astronomical! And counting. Rather than let that cause a swell of anxiety, students should channel that energy into productive focus. For example, here is a friendly description of fixed versus variable costs in a budget: Pant, Paula, March 12, 2019, "What's the Difference between Fixed & Variable Expenses," The Balance, retrieved from https://www.thebalance.com/what-s-the-difference-between-fixed-and-variable-expenses-453774.
- We find these kinds of articles tremendously helpful for forming a budget that will support a desired lifestyle. The web features numerous tips for college students on how to think about budgets. Here is one example: "College Student Budget Mini-Lesson," 1996, Indiana Department of Financial Institutions Consumer Education, retrieved from http://www.in.gov/dfi/CollegeStudBudgetMini.ppt.
- Here is another example: "Quick Guide: College Costs," 2019, CollegeBoard Big Future, retrieved from: https://

bigfuture.collegeboard.org/pay-for-college/college-costs/
quick-guide-college-costs.

- Here is one that comes with a budget spreadsheet
  template: Hong, Naomi, "Budgeting Basics for College Students,
  Plus Example Spreadsheet," College Express, retrieved from
  http://www.collegexpress.com/articles-and-advice/student-life/
  articles/living-campus/budgeting-basics-college-students-plus-
  example-spreadsheet/.
- However students choose to explore the subject, we recommend
  spending some time getting on top of finances now in order to
  avoid paying the price later.

## NOTES

1.  Stevens, Mitchell. 2013. "A School in a Garden." In Susan J. Ferguson (Ed.), *Mapping the Social Landscape: Readings in Sociology* (7th ed., pp. 564–577). New York: McGraw-Hill Education.
2.  Glassner, Barry. 2013. "The Culture of Fear: Why Americans Are Afraid of the Wrong Things." In Susan J. Ferguson (Ed.), *Mapping the Social Landscape: Readings in Sociology* (7th ed., pp. 105–112). New York: McGraw-Hill Education.
3.  Adler, Patricia A., and Peter Adler. 2013. "Peer Power: Clique Dynamics among School Children." In Susan J. Ferguson (Ed.), *Mapping the Social Landscape: Readings in Sociology* (7th ed., pp. 179–193). New York: McGraw-Hill Education.
4.  Domhoff, G. William. 2013. "Who Rules America? The Corporate Community and the Upper Class." In Susan J. Ferguson (Ed.), *Mapping the Social Landscape: Readings in Sociology* (7th ed., pp. 253–265). New York: McGraw-Hill Education.
5.  Marx, Karl, and Friedrich Engels. 2013. "Manifesto of the Communist Party." In Susan J. Ferguson (Ed.), *Mapping the Social Landscape: Readings in Sociology* (7th ed., pp. 43–47). New York: McGraw-Hill Education.
6.  Ehrenreich, Barbara. 2013. "Nickel-And-Dimed: On (Not) Getting By in America." In Susan J. Ferguson (Ed.), *Mapping the Social Landscape: Readings in Sociology* (7th ed., pp. 278–290). New York: McGraw-Hill Education.
7.  Edin, Kathryn, and Maria Kefalas. 2013. In Susan J. Ferguson (Ed.), *Mapping the Social Landscape: Readings in Sociology* (7th ed., pp. 598–605). New York: McGraw-Hill Education.
8.  Alexander, Karl, Robert Bozick, and Doris Entwisle. 2008. "Warming Up, Cooling Out, or Holding Steady? Persistence and Change in Education Expectations After High School." *Sociology of Education* 81(4): 371–396.

Blustein, David L., Anna P. Chaves, Matthew A. Diemer, Laura A. Gallagher, Kevin G. Marshall, Selcuk Sirin, and Kuldhir S. Bhati. 2002. "Voices of the Forgotten Half: The Role of School-to-Work Transition." *Journal of Counseling Psychology* 49(3): 311–323.

Bozick, Robert. 2007. "Making It Through the First Year of College: The Role of Students' Economic Resources, Employment, and Living Arrangements." *Sociology of Education* 80(3): 261–284.

Goldrick-Rab, Sara. 2006. "Following Their Every Move: An Investigation of Social-Class Differences in College Pathways." *Sociology of Education* 79: 61–79.

Hole, Jason N. 2013. "Disparities in Debt: Socioeconomic Resources and Young Adult Student Loan Debt." *Sociology of Education* 87(1): 53–69.

Massey, Douglas S., and Stefanie Brodmann. 2014. "Transitions to Adulthood." In *Spheres of Influence: The Social Ecology of Racial and Class Inequality* (pp. 266–303). New York: Russell Sage Foundation.

Terriquez, Veronica, and Oded Gurantz. 2014. "Financial Challenges in Emerging Adulthood and Students' Decisions to Stop Out of College." *Emerging Adulthood*: 1–11.

Torche, Florencia. 2011. "Is a College Degree Still the Great Equalizer? Intergenerational Mobility across Levels of Schooling in the United States." *American Journal of Sociology* 117(3): 763–807.

9. Bourdieu, Pierre and Jean Claude Passeron. 1977. *Reproduction in Education, Society, and Culture*. London: Sage.

Bourdieu, Pierre. 1984. *Distinction: A Social Critique of the Judgement of Taste*. Cambridge, MA: Harvard University Press.

Bourdieu, Pierre, and Jean Claude Passeron. 1977. *Reproduction in Education, Society, and Culture*. Thousand Oaks, CA: Sage Publications.

Bourdieu, Pierre, and Richard Nice. 1977. *Outline of a Theory of Practice*. Cambridge, UK: Cambridge University Press.

Johnson, Monica K. 2002. "Social Origins, Adolescent Experiences, and Work Value Trajectories during Transitions to Adulthood." *Social Forces* 80(4): 1307–1340.

Swartz, David L., and V. L. Zolberg. 2004. *After Bourdieu: Influence, Critique, Elaboration*. Boston: Kluwer Academic.

10. Lareau, Annette. 2013. "Invisible Inequality: Social Class and Childrearing in Black Families and White Families." In Susan J. Ferguson (Ed.), *Mapping the Social Landscape: Readings in Sociology* (7th ed., pp. 606–622). New York: McGraw-Hill Education.

11. Auerbach, Susan. 2007. "From Moral Supporters to Struggling Advocates: Reconceptualizing Parent Roles in Education through the Experience of Working-Class Families of Color." *Urban Education* 42(3): 250–283.

12. Stuber, Jenny M. 2011. "Inside the College Gates: Education as a Social and Cultural Process." In *Inside the College Gates: How Class and Culture Matter in Higher Education*. New York: Lexington Books.

13. Mills, C. Wright. 2013. "The Promise." In Susan J. Ferguson (Ed.), *Mapping the Social Landscape: Readings in Sociology* (7th ed., pp. 1–6). New York: McGraw-Hill Education.

14. Arnett, Jeffrey Jensen. 2015. *Emerging Adulthood: The Winding Road from the Late Teens Through the Twenties* (2nd ed.). New York: Oxford University Press.

15. Stuber, Jenny M. 2011. "Inside the College Gates: Education as a Social and Cultural Process." In *Inside the College Gates: How Class and Culture Matter in Higher Education*. New York: Lexington Books.

16. Reynolds, John R., and Chardie L. Baird. 2010. "Is There a Downside to Shooting for the Stars? Unrealized Educational Expectations and Symptoms of Depression." *American Sociological Review* 75(1): 151–172.

17. Seider, Scott. 2008. "'Bad Things Could Happen': How Fear Impedes Social Responsibility in Privileged Adolescents." *Journal of Adolescent Research* 23(6): 647–666.

# Taking Risks and Forming Identity

Chapter 4 integrates these topics by advising students to consider the ways that students exercise personal agency in making key decisions during college, while warning students to appreciate the difficulty of these choices and pay attention to the realities of the options they have available to them. The fourth chapter explains how exploring and forming a personal and social identity is vital to navigating college. In chapter 4, students learn that one key to college success is taking ownership of learning and exposing themselves to a variety of classes and majors in order to decide which is the best fit for them.

This chapter discusses the ways that social context and personal choices interact to shape individuals' paths through college and life. We discuss the importance of self-efficacy and ownership of learning in making important college decisions. In considering these ways to gain a sense of control over where one's life is headed, we also address how *feeling* that one has control is a mixture of belief and circumstances. In other words, it

*The Science of College.* Patricia S. Herzog, Casey T. Harris, Shauna A. Morimoto, Shane W. Barker, Jill G. Wheeler, A. Justin Barnum, and Terrance L. Boyd, Oxford University Press (2020) © Oxford University Press.
DOI: 10.1093/oso/9780190934507.001.0001

is hard to feel one has control if opportunities are limited, but even when opportunities abound, people might not believe that they have the ability to change their circumstances. Making choices, then, entails a complex balance between owning one's decision-making and accurately recognizing which opportunities one has (or does not have) available. Emphasizing personal transformation as a way to deal with all that life throws one's way can burden students with an excessive sense of responsibility for how their life turns out. We want to avoid this pitfall. At the same time, it is important not to accept a passive role in one's life, either. We talk through how to balance those ideals in creating value orientations that will help students choose a path with intentionality, ultimately making a meaningful life. Students must accept that, as with navigating via a GPS, they remain responsible for choosing a direction to travel, although there are many possible routes, and occasional "rerouting" is normal.

## STUDENT STORIES: WHAT WE EXPERIENCE

The student stories in this chapter highlight how students establish their identities in a variety of ways in college: through sororities or fraternities (**Abby**), deciding not to pledge (**Austin**), or in other ways finding self identity (**Kyndal**), especially by breaking out of high school cliques (**Emma**). Other students describe questioning the future of their childhood dreams (**Melissa**), including whether it is time to switch majors (**Chikako**), choosing from a myriad of interesting options (**Camille**), and considering how to commit to a major that will lead to a desirable career (**Mateo**).

---

**#greeklife #IamASororityWoman**: Best day ever! I am so proud of all the girls for rallying today for the pledges. The letters looked fantastic, and the photo booth was a definite hit. Here's to another great year together as sorority sisters ☺

**Abby** said the following about her identity as a sorority member:

Ever since I was little, I had dreamed of joining a sorority just like my mom, aunt, and older cousins had. Recruitment was incredibly rough and very much felt like being excluded by new people each day. However, on bid day I was welcomed home into the sweetest girls' arms . . . Within a few weeks of being part of the sorority I had found my best friends. We were thrown right into freshman sessions once a week, chapter once a week, and pep rallies most Fridays. We were taught how to act and carry yourself appropriately and were given numerous rules to follow. Not so surprisingly, I have found that almost all of my best friends are in my sorority. I hang out with these women almost every day of the week and have so much pride being able to wear our letters and throw our sign.

**#notgoinggreek #onbeingme**: To all the brothers who made pledge week so much fun, THANK YOU! Even though I decided not to go Greek, I had a blast this week and hope we can keep the good times going anyway. Who's up for going to check out a concert next weekend?

**Austin** described his decision not to go Greek in the following words:

My father works in a factory, and my mother is a social worker. I was never embarrassed by my . . . class origins until coming to college. The summer before my first semester, I decided I was going to rush. When you first decide to rush, you have to pay a substantial sum just for the chance to rush and then they give you a list of recommended outfits and items to bring for the occasion. I spent entire paychecks buying name-brand shorts and shirts that summed up who I was [supposed to be] as a person—having stains on them [implying that the person I was, and the clothes I wore, weren't good enough]. I did everything in my power to cover up my middle-class background to get into an organization that, three days after rush began, I decided was not for me. The pressure to be something I was not and conceal my origins was exhausting, and not how I wished to spend my college years. *College is the first time many get any true independence to make their own life decisions* [emphasis added]. I didn't want to give up my first chance to control my own life, to have some organization tell me how to dress, where to go, and how to live.

**#collegeainhighschool #findingyourself**: To all y'all back home, I miss you! College is so different than life back in YoJo!! For better and for worse. But I think I am starting to figure this whole college thing out and learning a lot about myself in the process.

**Kyndal** also reflected on the identity work involved in starting college:

The biggest change in my life in every way, shape, and form came when I moved to college. College is a shell shock to everyone because for the first time everyone is on their own without the reliance of their parents. I was so used to following the rules of my parents; I was also used to the culture of my hometown because I had never moved anywhere in my entire life . . . As I look back and compare high school Kyndal to college Kyndal there is a clear shift in identity. My high school definitely relied heavily on materialistic mindsets and popularity . . . My town is commonly referred to as the "YoJo bubble" . . . Most of the families that live in "YoJo" are ones with a lot of money, even more so, wealth matters more which is why the average car that was driven at my high school was either a Jeep, Lexus, or BMW . . . The "popular" kids had parents who had some form of high paying job who would buy them the newest fad the second it came out, making those who did not have those things, like myself, feel like an outsider, or like I did not belong. The "popular" kids through all four years of high school maintained the exact same friend group the entire time, something Adler and Adler (2018) call cliques.

College culture is one that really does not have a "set norm." Everyone in college does their own thing. No one really tries to impress anyone because some days I will see girls wearing onesies to class because it is just "one of those days." Everything you once knew as normal almost goes out the window once you go to college, because it is a fresh start and very few, if not anyone, knows you or your "reputation." The biggest thing that college throws at everyone, but mainly girls, are frat parties. The third day after I moved in, my roommates and I saw that everyone was going out, so we felt pressured to go out too. I never really partied a lot in high school, so experiencing a frat party for the first time was something new that I knew I would have to adjust to . . . *College comes with many new hardships and struggles, but I firmly believe college is where you find yourself; I have found myself*" [emphasis added].

**#findingnewfriends #nomorecliques**: So some people in my Friday class act like they are still in high school. First off, that's annoying! Please stop. Ok, but second, that reminds me how the rest of college is so different than high school. Cliques are so over with, and I couldn't be happier about that. To all my new friends, follow me, and I'll follow you back.

Also noting the monumental changes that college can bring to social identities, **Emma** had this to say:

[High school] freshman year friend groups included many girls, as everyone was trying to get to know each other. As the years went by, groups got smaller as people started to realize who they related to more . . . This year in college I started to grow apart from my [old] friend group and became closer with girls from a different clique. I quickly noticed how much more I related to them, and so I began to try and hang out with them as much as possible, to grow stronger friendships . . . I have quickly become very close, and consider them some of my best friends. However, there are numerous ways in which I have [also] experienced exclusion . . . In a high school setting, many girls are learning a lot about themselves and differences between others can be very apparent. Thus, I feel many cliques leave out outsiders because they are nothing like the other members of the group. Personally, I have experienced exclusion in that my friend group kicked out a girl because of constant fights and disagreements that were built up with multiple members of our group. Certainly, the exclusive and inclusive tendencies of friendship cliques have played a major role in my social life. *Although I have been in college for barely a year, many of my social experiences have already reshaped my life as a whole* [emphasis added].

**#whatamidoingwithmylife #stilldreaming**: Have I settled for the "easy" way out? Ever since I was little I have had a dream for what I wanted to do with my life, but everyone keeps telling me to be more "practical." Is it practical to give up on a dream, or is it selling out for safety?

**Melissa** shows how these social identity issues can affect decisions surrounding what to study and how that will affect life after college. As far back as Melissa can remember, she's been a dancer. Her mom often tells her she could do a perfect pirouette before she could spell her name. Melissa shows so much passion and talent when she dances. She is torn between wanting to pursue dance as a career and going the "practical" route of getting a traditional college degree. Melissa knows it is tough to make it in dance. She decided to enroll at her local university where she could remain a part of her dance company while completing college basics. As the first year draws to a close, she finds herself growing more comfortable with the idea of finishing college and letting go of her dream, but she struggles with wondering what will come next for her.

**#wrongmajor #wronglife**: I've told people for years that I'm going to be a lawyer. Now I find myself wondering if this is what I really want to do. Some of the classes are such a drag, and hard, because I'm just not that into it. There are so many other classes and majors that seem infinitely more interesting. Should I switch?

Both **Chikako's** mom and dad are lawyers, and it's always been assumed that he will follow in their footsteps. But to be honest he's never liked the idea. He hates his ethics class (just as a student aspiring to be a doctor might find he or she hates biology), but he likes his volunteer work at the local elementary school. He's a member of a fraternity and organizes all of their functions. He's thinking of switching to an education major, and he is trying to figure out how best to break the news to his parents. Luckily, he has a great relationship with one of his professors and has frequently visited during office hours to discuss his new path and how to approach this issue with his parents.

**#toomanychoices #howdoidecide**: Do you wonder where you want to end up? I keep hearing everyone else talking about their career plans, and I just don't have it figured out like they do. Everything interests me! How do you decide when there are so many exciting options?

**Camille** is a good student. She has always been a good student. In high school, she did well and made the grades that everyone expected. In fact, she did well in all subjects, and that is the problem. She is in her first semester and taking university core classes. While they are all going well, there isn't anything that she can see herself studying for the next four years. Her lack of direction is a constant weight on her shoulders. It seems like everyone she meets asks her how the semester is going and quickly follows it up with, "What's your major?" Her parents find a way to bring it up in every conversation, and she's started screening their calls because she doesn't have the answer they want. Her advisor assures her that this is normal and suggests she take some interest inventories and meet with a career counselor to guide her to a possible major. She has made those appointments, but secretly she worries that they won't help and wishes someone else could just tell her what to do.

Similarly, since high school, **Mateo** has been interested in a lot of different things and has generally found something he likes in each of his classes. While registering for his first semester, he picked a major in history because he really loved his high school history class the year before. He's doing well now and has been pretty happy with his choice. However, he has a friend who is studying computer science, another in engineering, and another working on a criminology degree. When they talk about the classes they're taking, they all seem really interesting, and he could see himself taking all of those classes too. He thinks, "I'm at a university with dozens of majors and hundreds of courses to choose from . . . am I choosing the right major? What happens if I finish my degree, and I would have been better off with one of the other majors?" The choices seem overwhelming and irrevocable. He wishes there were an easier way to sort it all out.

## SCIENCE: WHAT WE KNOW

It is important to note, after the discussion of chapter 3, that family backgrounds are not *determinative*: one's resources play a major role in individual experiences but do not prevent individuals with similar resources from acting differently. Connecting earlier discussions of cultural inequalities with the identity construction process of emerging adulthood, we think this is why *self-efficacy* and *ownership of learning* are important predictors of college success. We prefer the term "social self-efficacy" because the concept refers to having confidence in one's competence to acquire and respond to the social norms of different settings—for example, college. In this sense, feeling that one has control over one's life is a mixture of belief and circumstances. Ownership of learning, or a sense of personal involvement and investment in one's education, is "not sufficiently taught or measured" in college, but it "can be developed systematically" and has the greatest effect on students for whom college is a challenge initially (Wright, Jenkins-Guarnieri, & Murdock 2013: 1019).[1] Wright and colleagues find that these "extra-cognitive" factors are becoming more important in navigating college because of increasing class sizes and a heightened focus on independent learning. In other words, academic knowledge of class content is necessary for success in college, but it is not sufficient. Students also need general skills for directing their college experiences. It turns out these skills also promote improved health and well-being.[2]

It is important, then, to understand that college presents students with the freedom to make decisions and have fun while taking into account their particular social and economic circumstances. As **Kyndal** illustrates, students can experience a culture during their first year that is quite different from what they are used to. Learning to thrive in this new culture involves figuring out who to ask for help when needed and how to ask for it. The challenge for new college students is to adapt to a new culture without feeling like they have lost their fundamental character. This process is among the most exciting and rewarding experiences of college for many students—learning how to adapt while also learning more about who one is and establishing who one wants to be. Many of the student stories in this chapter demonstrate the importance of selecting which groups of friends to have and what activities to get involved in. On every campus there is a wide array of options. Finding the right fit can promote well-being.[3]

Moving beyond the overview of social class and cultural inequality dynamics that we summarized in chapter 3, we focus in this chapter on the ways that social experiences affect our everyday decisions. This is most in line with a branch of social theories that is referred to as *symbolic interactionism*, as well as with the sociology of culture. This branch of social thinking pays attention to the subjective meaning we derive from everyday experiences, and the interaction between the circumstances that people are in (*social structure*) and the choices they make in response to these circumstances, which also can change their circumstances over time (*agency*).[4] In interpreting social interactions, people react based on a combination of their view of themselves and what they think others think about them. Focusing on this iterative process highlights that people do not form their identities in a vacuum. Someone could think they belong in a certain social group, but if people do not accept them in that group, then they will likely reevaluate whether they want to belong in it. For example, students could enter college thinking they want to be lawyers, but if spending time in the pre-law group makes them feel like outcasts or gives them the sense that they are different from the other students in that group, then they may reconsider whether they truly want to be lawyers.

Having these kinds of experiences can result in what Dalton Conley[5] refers to as the "*intravidual.*" The term conveys the idea that we as individuals are penetrated by society, meaning even our most personal thoughts and feelings are punctuated by our experiences within multiple social groups. This is why it is important to think of self-efficacy, and well-being generally, as situated within a social context that presents challenges for personal integration. Conley describes modern life as presenting a "competing cacophony of multiple selves all jostling for pole position in our mind" (Conley 2013: 169), In the face of such a cacophony, it is important for students' well-being to do the work of self-reflection, and to focus on how to gain self-efficacy in navigating their lives effectively. For example, **Aaron** of chapter 5 describes the following:

> Even though I began to conform to the ideals of the upper class, I still interacted with people of the middle to lower class through my church. These people had completely different ideals and values than the people of the upper-class that I interacted with daily at school. Because of this difference, I would act different at school than I would at church.

Aaron continues by explaining how multiple interactions can cause a sense of fragmentation:

> My "self" had become fragmented because I was being socialized by two different groups, and this made me an intravidual (Conley 2013). Because of this, I almost never brought the two groups together. On occasion, I brought my school friends to church, or I would bring someone from church to a school dance or football game. When this did happen, I was confused on how to act. Although my personality

did not completely change when I switched groups, I still acted different in the slightest way, and this caused friction.

Reflecting on his experience of fragmentation, he connects this to his prior family experiences:

> Not only was I fragmented between my friend groups, but it also happened between my divorced parents' houses just like Conley pointed out (2013). While one parent would be strict in one area, the other parent would be relaxed in that area. This caused many fights between me and both of my parents. After realizing this difference in the enforced norms in each home, I began acting differently around each of my parents, just as I did between my different friend groups.

Conley explains that growing up in a highly networked era, with social media connecting people across the globe, confronts individuals with limited participation in a broad array of social groups. We can get the sense that we are one self when we interact in one group, and another self when in other groups. When we think about all these different groups together, we may feel that they do not add up, that we have "lost ourselves" in the bustle or have to devote concerted effort to "finding ourselves." This experience of fragmentation can be profound for college students, who may be confronted on university campuses with a greater range of options in terms of who to be, who to hang out with, and what to do. For example, **Troy** (a student discussed in chapter 2), reflected on the dramatic change from high school to college, stating the following:

> Pieces of myself are still invested back home in my family and friends, but at the same time, I am actively expanding my individuality in town through clubs, school, and the new people I have met. This expansion has led to a feeling of fragmentation because the intra-individual pieces of myself are much more distant than they were in the past. Luckily, I found other things to invest myself into.

These sentiments from Troy represent a healthy way to respond to a moderate degree of fragmentation in a fairly normal college experience.

A degree of fragmentation, and distress over the challenges of reintegration, can be normal during college, and in life generally. For some, however, this issue can become overwhelming. Long-term fragmentation in the absence of integration can be linked to disorganized thinking, which is a key aspect of what psychologists call schizophrenia. The key then is to acknowledge the normality of experiencing fragmentation in modern societies, with such a diverse array of interactions, while also understanding that moderation is the key differentiator for health and well-being. Becoming stuck in fragmentation, being overwhelmed by the task of reintegration work, or ruminating for long periods of time over the difficulties inherent in fragmentation can be well-being issues. From a sociological approach, schizophrenia and other mental health issues can be understood as an outcome of the modern condition, which can promote too high a degree of social disorganization.[6] This approach is important for recognizing factors in the broader social context that create negative, and positive, personal experiences. From a psychological approach, schizophrenia and other mental health issues can be viewed as an individual condition, which needs medication and personal reconstruction to treat.[7]

As discussed in chapter 1, sociologists describe the *socialization* process as meaning "that societal values, identities, and social roles are learned, not instinctual" (Granfield 1991: 145).[8] To the extent that higher education boosts social mobility (as discussed in chapter 3), it provides students with a greater sense of control of their lives. Here is a student description that exemplifies this sense of control:

> Controlling one's own life means exercising authority and influence over it by directing and regulating it oneself. People vary in the control felt over their own lives. Some feel they can do just about anything they set their minds to. They see themselves as responsible for their own successes and failures and view misfortunes as the results of personal mistakes. Others feel that any good things that happen are

mostly luck—fortunate outcomes they desire but do not design. They feel personal problems mostly result from bad breaks or the callous selfishness of others and feel little ability to regulate or avoid the bad things that happen . . . Sociologically, the sense of personal control reflects the real constraints and opportunities of one's ascribed and achieved statuses (Mirowsky & Ross 2007: 1340–1343).[9]

Education, especially during college, builds a greater sense of control, which is a key aspect of long-term well-being. While other adults experience a diminishing sense of control as they age, those with a college degree feel an increasing degree of control. The reason for this difference seems to be that college regulates access to opportunities, and access to opportunities facilitates a general sense of control over the direction one's life is headed.

Part of acknowledging the importance of students' different social and economic resources (discussed in chapter 3) is recognizing how class backgrounds can affect cognition and thus shape decision-making. For example, **Chen** of chapter 5 reflects on differences in social resources by describing the emotional labor of her childhood:

Emotional labor, as defined by Loe, "requires one to induce or suppress feeling in order to sustain an outward countenance that produces the desired state of mind in others" (2013: 83).[10] I had no term for what I was doing [back then], but I was learning to do emotional labor in all parts of my life, even my home. It is easy to see how it became difficult for me to express anger in the way an adult would because I learned how to conceal anger.

Research finds that students from less resourced backgrounds can use "resistance strategies"[11] that are intentional efforts to conceal any ways they may not fit into the middle-class culture of college. Jennifer M. Silva[12] refers to this as a "mood economy," in which students—especially those from working-class backgrounds—adhere strongly to the idea of therapeutic self-transformation:

The need to continuously recreate one's identity—whether after a failed attempt at college or an unanticipated divorce or a sudden career change—can be an anxiety-producing endeavor. In a world of rapid change and tenuous loyalties, the language and institution of therapy—and the self-transformation it promises—has exploded in American culture (Silva 2013: 18–19).

Silva continues by explaining what is entailed in the therapeutic culture:

[The] therapeutic narrative . . . provides a blueprint for bringing a reconstructed, healthy self into being. It works like this: first, it compels one to identify pathological thoughts and behaviors; second, to locate the hidden source of these pathologies within one's past; third, to give voice to one's story of suffering in communication with others; and finally, to triumph over one's past by bringing into being an emancipated and independent self (Silva 2013: 19).

Contrary to the widely held belief that individuals can choose freely which path to take in life, the educational process presents a number of "institutional sorting mechanisms."[13] People do make choices, but these choices are not free-floating options. They are pathways; they are akin to a GPS's presentation of several preexisting routes. Choosing one versus another affects one's likelihood of getting stuck in traffic or having to take a detour because of construction. Anyone who has tried different map apps knows they are not all equally good at predicting which route is the best to take, in part because they rely on different sources of data, including potentially outdated information. Likewise, college pathways sort students in different ways.

As one example of thinking about how social class background and individual behavior affect the routes students take through college, Elizabeth A. Armstrong and Laura T. Hamilton[14] describe three college pathways: the professional pathway, the party pathway, and the social mobility pathway. They state, "Just as roads are built for types of vehicles, pathways are built for types of students. The party pathway is provisioned to support the affluent and socially oriented; the mobility pathway is designed for the pragmatic and vocationally oriented; and the professional pathway fits ambitious students from privileged families" (Armstrong & Hamilton 2013: 15). All these pathways return students skills, and which pathway students regularly engage in during college has ramifications for the kinds of skills they develop.

For those on the *professional pathway*, the university is a means for achieving a professional career. Students on this pathway typically come from affluent backgrounds and have set their sights on entering a profession as a career and life identity. They typically focus on studying during college and tend to form their friendship groups around their professional identity. Often hailing from the other end of the socioeconomic spectrum, those on the *mobility pathway* tend to see the university as a means for striving to be upwardly mobile. Although getting a college degree may be their end goal at this point, as they may not have settled on pursuing a certain job or career after college, students in this path tend to work hard and befriend others who do the same. Between the focus of these other two groups lies a third group, the *party pathway*, and students on this path tend to see the university as a means for socializing and fun. Armstrong and Hamilton describe how these students and the university have a "mutual agreement" to demand little of each other. Thus, many students on this path prioritize participating in campus life over attending classes.

Importantly, people on all three pathways can be successful after college, and people on all three paths can also struggle to carve out comfortable careers and lives after graduation. Students' post-college lives are determined less by the paths they select than by the degree to which their resources, choices, and behaviors align with the path that they are on. For example, the professional pathway is home to both "achievers" and "underachievers," in Armstrong and Hamilton's terminology. Achievers, who earn good grades in difficult classes, accomplish a relatively smooth transition into careers after graduation. The "underachievers" often struggle to balance their social lives on campus with the rigorous studies that the professional pathway demands. The post-college success of these students is mixed, depending on whether they switch course during college to better align their major and career path with their actual behaviors.

Likewise, there are more successful and less successful groups within the party pathway. In this case, the groups are "socialites" and "wannabes." Socialites make the most of their high degree of social engagement, and build strong networks during college that position them well for careers that rely upon networking. Advertising, PR, and other business positions, for instance, are well-suited for students on the party pathway. Wannabes, on the other hand, may attempt to take that pathway but never fully fit into the social scene, often due to a misalignment between their desires and the path they are traversing. In some cases, these students attempt majors that require strong academic performance, which proves incompatible with their entrenchment in the party scene. Students in this situation must often confront hard choices related to downgrading their expectations for their major and career to better align with their social participation. Other wannabes on the party pathway are the students who do not have enough resources to pay for the fashion, entertainment, and extra expenses involved in partying. These students struggle to fit in, and among the students Armstrong and Hamilton studied, their outcomes were sometimes worse than those of students on the social mobility pathway who were not trying to juggle multiple social identities.

For students on the third path, social mobility, results vary as well. All the students on this pathway are striving, motivated to establish a better life than they had growing up. Armstrong and Hamilton describe such students in this way: "They came 'motivated for mobility,' making it to college despite considerable odds and leaving communities where college attendance was far from the natural next step in life" (Armstrong & Hamilton 2013: 148). Some of these students are "creamed" from the group, referring to the "cream of the crop." In other words, the best students are plucked from the mobility pathway by intervention programs designed to facilitate their move into the professional pathway. Many others on this mobility trek find the path to be "blocked." Weighed down by the struggle to cover everyday expenses, they come to feel isolated in their attempts to handle financial difficulties while matching the academic accomplishments of their peers on the professional path or finding the resources to socialize with their peers on the party path.

Key for our purposes, those students who best align their interests, desires, social capital, and other resources with the path most likely to reward them are more likely to be successful. In tracking the post-college trajectories of the students they followed, Armstrong and Hamilton found that the achievers of the professional pathway made a quick and smooth entry into professional job markets or graduate programs, successfully reproducing an upper-middle-class trajectory. Meanwhile, the underachievers of that same path struggled with underemployment or unemployment and continued to depend on their parents financially, facing a risk of downward mobility. Among those on the party pathway, the socialites secured solid jobs in big cities thanks to the connections and continued support of their parents, reproducing their middle-class standing. The wannabes, however, struggled with unemployment due to underqualification, and they lacked the parental funds or social ties to support their trajectory, placing their future class standing in jeopardy. Finally, the results of graduates of the mobility pathway also diverged. Students who were successful on this pathway (the creamers) landed jobs that launched them from working-class to middle-class lifestyles. In contrast, those who were less successful (the blocked) often ended up encountering difficult financial situations that undermined their chances of upward mobility. In many cases, they ended up back at home in jobs that did not require a bachelor's degree. Thus, pathways through college reflected a combination of the following: parental resources upon which students could rely; the particular pathway selected; and the ways students aligned their everyday choices (or not) with the pathway they were attempting to take.

Another college navigational choice relates to the degree of engagement online, especially social media interactions. For emerging adults, friendships are fluid and disjointed and social networks are loose.[15] In studying the role of social media sites on friendships, scholars found that these sites help emerging adults maintain large and dispersed networks of friends.[16] The increased mobility, use of social network sites, and the overall casual attitude toward friendships can benefit emerging adults through expanding their social networks and increasing their connections to many people who have access to a wide variety of social and economic resources.[17] Indeed, for socially anxious individuals, interacting online can provide greater support than interacting face-to-face, resulting in improved well-being.[18] However, there are eventually diminishing returns to the number of friends on social media, and likewise drawbacks to obsessively posting on social media.[19] Plus, researchers have found that intense engagement on social media is related to lower levels of academic engagement and to less involvement in extra-curricular activities during college.[20] Thus, the results of social media in college are mixed.

In summary, navigating college well requires continual work to align and realign one's progress as an individual with one's structural position within the institution of higher education. When navigating by a GPS, it is not wise to take a route plotted for a car if one does not have a car. However, there are many ways to get to every destination, and taking public transit, riding a bicycle, or using a ride share app can prove just as effective, as long as the navigator understands that is the method they need to choose and acquires skills for using it. Technology enabled navigation systems are one of the beauties of modern existence. Nevertheless, there is something to be said for getting lost. One of the most "adulting" experiences one can have is to drive to a new city with only a paper map and the willingness to ask people for directions. As hard as it is to believe, many people made it into adulthood without having a cell phone, let alone with a navigation device. This sense of being untethered,[21] on one's own two feet without constant access to calls or lookups for help, may be one of the best ways to craft a path into adulthood.

## ADVICE: WHAT WE (CAN) PROVIDE

This advice section switches from the previous voices of faculty members to the voices of student development and student support practitioners that follow. To some extent, the advice offered here is a bit generic, as it must be general in order to write to a wide variety of readers. But tailoring different pieces of advice toward particular student stories can aid students in understanding how and why to access different resources on college campuses. In our experience, students are smart people who generally know about the existence of campus resources. Typically, the problem is not ignorance of their existence, which seems to be presumed by many available books that just provide students with lists of campus resources. Rather, we find the problem to lie with students knowing which resources can be helpful for what sorts of problems. Thus, in what follows we offer examples of the kinds of support that students can seek, relative to the kinds of issues they face. In reality, the support that real students receive would be even more personalized than these general pieces of advice suggest, which is why this book does not replace students actually reaching out for real support. Our aim instead is to help students feel less embarrassed and more knowledgeable about who to go to for what, and ultimately to feel empowered to ask for the help that they need.

**#greeklife #IamASororityWoman** The first student in this chapter, **Abby**, has a story that is relatable for many students. She does not mention that academics are difficult for her, and she does not mention any particular problems. She enjoys following the rules that her sorority sets for her. She has found a place within her sorority and appears to be on the party pathway. Though it sounds like she is well-aligned with this route, we encourage students like Abby to meet with an advisor to ensure they balance their effort and attention between academics and their social lives. In addition to making connections that can become lifelong friends, it is key to keep track of academic deadlines, attend classes, complete assignments, and prepare adequately for exams. Academics will help Abby, and students like her, to wind up with a degree along with valuable network connections. Both will be important for launching her career.

**#notgoinggreek #onbeingme** In contrast to Abby, the second student, **Austin**, appears to be on the mobility pathway. He attempted to get on the party pathway by seeking to join a fraternity but realized early on that he was not meshing well there due to his limited finances. As Austin's situation illustrates, students have choices; they can still participate in the social scene as long as they have enough awareness to recognize whether heavy participation will set them up for misalignment. Austin could have become a "wannabe," but instead he makes a choice to have intermittent involvement in the social scene while focusing on making sure he is upwardly mobile. We advise students like Austin to consider with care what their ideal fit is within different student organizations.

At most universities, there is a group for every kind of student, so even though it was good for Austin to pull back from fraternity life, he should still scout out other options. Also remember that there are many other students on campus who have similar challenges, concerns, and desires. Next, we encourage students like Austin, who do not benefit from the informed guidance of family members who graduated college, to be mindful that it is especially vital for them to meet with an advisor who can help them manage their class schedules and direct them to people on campus who can help set up tuition and other payments, such as financial aid counselors. Many campuses feature ways to set up automatic payment reminders and other resources that can help a student like Austin ensure that he keeps on top of things. Plus, students often find that these advisors and counselors can be good sounding boards, providing someone besides fellow students to discuss these issues with more comfortably.

**#collegeainthighschool #findingyourself** With **Kyndal**, it is clear that she shares aspects in common with both Abby and Austin. Like Abby, Kyndal appears to be on the party pathway, especially since she does not mention a professional identity. However, like Austin, Kyndal mentions her socioeconomic background and alludes to how it has barred her from certain cliques. Drawing on Kyndal's description of her background, it seems that she comes from the middle class, but perhaps she is not as affluent as the students that surrounded her in her hometown. Now she is in college, and it sounds like she may feel some of the same pressures to fit in among college circles who also may be more affluent than she is.

As an advisor, we would be interested in talking more with Kyndal about the ways she has "found herself" in college. One concern her story raises is whether participating in the social scene, attempting to be on the party pathway, is the best fit for her. We would ask Kyndal to reflect on whether she may instead be best aligned with the mobility pathway.

Perhaps, like Austin, she would benefit from investing less in the social scene and instead finding student organizations in which she could be her authentic self and gain support from other less affluent students. Or she may be interested in finding an organization in the community that she can participate in or volunteer for, working with people outside the "university bubble." Stepping back from the social scene would also give Kyndal more energy to devote to academics and to cementing a secure career path.

By whichever route, we advise students like Kyndal to find a group or activity in which they feel some ownership, and where they feel like they truly fit in. Doing so is part of navigating their own pathway. Not only will this generally feel better and be more enjoyable in the long run, but it may also boost their chances of completing college and launching a successful career afterward, as the research summarized in this chapter suggests. This knowledge can empower students to navigate their own way, with others, but without feeling like they have to do what they think everyone else is doing. Finally, we advise students like Kyndal not to attempt to do everything at once and instead to understand the first year of college as a critical time to lay a strong foundation for success in the years to come. It is important for Kyndal to remember why she came to college in the first place, and to avoid getting too caught up in what everyone else is doing.

**#findingnewfriends #nomorecliques** Sharing similar experiences with Kyndal, **Emma's** story shows students that they are not the only ones who feel like they do not always know how to belong. We can imagine that, by exploring other organizations and opportunities on campus, students like Emma could wind up participating in the same student club, or volunteering together. They could find common ground in that they have not really been on the professional pathway but are also having trouble along the party pathway. Of course, they would probably not use those terms, but they could share that—unlike everyone else, it seems—they do not know what career they want to have, and though they have tried going out, they find it hard to keep up with the social scene without falling behind in their classes. We recommend that students like Emma and Kyndal complete the activity described in the next section so they can discuss with others their experiences with feelings excluded. This is one way to find people who are like-minded, and to form a group of friends who can support each other's academic success by studying together, instead of, or before, going out together.

We also advise students like Abby and Kyndal to recognize the ways that college is different from high school, and also how college presents opportunities to break out of previous patterns. Most students attend universities that are larger than their high school, which means there are more of every kind of student, making it easier to find an entire subgroup of friends that are not the typical kind of student that, it seems, everyone else is. As a point of reference, we have taught many students in class who confide in us as professors that they are different than the "typical student in here," but we look around and think, "that is what nearly every student in this class has said." Be mindful that the typical college scene actually entails many different kinds of student groups, and that some may simply be more visible than others, especially early on in the first year. Our main piece of advice, then, would be to reject the assumption that everyone is the same and instead talk with people to find out about the many groups on campus. All phases of life involve cliques and subgroups, so college is the perfect time to gain skills in navigating group dynamics. (Notably, students who find these relational tasks to be exceedingly difficult should consult counseling services and other coping strategies, such as group therapy.)

All these students, and the four to follow, should know that it is common to be swept up in what everybody else is up to, or what it seems like everyone is doing, when college begins. But now is the time to take ownership of this journey. It is no fun being bored, so explore what is exciting, and find those personal passions. Perhaps surprisingly, researchers find that exploring (switching majors and switching jobs) during college is linked to *better* outcomes after graduating.[22] But job-hopping while not enrolled in college is linked to worse outcomes. So now is the time: explore with the protection of the college safety net.

**#whatamidoingwithmylife #stilldreaming** An example of a student who is on the professional pathway, **Melissa** is clearly focused on choosing a professional identity. However, she is having doubts about whether she needs to change career plans from the dream she thought she had. That too is a very normal part of college, and it does not mean that Melissa is getting off the professional pathway. Students can still take that route without knowing exactly which profession they will enter. The key is that figuring out that professional identity is core to their college experience. It is common for students to enter college with a dream of something they have long seen themselves doing and then have that dream shaken. We advise students like Melissa to meet with an advisor to discuss these questions about changing their intended career.

As an advisor, we would ask Melissa what it is about dance that makes her feel good. What is she drawn to—the performance, the freedom of her body movement, or something else? We would then help her to consider other career options that may provide her some of the same rewards, but perhaps in a different way. One option, for example, would be to become a dance teacher. To explore whether she would enjoy and gain the same satisfaction from teaching dance, we would advise Melissa to check into dance programs in the community, and to investigate whether she could get involved in one. More generally, we encourage students like Melissa to view changing their mind about their childhood dreams to be a normal part of the college experience and to explore other options. All the answers do not have to be clear from the beginning. It may have been nice at earlier ages to tell friends of the family and teachers about a clear dream or career path, but students do not have to cling to that plan in college merely because that is what they always said.

College is a journey. It does not begin and end in a single semester. Students need to be able to test different options and find what truly motivates them and channels their passion. Typically college is not strictly vocational in nature. The skills that students gain throughout their education, in coursework and through other experiences, can serve them well in many areas of life after college. Enjoy the fact that college presents the chance to explore; take in all the skills and experiences possible; and think about how to translate those attributes into viable options that still fulfill one's dreams. For example, maybe one day Melissa will open her own dance studio, and in the meantime, she can take some education courses to learn techniques for teaching and some business courses to learn how to manage a small business. Classes in the social sciences would teach her more about working with people, and those in the arts would enliven her passion. All of these courses can culminate in her living her dream, in a different way than she imagined.

**#wrongmajor #wronglife** In a story somewhat similar to Melissa's, **Chikako** is on the professional pathway while reconsidering which particular career option to pursue. Chikako was raised in an affluent background, and he feels pressured to match his parents' status. There are many students who do the same—arrive to campus with a declared major and a plan that was never really declared by them. We encourage students in the same boat as Chikako to meet with an advisor to discuss more options. Chikako's dislike of his ethics class is an indication that law may not be the right fit for him (the same is true for someone who detests a biology class and is a pre-med major, and so on). A college degree provides beautiful flexibility in that students can check out a variety of class options to explore other departments, majors, and careers. We advise students to take the courses that look most interesting to them, seizing the opportunity to talk with the instructors of those courses about related career options.

We also recommend that students inquire about ways to shadow a professional or conduct an informational interview with someone in the career that interests them. See what it would really be like to be a lawyer, or a doctor, or a teacher. Do not assume that the TV version is accurate. In fact, it is best to assume it will not be nearly as exciting as those sensationalized portrayals. Long-term excitement comes rather from being authentically passionate about a career, which depends on "gelling" with the reality of that profession. Shadowing someone in a student's intended career can also provide him or her with material for explaining to parents what is attractive or unappealing about career options, rather than attempting to explain less informed ideas about this to parents, which may raise their concerns regarding whether the student has really thought through a change of plans. Taking the initiative to scope out a future career and relaying specific information goes a long way to reassuring most parents that the student is being responsible and thorough. When it comes down to it, most parents simply want their children to be successful, happy, and secure. Showing parents how the path they are charting can achieve those goals, even if it is different from what the parents have in mind, may go a long way toward relieving the pressure students like Chikako feel. It also helps parents to be supportive, as they can feel assured their children have "done their homework."

Another piece of advice for students in a similar situation to Chikako is to develop a network of people who share their passions. Like shadowing a professional, spending time with other students who intend to pursue the same profession can be revealing. This step can help students distinguish between not enjoying a single class, which they may have to just get through, and an indication that there is something about the overall profession that does not fit. Student groups devoted to a given profession are a decent representation of the people who practice that profession, so this is a great way to get a sense for whether these are the people with whom one wants to interact regularly for the foreseeable future. If students do not enjoy the company of the other people in a pre-professional group for their intended career, it is time to consider a switch. If this non-enjoyment of social interactions is a long-term pattern across multiple groups, regardless of the professional and social interests of that group, then students should seek more intensive changes, such as individual counseling or social group therapy.

**#toomanychoices #howdoidecide** To **Camille,** the possibilities seem endless, and that is keeping her up at night. With every semester and each course she takes, though, she is figuring out who she is and what she wants out of life. While it may not feel that way to her right now, emerging adulthood is giving her the freedom to gain exposure to what, until recently, she may have seen as unusual education choices or simply never have heard of. That she is comfortable in so many different disciplines allows her the opportunity to try out the possibilities until she finds the right path for her.

A caring adult in her life could help Camille to see her confusion not as a problem but as an understandable and desirable part of the process of figuring out what major and career will fit her newly forming identity. Research shows that the "cost" of a mistake, such as initially choosing the wrong major, is relatively low during this time in life, so a caring adult could assure Camille that—while enrolled in college—she has the flexibility to explore without the pressure of believing that every step she takes is set in stone. We recommend that Camille visit an advisor to discuss the pressures she is feeling. College offers a bewildering array of choices, but of course making choices doesn't end after graduation. We encourage students to think of college as a time to take charge. Now Camille gets to be the one who decides what she will study. An advisor can work with her on ways to get engaged outside the classroom, reminding her that college is more than the content of her particular courses. Getting involved in student government, or housing, or any of the different options available could give her an idea of where to head next.

#toomanychoices #howdoidecide Along with Camille, **Mateo** represents how having seemingly infinite options can be overwhelming. Emerging adulthood is a time of possibility and hope—a period of "unparalleled opportunity to transform." Nevertheless, the instability of this period can be stressful.[23] Mateo's struggle to settle on a major reflects the broader challenge of shaping one's present identity and simultaneously creating a plan for the future. Both Camille and Mateo fear that even routine choices may have long-lasting consequences. Yet emerging adults usually pay a lower price for their choices than adults do. We thus advise students like Mateo and Camille to think of their choices as explorations, not permanent decisions. Picking a major, even completing a college degree in a certain field, does not mean that one cannot change one's life plan again. Instead of worrying about that, it is better to focus on developing basic academic and social capabilities, as those open doors to many career options. Research comparing college students making such changes to college graduates or young people not enrolled reveals that college is like a protective bubble in which young people can actually *benefit* from changing their majors or career paths without major problems, but, in fact, with benefits. Conversely, people not in the protective environment of college making these changes tend to fare worse. Knowing this information, Mateo and Camille can continue to explore during college, and the adults in their lives can relax knowing that they are "on track" for success.

Mateo's concern about the appropriateness of his major, as for many other students, probably stems from a combination of general indecisiveness and the social and cultural skills he brought to campus. In chapter 3 we summarized how Stuber (2012)[24] notes that social class background structures a student's ability to navigate their campus life. Whereas privileged students typically begin college with the necessary tools to guide their academic decision-making, "less privileged students are often less equipped for the journey" (Stuber 2011: 12). As a result, middle- and upper-class students may seem more likely to "have it all together" than students who are from working- or lower-class families. One solution for Mateo might be to speak with his professors and advisors, all of whom can equip him with new skills and ideas for navigating college life inside and outside of the classroom. They may say, "Now is the time to try out different things within the safer confines of college, and engaging adults across campus can help you (a) identify the right places to build social and cultural tools and (b) use them to make more strategic decisions about your major." Rather than beating himself up for feeling indecisive and unsure of his career trajectory, Mateo needs to recognize that other students may have worked through the same processes prior to coming to campus, and that he can master the same skills before he graduates.

Important here is to recognize the difference between a short-term setback and a longer-term debilitation. Short-term setbacks and failures of various kinds during college can provide important opportunities to recalibrate and shape oneself in better and more positive life directions, which will ultimately promote better health and well-being outcomes. For a subset of young people, however, what could be short-term setbacks instead preempt longer-term debilitation, rumination, and other personal problems. Rising to the challenge is a key differentiator for encountering the normal failures of college as opportunities for positive growth, or not. If students find themselves consistently unable to overcome short-term setbacks and repeatedly find themselves responding in destructive patterns to these opportunities for growth, then more intensive personal interventions may be necessary. In the absence of debilitating personal issues, the challenges and opportunities afforded by college experiences present young people with new chances to figure out what fits them and to construct a balanced life.

The challenge both Mateo and Camille face in finding a major that "fits" them is, in fact, a valuable exercise that will pay off in the future. Many students feel anxious about such decisions for a wide variety of reasons. Perhaps they have limited budgets that constrain the time available to explore different majors, or maybe pressure from their family to choose a particular field of study weighs on them. Yet one of the goals of higher education is to provide the skills and resources to shape one's own life. Not every student arrives with the same familiarity and social/cultural tools for finding the right discipline, and some students may need stronger social support networks to navigate these choices. Yet, coupled with insights from our discussions of cultural inequalities and emerging adulthood, we would give Mateo and Camille the same advice: this is part of the process of developing competence and confidence to respond to different expectations in diverse settings. Put simply, they are both being asked to take ownership of their learning, and to achieve what sociologists would term social self-efficacy. Both of them will have to make many decisions on their own in the future, and college is one place where they can practice doing so with fewer consequences. In summary, the point for many of these students is to reflect on what they want and own it. This can be especially important for students who want to take the professional pathway or the social mobility pathway: having a clear plan will ensure they do not get swept up in the party pathway, only to realize later that their lifestyle is incompatible with their goals.

## FURTHER READING ONLINE

- For additional reading, here is a book chapter available online that offers short quizzes and other activities to understand the values students hold in college and how those interact with their personal and social biography: Smith, Wayne, "You and Your College Experience," OpenCourseWare, retrieved from http:// ocw.smithw.org/univ100/textbook/beiderwell.pdf.

- Here is a values worksheet that helps students identify their highest values: Brown, Duane and R. Kelly Crace, 1996, "Life Values Inventory." Life Values Resources. Retrieved from: https:// bhmt.org/wp-content/uploads/2016/04/BHMT_CC_Life-Values_Inventory.pdf.

- After completing the personal values worksheet, students can use this worksheet to assess their highest work values: "Work Values Inventory," Humanists at Work, retrieved from https://humwork.uchri.org/wp-content/uploads/2015/01/ Workvaluesinventory-3.pdf.

- Here is an example of a person owning their story, even the messiness of their life, to make it into something of their own— in this case a profitable business: Carles, Mayi, 2019, "Life Is Messy Bootcamp," http://lifeismessybootcamp.com/. We are not endorsing this business, or even this approach, but we do more generally see this as a way of thinking about how to own your own story.

- After spending time analyzing personal and work values, the next step for students is to assess changes that they may need to make to actualize those values. In other words, it is one thing to have an ideal but quite another to carry it through. Some of the common barriers to becoming the people we intend to be are conflicts of time and competing priorities. In order to evaluate what tweaks need to be made to prevent these barriers from getting in the way of goals, here is one way to assess time management skills: "Assessing Your Time Management

Skills," Aventri, retrieved from https://www.eiseverywhere.
com/file_uploads/a071b60da1a6ed23b6008fbe5cda8294_
AssessingYourTimeManagementSkills.pdf.

- Along similar lines, here are tips for scheduling
strategies: Sicinski, Adam, "How to Manage Your Time and
Boost Your Levels of Productivity," IQ Matrix, retrieved from
http://blog.iqmatrix.com/manage-your-time.

- To think about how to prioritize tasks relevant to different
kinds of student situations (for example, being a student with
children, athlete students, and so on), we recommend this
resource: "Organizing Your Time: Learning Objectives," Lumen
Learning, retrieved from https://courses.lumenlearning.com/
freshmanexperience/chapter/2-3-organizing-your-time/.

- Some recommend thinking about time as a "life pie" with a
balance between school, work, and leisure. See here for more on
this: Wong, Linda, "Essential Study Skills. Chapter 3, Interactive
Pie of Life: Leisure," Cengage Learning, retrieved from http://
college.cengage.com/collegesurvival/wong/essential_study/5e/
students/additional/pie/leisure.html

- As a last suggestion related to time management, we recommend
completing an evaluation such as this one on the aspects of
timing and scheduling that seem most changeable: Chapman,
Alan, 2002, "Time Management Questionnaire," Business
Balls, retrieved from http://www.businessballs.com/
timemanagementsurvey.pdf.

- Related to discussion in this chapter on anxiety, alcohol or
drug abuse, eating disorders, unwanted sexual activity, and
other issues that many college students face, we recommend
completing a wellness inventory, such as this one: "TestWell—
Making Life Easier," retrieved from http://www.testwell.org/.
This kind of activity can be completed alone as a way to learn
what kind of help and support students may need to seek. There

is absolutely no shame in visiting with counselors through a campus health center.

- For academic integrity, we encourage students to search on their university website for the academic policy. Most universities make this publicly available. Some are written by students, some by faculty. Make sure to read this statement for an explanation of how particular campuses treat academic integrity. Many classes will also include academic integrity statements in the course syllabus that provide the particulars of each instructor. Many online resources give more general understandings of academic integrity. Here is one we recommend: International Center for Academic Integrity, "What Is So Important about Academic Integrity," May 23, 2012, YouTube, retrieved from https://www.youtube.com/watch?v=xSfmWIlEhSg.

- For considering the student expectations and experiences in the digital environment: Beetham, Helen, June 10, 2014, "Students Expectations and Experiences of the Digital Environment," Glasgow Caledonian University, retrieved from https://digitalstudent.jiscinvolve.org/wp/files/2014/06/Outcomes-from-Glasgow1.pdf.

- Also here for research-informed ideas on forming a personal and professional brand online: Philbrick, Jodi L. and Ana D. Cleveland. 2015. "Personal Branding: Building Your Pathway to Professional Success." *Medical Reference Services Quarterly*, 34(2): 181–189. Retrieved from: https://www.tandfonline.com/doi/abs/10.1080/02763869.2015.1019324.

## NOTES

1. Wright, Stephen L., Michael A. Jenkins-Guarnieri, and Jennifer L. Murdock. 2013. "Career Development among First-Year College Students: College Self-Efficacy, Student Persistence, and Academic Success." *Journal of Career Development* 40(4): 292–310.

2. Meca, Alan, Rachel A. Ritchie, Wim Beyers, Seth J. Schwartz, Simona Picariello, Byron L. Zamboanga . . . Cynthia G. Benitez. 2015. "Identity Centrality and Psychosocial Functioning: A Person-Centered Approach." *Emerging Adulthood* 3(5): 327–339.

    Nelson, Larry J., and Laura M. Padilla-Walker. 2013. "Flourishing and Floundering in Emerging Adult College Students." *Emerging Adulthood* 1(1): 67–78.

3. Creed, Peter A., and Trinette Hughes. 2013. "Career Development Strategies as Moderators between Career Compromise and Career Outcomes in Emerging Adults." *Journal of Career Development* 40(2): 146–163.

4. Hunter, Chris, and Kent McClelland. 2013. "Theoretical Perspectives in Sociology." In Susan J. Ferguson (Ed.), *Mapping the Social Landscape: Readings in Sociology* (7th ed., pp. 33–42). New York: McGraw-Hill Education.

5. Conley, Dalton. 2013. "The Birth of the Intravidual." In Susan J. Ferguson (Ed.), *Mapping the Social Landscape: Readings in Sociology* (7th ed., pp. 169–178). New York: McGraw-Hill Education.

6. For a sociological approach to understanding the ways the modern condition can promote mental illnesses, see for example, Pescosolido, Bernice A., and Beth A. Rubin. 2000. "The Web of Group Affiliations Revisited: Social Life, Postmodernism, and Sociology." *American Sociological Review* 65(1): 52–76.

7. For a psychological approach to medication and individual-level healthy responses to mental illnesses, such as schizophrenia, depression, and bipolar disorders, see for example:

    Correll, Christoph U., Johan Detraux, Jan De Lepeleire, and March De Hert. 2015. "Effects of Antipsychotics, Antidepressants, and Mood Stabilizers on Risk for Physical Diseases in People with Schizophrenia, Depression, and Bipolar Disorder." *World Psychiatry* 14(2): 119–136.

    Kane, John M., William H. Carson, Anutosh R. Saha, Robert D. McQuade, Gary G. Ingenito, Dan L. Zimbroff, and Mirza W. Ali. 2002. "Efficacy and Safety of Aripiprazole and Haloperidol versus Placebo in Patients with Schizophrenia and Schizoaffective Disorder." *Journal of Clinical Psychiatry* 63(9): 763–771.

    Pope, Harrison G., Joseph F. Lipinski, Bruce M. Cohen, and Doris T. Axelrod. 1980. "Schizoaffective Disorder: An Invalid Diagnosis? A Comparison of Schizoaffective Disorder, Schizophrenia, and Affective Disorder." *American Journal of Psychiatry* 137(8): 921–927.

8. Granfield, Robert. 2013. "Making It by Faking It: Working-Class Students in an Elite Academic Environment." In Susan J. Ferguson (Ed.), *Mapping the Social Landscape: Readings in Sociology* (7th ed., pp. 145–157). New York: McGraw-Hill Education.

9. Mirowsky, John, and Catherine E. Ross. 2007. "Life Course Trajectories of Perceived Control and Their Relationship to Education." *American Journal of Sociology* 112(5): 1339–1382.

10. Loe, Meika. 2013. "Working at Bazooms: The Intersection of Power, Gender, and Sexuality." In Susan J. Ferguson (Ed.), *Mapping the Social Landscape: Readings in Sociology* (7th ed., pp. 79–94). New York: McGraw-Hill Education.

11. Radmacher, Kimberley, and Margarita Azmitia. 2013. "Unmasking Class: How Upwardly Mobile Poor and Working-Class Emerging Adults Negotiate an 'Invisible' Identity." *Emerging Adulthood* 1(4): 314–329.

12. Silva, Jennifer M. 2013. *Coming Up Short: Working-Class Adulthood in an Age of Uncertainty*. New York: Oxford University Press.

13. Elman, Cheryl, and Angela O'Rand. 2007. "The Effects of Social Origins, Life Events, and Institutional Sorting on Adults' School Transitions." *Social Science Research* 36(3): 1276–1299.

14. Armstrong, Elizabeth A., and Laura T. Hamilton. 2013. *Paying for the Party: How College Maintains Inequality*. Cambridge, MA: Harvard University Press.

15. Settersten, Richard, and Barbara E. Ray. 2010. *Not Quite Adults: Why 20-Somethings Are Choosing a Slower Path to Adulthood, and Why It's Good for Everyone*. New York: Bantam.

16. Grieve, Rachel, Michaelle Indian, Kate Witteveen, G. Anne Tolan, and Jessica Marrington. 2013. "Face-to-Face or Facebook: Can Social Connectedness Be Derived Online?" *Computers in Human Behavior* 29(3): 604–609.

    Steinfield, Charles, Nicole B. Ellison, and Cliff Lampe. 2008. "Social Capital, Self-Esteem, and Use of Online Social Network Sites: A Longitudinal Analysis." *Journal of Applied Developmental Psychology* 29(6): 434–445.

17. Brooks, Brandon, Bernie Hogan, Nicole Ellison, Cliff Lampe, and Jessica Vitak. 2014. "Assessing Structural Correlates to Social Capital in Facebook Ego Networks." *Social Networks* 38 (July): 1–15.

    Ellison, Nicole B., Rebecca Gray, Cliff Lampe, and Andrew T. Fiore. 2014. "Social Capital and Resource Requests on Facebook." *New Media & Society* 16(7): 1104–1121.

18. Indian, Michaelle, and Rachel Grieve. 2014. "When Facebook Is Easier than Face-to-Face: Social Support Derived from Facebook in Socially Anxious Individuals." *Personality and Individual Differences* 59 (March): 102–106.

19. Bohn, Angela, Christian Buchta, Kurt Hornik, and Patrick Mair. 2014. "Making Friends and Communicating on Facebook: Implications for the Access to Social Capital." *Social Networks* 37 (May): 29–41.

20. Junco, Reynol. 2012. "The Relationship between Frequency of Facebook Use, Participation in Facebook Activities, and Student Engagement." *Computers & Education* 58(1): 162–171.

21. Turkle, Sherry. 2012. *Alone Together: Why We Expect More from Technology and Less from Each Other*. New York: Basic Books.

22. Konstam, Varda. 2015. "Floundering or Experimenting: Finding a Vocational Home." In *Emerging and Young Adulthood* (pp. 95–113). Advancing Responsible Adolescent Development Series. Cham, Switzerland: Springer International.

23. Tanner, Jennifer Lynn. 2006. "Recentering during Emerging Adulthood: A Critical Turning Point in Life Span Human Development." In J. J. Arnett and J. L. Tanner (Eds.), *Emerging Adults in America: Coming of Age in the 21st Century* (pp. 21–55). Washington, DC: American Psychological Association.

24. Stuber, Jenny M. 2011. "Inside the College Gates: Education as a Social and Cultural Process." *Inside the College Gates: How Class and Culture Matter in Higher Education.* New York: Lexington Books.

# Resiliency in the Face of Setbacks

Resiliency, or how students can bounce back from personal and structural challenges to build a successful college career is the focus of chapter 5. This fifth chapter explores the value of having challenging experiences during college as a way to build this resiliency for life after college. College presents the opportunity to reflect on earlier experiences in families, cultures, groups, and within organizations. For students, reflecting on how their backgrounds affect current choices is crucial for shaping a personal and professional story that can guide choices in college, frame personal statements, and point toward potential career paths after graduation.

This chapter focuses on *resiliency*—rising to the challenges that life in college (and after) brings. Whether it is intense trauma, struggles with finding groups to belong with, or challenges in academics, part

*The Science of College*. Patricia S. Herzog, Casey T. Harris, Shauna A. Morimoto, Shane W. Barker, Jill G. Wheeler, A. Justin Barnum, and Terrance L. Boyd, Oxford University Press (2020) © Oxford University Press.
DOI: 10.1093/oso/9780190934507.001.0001

of college is figuring out how to overcome hurdles. Building on our basic introduction of this concept in chapter 2, the key to having resiliency is understanding the life course as a *social construction*, with college as a pivotal time when emerging adults learn how to balance their personal agency with an awareness of social influences. In order to construct a personal and professional biography, students should think critically about their prior experiences and evaluate what they want to repeat or continue doing, and what to change now that college provides the opportunity to do so. Important in this process is not giving society too much credit in defining who students are and can be, nor framing individuals as totally free agents with complete freedom to create anything, nor total responsibility for the outcomes of the choices they make. Life combines personal agency and social support, with occasional limits and setbacks, and college is the perfect time to strike the right balance of finding one's own path, coupled with awareness of the limits of the self and reliance on others for help when needed.

## STUDENT STORIES: WHAT WE EXPERIENCE

In the following student stories, **Aaron** discusses the fragmentation he experienced between different peer groups, as well as within his family after his parents divorced. **Alexa** also describes her divorced parents and their social class distinctions, and tells about her struggle to balance everything as she carves out her own identity. **Chen** likewise discusses struggling to fit in to different social settings, but she experiences these struggles as someone who is shy and who internalized her parents' instructions to "hold her tongue." Resilient in the face of an emotionally abusive relationship, **Michalyn** reports how she is working to release herself from the bonds of others' expectations for her. **Connor** is a student who is "just not getting it." He is doing everything in his power to earn good grades, but having difficulty figuring out what class content is important and where he should focus most of his energy.

**#outsider #identitycrisis**: Who are you? They ask. I am what I want to be, or you want me to be, or you are who I want you to be. No one knows. But I know one thing, it's time to find out!

**Aaron** describes how the identity questions of the last chapter can come to a head during emerging adulthood, especially as students experience different cultural values and sort out social groups. He explains:

Another area of my life [in which] I had to prove myself, because I was seen as an outsider, was my Catholic, private high school. Before transferring to this high school, I went to a Baptist, private school where the culture held values [that] were quite different. Many families were middle class and working lower end jobs, and this mirrored my family structure; therefore, we shared the same values and were from the same culture. Once I transferred to the Catholic high school, I was immersed in a new culture that was full of values that were strange to me. Indeed, many of the families that had children there, were upper class and had nice houses, cars, and designer clothes. The spring before starting this high school, I went to an event that the high school hosted called the freshmen fire-up. While everyone around me was dressed in nice outfits, I had shown up in my middle school uniform, and the stares were enough to convey the fact that I had broken a norm of this upper-class school. Another piece of my middle-class life that broke a norm was my dad's truck that took me to high school for two years. While other students were brought to school in Mercedes, Land Rovers, and Cadillacs, I was brought to school in a rusting Chevy truck that was older than me. After seeing the other parents' cars, I began to make my dad drop me off down the street because I knew I was breaking this norm of the upper-class world, and I did not want to be embarrassed by this lack of a nice vehicle . . . If I was ever asked what my parents did, I would twist their job titles to make them sound more professional and hide the fact that neither of them went to a four-year college. Until junior year, I lived in a double-wide trailer with my mom and a single-wide trailer with my dad. I was embarrassed by this, so I never invited people over to my house, and instead, I went to my friends' houses.

**#recentering #notbrandname**: Learning an important life lesson. I just keep trying to fit in instead of being myself. I have to learn to do me, regardless of what people think. #nologo

**Alexa** also reflects on identity fragmentation in families and friend groups. She describes it this way:

As I got older, many things began to happen in my life that were not necessarily good things. My parents got divorced when I was in fourth grade, and that started a whole new path and way that I experienced life. Since I was going back and forth between my mom's and my dad's, that also entailed having two completely different life styles. When I was at my mom's house everything was how it was before they got divorced, but when I was at my dad's it was completely different. He did not have very much money, or at least acted like it, and so everything at his house was very downgraded. A pretty crappy house, old junky car, and the things I wore were also a representation of this. I was not used to living like this, especially where I was from, so I was constantly worried about what other people thought of me and how this would affect my future. So, I began to act like I was part of the upper class and avoid all confrontation of the fact that my dad did not have much money. I wanted to fit in with all the other kids at my school and I was embarrassed when I came to school in off-brand clothing and was dropped off in a crummy car.

**#shy #followingtherules**: Sometimes I feel like I'm watching a movie starring other people. I'm tired of following the rules and waiting for other people to speak.

**Chen** describes how the cultural approach of one's family can affect the type of person that one is as an entering college student:

I am the type who always follows the rules because, especially as a child, I was terrified of getting in trouble. The rule that determined how much I spoke had to do with when I was allowed to speak. It was the "don't interrupt me when I'm speaking" rule [that] I was given by my parents and teachers. I was told that was a rule I had to follow, so I tried my best to save my responses until after people finished talking. My problem with this was that no one shut up for long enough to let me say anything. I broke that rule many times. When it came to adults, though, I tried my hardest to not interrupt but I ended up with comments like, "you sure are a quiet one, ain't cha" or "cat got your tongue?" It did not take long for me to get used to those comments . . .

I misunderstood that not interrupting was a good rule for the classroom, or with adults I needed to respect, but it was more of a courtesy in regular conversation than a necessity. My silence was also questioned by peers and, when I had no good answer for them, they left me alone. Being on my own was fine with me, though it kept me out of cliques and limited the amount of friends I had. Silence became my way of excluding myself from cliques . . . Another rule that led me to being reserved was "don't take that tone with me" or "there's no need for those crocodile tears." I got these mainly at home. They were reminders that it was "always my decision about how I acted," as my mom would tell me if I got angry or sad. I know now that she was trying to teach me that my reactions should not be overdramatic and that it mattered how I responded, but as a child I believed she was telling me not to show what I was feeling. Through a process that took me years, I learned to conceal anger, sadness, and pain so well that my parents could hardly tell what I was feeling . . . I am not open about my opinions or how I feel. [This is] partially because I am naturally reserved;

it is also because I did not feel comfortable being open at home. It became easier to act like nothing hurt me than it was to voice how I felt . . . All this was not helped by the fact that I was a shy child. It is difficult to say if my childhood shyness was caused by my socialization at home and at school or if it was my nature . . . It is unclear, even to me, whether I was labeled quiet because of how I acted or if it was an expectation I learned to live up to . . . I was trying to get an answer to a question or ask something I needed without breaking the "don't interrupt me" rule which often was impossible . . . How was I supposed to not interrupt, but also get help from busy adults? Most of the time I ended up avoiding the problem or I tried to deal with it myself; it was not fun at the time but it taught me to be independent and solve my own problems. A downside to this was that I did not break out of my shell until junior high, and when I did, I still found it difficult to tell others what I needed or what I thought.

**#movingon #emotionalabuse**: i think i'm done with this whole heartbroken thing. accepting what is. letting go of what was. believing in what is to come.

**Michalyn** explains how she weathered an emotionally abusive relationship and is finding her resiliency while moving on and beginning to heal.

After I finished my first year of middle school, I began taking my first clarinet class in school and I remember being so happy to be able to be a part of a larger group in school. I kept making new friends for the next couple of years until one day I met this boy. And it was during my last year of junior high that we began dating and we continued to date for two years. At the beginning things felt as though they were going perfectly. I spent almost every day with him and became close to him and his family. It was not until the second year of our relationship however that things began to fall apart. He became emotionally abusive to me and began trying to push me emotionally to my limits by trying to upset me on purpose. Following that he began pushing me to convert because his family believed I was going to hell if I did not. I remember having a solid four months of crying every night because of how broken I felt and I tried to do everything I could to make him happy. I began to lash out at those around me because of how unhappy I was, which led my father to stop talking to me and hate the person I was with. I became engulfed by the pain he caused me, to the point I could not pull myself out. When the relationship finally ended, however, I began to heal. I stopped being horrible to those around me and started making new friends and living my life how I wanted, which was something I was not used to.

**#notgettingit #saywhat**: I just got a bad grade on an exam that I thought I was going to ace, and everyone says it was easy and understood everything. What gives?!

**Connor** never misses physics class, always takes notes, and tries to follow along with the lecture as best he can. A few days before the first exam, he joins a study group and quickly realizes that he is not getting the major concepts the same way his friends are. Everyone else seems to have somehow gotten the most important points of the chapters and lectures, while he took tons of notes on what seems unimportant now. His friends all quickly answer the problems with the correct information, while Connor is still digging through his notes trying to figure out what is relevant. He feels lost and wonders how he can sit in the same class with these students but not get what they did. Should he keep being a physics major if he is just not getting it?

## SCIENCE: WHAT WE KNOW

All these students are confronting issues from their childhood that they must understand and come to terms with now that they are in college. Whether these are personal questions about identity and behavior, questions about navigating unequal class or racial structures, overcoming academic struggles, or healing from the trauma of an abusive relationship, challenges shape who young people are. Resiliency—or the ability to bounce back from these difficulties—will help them overcome these challenges. More than just "moving on" or "getting over it," resiliency comes more naturally with some understanding of the concept of social construction.

In a book entitled *Social Problems across the Life Course*, Lopata and Levy (2003)[1] draw upon the scholarship of Glen Edler (1974)[2] in describing the life course as a *social construction*, which refers to an issue, experience, or phenomenon that is actively shaped in response to different cultures, places, and social groups. This does not mean the life course is made up, or in some way not real. Rather, it means that the path we follow as we grow and mature is fashioned by the choices that people make, which are influenced by the markedly different ways that those potential choices can be understood and experienced. Understanding the life course as a social construction means focusing on the ways that human lives intersect with historical, political, economic, and cultural circumstances. Viewing people as within a life course development process means thinking about how people view different ages and age-related roles, such as transitions into adult roles as parents, college graduates, or professionals. Another way that the life course is socially constructed is through the major events that shape generations in distinct ways. For example, people who were adults before the terrorist attacks of 9/11 (or, in earlier generations, World War II or the Vietnam War) have a "before" and an "after" that sets them apart from people born after that time, or who were very young at the time of the attacks, and who thus only have an "after." Understanding this generational distinction means recognizing that individuals are shaped by their social environments. However, viewing the life course as a social construction also entails the ways that people make free choices that shape society in turn. Moreover, the social construction of the life course emphasizes the interdependence of lives, and the ways relationships among people mutually shape each other.

In essence, there are two sides to the equation of the life course as a social construction: (1) the ways people shape themselves and society as they develop into adults, and (2) the ways society shapes what it means to be a person of different ages, and how transitions across life stages are understood within distinct cultures and groups. The key is to maintain the delicate balance between these two sides of the equation. Emphasizing one over the other often has negative consequences. In particular, at-risk factors for lack of student success and retention often fall within what are referred to as low "meta-cognitive" skills: limited ability to reflect on one's self, think about, and articulate the process one uses to make decisions. On the one hand, being too hard on oneself can be a problem, as students can underrate their ability to perform academic tasks, leaving them feeling powerless. In this case, students often hear feedback, however constructive, as confirming their negative self-image and confirming their belief that they are not smart enough to achieve. Yet, in reality metacognition is a far better predictor of academic success than intelligence, often referred to as IQ. One of the key factors in metacognition is having a growth mindset rather than a fixed one. A student with a fixed mindset views feedback and grades about low performance to be permanent; whereas a student with a growth mindset embraces feedback and treats a low-performance critique as an opportunity to rise to the challenge, to grow in response to learning. Indeed, if students view intelligence as malleable, rather than set, they exert more effort on academic tasks.[3]

Particularly important in effective social construction of college navigations is a concept called "grit." Grit combines several personality characteristics, including conscientious, self-control, and persistence. Conscientiousness is a person's ability to be organized, follow through, and be self-reflective. Self-control is the ability to resist the urge for short-term gains in pursuit of long-term gains. Persistence is the ability to overcome obstacles in order to pursue and achieve goals. As the combination of these characteristics, grit is often described as combining passion with perseverance in pursuing long-term goals. Grit is more predictive of academic success than IQ. Indeed, gritty people maintain commitments to a variety of life goals, not purely educational. Perhaps one of the most important aspects of grit is that gritty people persist even in the absence of positive feedback. In fact, gritty people seek out long-term goals without achievement orientations, meaning they can pursue their goals without being reliant on others to give them continual praise for their efforts.[4]

Receiving praise for efforts exerted, rather than the actual quality of those efforts and their outcomes, can result in a sense of entitlement. "Academic entitlement" refers to a student perception that demands positive marks and feedback, regardless of whether the quality of work was deemed worthy of positive evaluation by faculty.* Students with academic entitlement view themselves as having a right to high grades with minimal effort and discomfort, often combined with an externalizing sense that faculty are responsible for awarding good grades, rather than providing students with constructive feedback for how to improve. When students have high levels of academic entitlement, they may demand that faculty change their grades, especially when they are close to the next letter grade, have completed extra credit assignments, or because missed classes hurt their scores. In some cases, academically entitled students can be overtly hostile, even belligerent, in confrontations with faculty, expecting professors to bend to their will whenever they are dissatisfied.

Academic entitlement is linked to externalizing behavior generally, including an external locus of control, which refers to viewing others to be the actors in any situation, rather than seeing one's own role. Often accompanying externalizing is blame deflection: seeing others as at fault rather than acknowledging how one has personally contributed to a negative

---

* Typical measures of academic entitlement include high levels of agreement with the following statements: "If I have explained to my professor that I am trying hard, I think he/she should give me some consideration with respect to my course grade"; or "My professors should reconsider my grade if I am close to the grade I want." These are the reverse of a mindset that says, "I believe that it is my responsibility to seek out the resources to succeed in college"; and "If I miss class, it is my responsibility to get the notes."

outcome. Students high in academic entitlement can view themselves to be victims of unfair grading policies, since they perceive that they received a poorer grade than they expected due to a problem with the faculty member's unjust grading policy, rather than a fair assessment of low quality. Alternatively, students with a growth mindset view poorer-than-expected marks as an opportunity to learn and improve in future endeavors.[5]

In combining grit with academic entitlement, the key for students is to develop a growth mindset that balances an understanding of the self with the feedback of others. A healthy balance achieves a moderate understanding of the power of one's self. Students should view themselves as capable of persisting through conscientious effort—grit—while understanding the importance of feedback from others. Having a self-concept as a worthy person, who is smart and capable, is crucial for taking feedback constructively, rather than becoming offended over self-perceived entitled rights, or alternatively being debilitated by self-doubting confirmations of low worth. Students need to learn to cope with less-than-perfect grades, and other forms of feedback regarding low-quality performance. Another important resiliency skill in college is to seek out feedback from faculty. Resilient and growth-minded students request to meet with faculty, not to complain or demand grade changes, but rather to learn why they received the marks they did and acquire strategies for improving on subsequent exams and assignments. Especially helpful in fostering these skills in college are mentoring and research assistant relationships. In fact, students with the lowest levels of ability benefit the most from additional forms of academic engagement, returning even more significant returns to academic outcomes than those who began with higher levels of ability. Hard work can pay off, if students are willing to couple their hard work with responsive changes based on feedback from expert others, such as faculty. The most important first step is acknowledging personal responsibility for a student's own learning. The second step is to take responsibility for seeking out opportunities to develop from others.[6]

One way for students to accept personal responsibility is to reflect on the ways they have been socialized in prior experiences to view themselves in certain ways. Families, prior school experiences, friend groups, and social media all socialize people to view their self in certain ways. As an example of this kind of self-reflection on self and other expectations, **Chen** reflects on how gender expectations affect her self-interpretation, saying that "I fall on the masculine side of the scale when it comes to how much I express my emotions, even though how I express them appears more feminine." In doing so, she refers to a reading by Emily Kane (2013)[7] entitled " 'No Way My Boys Are Going To Be Like That!' Parents' Responses to Children's Gender Nonconformity." Kane emphasizes the likelihood that one's own gender identity is influenced by one's parents. At the same time, Kane emphasizes that children are not merely passive recipients of gender socialization by parents and society. Rather, children are active agents in forming their understanding of gender in relation to the ways their parents (and others) socialize them. Furthermore, parents often socialize gender in unconscious ways, based on what they were taught as children, but they too can become conscious of their actions and think critically about what ideas they want to pass on. Likewise, the fact that Chen is becoming aware of the ways she does and does not fit into gender stereotypes regarding emotional expression means that she has the opportunity to more actively shape her femininity, and to begin to harness her ability to mold the impressions others have of her.

Donna Gaines (2013)[8] studied a more extreme example of how society shapes what it means to be an individual: teen suicide pacts, when a group of teenagers decides to end their lives together, simultaneously. Gaines attributes these atrocities to intense forms of societal neglect, in which the individuality of teens is ironically both ignored, in terms of personal care and compassion, and simultaneously informally controlled, through strict expectations regarding acceptable teenager behavior. Teens who do not conform to society are considered deviant, separated, removed from contributing to society—labels that produce angst and despair. When social messages about and to teenagers convey these types of labels, it is not entirely surprising that some respond by actualizing their removal from society by ending their lives. This is not to condone, approve, or encourage teen suicide. The point is instead to move beyond the impulse to villainize such teens by attributing their actions entirely to individual deficits.

Surely there are individual imbalances, but also to blame are the societal imbalances that impact these teens' behavior. Removing free will and choice from teens, or from anyone, places the emphasis too squarely on the role of society and disempowers individuals from seeing the ways their own choices matter. On the other extreme, viewing personal choices as reigning supreme is also dangerous and places too much responsibility on individuals. For example, one of the students in chapter 6, **Jacob**, reflected on this reading by saying, "Labeling is a powerful influence that society can put on a person; this power is seen in 'Teenage Wasteland' as kids who are negatively labeled as 'burnouts,' 'druggies,' and 'troubled losers' are forced into feeling that suicide and 'crash[ing] to the bottom' of the social world were their only options in life (Gaines 2013: 7,11)." Likewise, one of the students in this chapter, **Chen**, refers to this reading in describing her socialization:

> Teenagers are labeled by adults and their peers, and it can be unclear as to whether they were labeled because of the way they act or [if they instead] act how they do because that is what is expected of them (Gaines 2013, 13–14). . . . *Those types of interactions I had with adults shaped the way I interact with others by socializing me to be more reserved* [emphasis added]. . . . When someone gave me a label, I found a way to fit into that role . . . Had I been socialized in a different way or given different labels during my childhood, I would have become a different person.

Chen is reflecting on to what extent she is making choices that reflect her personal desires versus acting in ways that mimic what she was taught to do. However, this is not an either–or choice.

A balanced perspective centers on recognizing that all personal choices are part *agency* (exercises of free will to be and do what one wants) and part *society* (informed, shaped, or controlled by social groups, cultural norms, and shared experiences). Focusing on this interplay, especially in the ways young people transition into adulthood, is key to having resilience in the face of adversity. Sometimes college brings difficulties, as does life more generally. Some college students experience the hardest moments of their lives during college, either through their academic pursuits or through relationships with their families and friends. Other students experience some of the best and most rewarding moments of their lives during college. Many students experience a combination of the best and worst. To navigate these dynamic times, young people must exercise resiliency, recognizing both the ways their personal biographies shape their current choices *and* the ways they can retool the person they are becoming and write their own personal and professional stories.

## ADVICE: WHAT WE (CAN) PROVIDE

**#outsider #identitycrisis #recentering #notbrandname** What resiliency looks like will vary tremendously by the individual and their specific challenges and circumstances. Students like **Aaron** or **Alexa** can focus on the issues of re-centering and identity they describe. One challenge that Aaron mentioned was the difference between his upbringing and that of his peers:

> My lacking in skills was due in part to the different childrearing techniques that my parents used compared to my classmates. My parents leaned towards more of a[n accomplishment of] natural growth technique, where I was the one in charge of my free time. Indeed, I was in some organized sports, but not in as many as my classmates were in, as their parents used concerted cultivation (Lareau 2013; see chapter 3 for a summary). Because I lacked these things, I experienced many embarrassing moments that began shaping me into an upper-class look-alike.

A professional counselor or other university support staff could help Aaron and Alexa to transition from allowing their high school identity to define their college experience and into exploring new opportunities and groups that college provides. The transition to adulthood involves thinking critically about prior social experiences and considering whether the dynamics of the past remain relevant in new social situations, such as college. Trying to fit into groups in which one feels unaccepted is tiring, and that energy may be better spent on finding new social groups that provide acceptance. Sometimes that requires changing the people with whom one associates, and other times it simply means changing the dynamics of interaction among the same group of people. In either case, we caution students like Aaron and Alexa against reliving their high school experience on campus. Often college provides opportunities for a fresh start and the chance to break old patterns.

We also advise students to seek ways to reflect upon, understand, and live *their truth*. This starts with understanding that in college, there are going to be people from the upper class. Yet there are also going to be students who are middle-, working-, or lower-class. Students do not need to feel pressured to fit into one group or another because it is possible to go between groups, to make friends with someone who is more well-off and with someone who is not. Aaron and Alexa could reach out to other people who identify the way they do. Instead of trying to "keep up with the Joneses," much less the Kardashians, we advise students to think critically about what they are capable of, given their social circumstances, and how to comfortably align their lifestyle with their long-term plans. If students like Aaron and Alexa let their real, authentic personalities come through, they will find friends that like them not because of what they do or do not have but because of who they are. This is the way to embrace the social construction of the life course, and to embed personal biographies into current social interactions in ways that create positive support channels and which help students become the people they desire to be. While students are no more able to change their structural circumstances or history than the rest of us, college life does give them the opportunity to make choices and move forward.

**#shy #followingtherules** We remind **Chen** that emerging adulthood is a period of identity exploration, when young people are becoming independent of their parents but are not yet financially self-supporting. It is a time when young people can explore the possibilities for their road ahead and make important life decisions. Both in terms of day-to-day living as well as long-term trajectories and outcomes, emerging adults have freedom to choose and decisions to make. For some people, such decisions naturally give way to clear pathways to achieve their desired outcomes: a major leads to a career, which leads to financial independence, and that in turn leads to establishing an independent household and later building a family. For others, such as Chen, these waters may be murky and harder to navigate, at least initially. When this is the case, and particularly when emerging adults lack social connections to a supportive community, they can experience this period as unstable and disconnected.

These problems are especially acute when students are living far from home or are the first in their family to attend college (like Chen), so their parents do not have experience navigating higher education. For Chen, the many decisions and choices could lead to confusion, a lack of direction, and feelings of isolation from those whose plans seem clear. Alternatively, the questions she is considering could also be compatible with having a reasonably clear plan for college and career. She is at a crucial juncture then, a point at which reaching out to the right people can make all the difference. If Chen were to reach out to a professor or another trusted supportive adult, the best research-based advice she could receive would be to get connected in an effort to find her voice. Some way, somehow, she needs to start making her campus her home. Many students do not realize what a wide array of resources there are for finding places where they can speak out and fit in on campus, especially for finding fellow students who may be underrepresented at the university. However, we guarantee there are other people like Chen on her campus; she and others like her must only work to find them.

Connecting to the content of chapter 3, Stuber (2012)[9] documents that "social class shapes students' experiences within the experiential core of college life, structuring their abilities to navigate their campus' social and extracurricular worlds. Indeed, privileged students typically arrive on campus with sophisticated maps and navigational devices to guide their journeys—while less privileged students are often less equipped for the journey" (p. 12). Thus it is natural for students whose parents did not

attend college or who come from a working-class background to fluctu-
ate between feeling enthusiastic and feeling lost. Importantly, scholars of
higher education remind us that *college is a process* that involves more
than educational outcomes. Students are also acquiring social networks,
along with cultural tastes and attitudes that carry over into professional
life. Since cultural competencies vary at the outset of college, they inform
the choices that students make while in college, which in turn shape life
after graduation, carrying over to decisions about careers and family.

As Stuber (2011) points out, although the ability to confidently navigate campus life leads to the reproduction of economic, social, and cultural capital, higher education also provides a means to contest existing
economic hierarchies. Doing so requires not simply choosing a major
that theoretically guarantees a given job, but also attending to both cur-
ricular and extracurricular ways to find their voice and learn what works
for them. Indeed, this aspect of college life makes it doubly important for
people like Chen to seek out opportunities to connect to groups and find
some way—social, cultural, academic—to participate more in campus life.
For Chen, learning how to speak up will steer her toward goals and an outcome that fits her interests and desires. Students who have specific goals
that they are able to articulate and put into action are much more likely
to achieve those goals, and the resulting sense of accomplishment or self-
efficacy leads to further success (Mirowsky & Ross 2007).[10]

For this reason, Chen's expressed concern about labeling is reflective
of not knowing whether she has control or feeling unable to see how the
path that she has chosen in college will lead to long-term success. As Chen
points out, it is not clear if she was labeled "shy" due to expectations of
her family or a result of her true personality. She indicates that "[t]his is
similar to dilemmas the teenagers Gaines studied dealt with in their town.
Gaines found their major problem was that they were told 'to be decent
human beings when nobody [seemed] to respect them or take them seriously' (2013: 12)." Since increased self-direction leads to greater success,
Chen will reap longer-term rewards if she seeks out resources to help her
define a path and break free of the label she had in high school. We advise
students like her to think critically about how to stand firm in articulating

what they value. Not every situation requires a response, of course, so Chen should still exercise her keen observational insights to understand what is going on before speaking.

We also advise students like her to view college as providing the opportunity to improve social skills. Seek challenging situations and find ways to offer comments and opinions when comfortable. This will build confidence and begin to crystalize passion and purpose. Importantly, students like Chen need to know that it is alright to ask for help. "Be quiet" is not a rule in college, unlike in Chen's past, and people on campus value hearing from students. As higher education professionals and faculty, we do not get annoyed when students ask us questions. Rather, asking questions is expected and welcome on the university campus. Another key opportunity in college is the chance to find groups of friends that can build confidence, and for Chen, this confidence is a critical part of resilience. It may start with being around people who have similar interests. As quiet students speak up among friends, they gain the experience for speaking up more generally.

**#movingon #emotionalabuse** As for Michalyn, we advise her to seek counseling. The experiences she has been through require professional counselors to understand, and there is no sense trying to go it alone. Most campuses have a counseling and psychology center, often within the health center, that provides students professional help with learning to manage negative emotions. Once Michalyn gains assistance in lessening the intensity of her experiences, she will be better equipped to focus on what they mean for the life she is shaping. She is rightly engaging in relationship management and realizing that some relationships are not good for her, and she is beginning to seek positive relationships. That is wonderful, and we advise students in similar situations to do the same critical evaluation of themselves and their social interactions.

At the same time, there is a broader issue that needs to be addressed: Michalyn's intense focus on the expectations of others. This risks tipping the delicate balance, described in the science section, too heavily toward the social control of others at the expense of the role of the self. Students like Michalyn would do well to achieve a better balance between the two, and to guard against only living in ways they think will fulfill the expectations of others. Professional counseling would help to address this overarching issue as well as promote healing from the emotional abuse in Michalyn's recent past.

In order to enhance her personal resiliency, we would advise Michalyn to make a list of the positive aspects in her life that affirm the positive feelings she is having now, as she begins to establish her personal freedom. Even after moving beyond negative emotions of past trauma, counseling services can provide regular check-ins on progress toward building the better life that Michalyn desires. Those efforts will help to restore her sense of personal agency over her social experiences. Ultimately, she can invest those skills in thinking about what kind of professional path she wants to carve, and what steps she needs to make toward it. For Michalyn, resilience will be an involved process, but well worth it.

**#notgettingit #saywhat** Interpreting Connor's story requires returning to the content of chapters 1 and 2. Recall that emerging adulthood is a time of instability, of "shifting choices," according to Arnett, where emerging adults "know they are supposed to have a Plan with a capital P."[11] Connor's trouble with zeroing in on the important concepts in class, and his difficulty focusing, may be signals to reconsider his Plan. The Plans of most emerging adults are subject to numerous revisions, and the goal of further development during this life stage is to learn from each set of revisions. We urge Connor to visit an advisor to discuss the academic challenges he is facing. Adept advisors would deepen Connor's awareness of the numerous career options available on campus, and the fact that faculty in roles besides the typical "doctor, lawyer, engineer" paths are likely able to relate to his experience. The advisor could offer Connor examples of other courses that he could take in order to assess whether he is on the right career path. After selecting some courses to explore whether those subjects would make more sense for him and better captivate his interest, the advisor could also encourage Connor to connect with the faculty teaching those courses, and to meet with them during office hours to ask about how they became interested in their career path and in their field of study.

We advise students like Connor to talk with others on campus about their experience feeling lost in a certain class and later finding other classes that animated them. Doing so orients students toward career paths aligned with who they want to be and what they want to do, instead of following a plan created by others. Instability during college should not be read negatively; rather, it is part and parcel of possibility and exploration—the liminal phase, where young people create meaning and discover identity. Connor's feelings of being lost, confused, and even scared are normal. Many advisors can relate to his experiences, and it is often the case that advisors did not at first know the ultimate goal of their own career path. The major lesson is that Connor can bounce back by embracing college as a time to gain exposure to the wide array of career options and to learn from people who hold positions that interest him.

We also advise students like Connor not to write off the professor of the course that is challenging them. If he reaches out to the professor of his physics class, Connor may find that there are ways for him to better connect with the content. Sometimes students literally show professors the notes they are taking during class to ask for specific feedback on whether they are absorbing the right content. This method, in contrast to a general statement like "I'm lost," can be an effective way to get concrete help from a professor. Some students do not realize that they can gain more individualized instruction through professors' office hours. Meanwhile, other students come by regularly to take advantage of this personalized "tutoring," which then bolsters their understanding of classroom instruction. Plus, there are many university courses for which additional tutoring is available, often provided by students who excel in those topics. If Connor takes advantage of these resources, he will gain an important life skill that stays with him beyond the immediate goal of doing well in that particular class. He will learn that the first impression of a social circumstance does not have to be the last: he can be resilient amid confusion.

## TOGETHERNESS: WHAT WE (CAN) SHARE

Next, we offer a possible dialog between several of our case studies. Faculty and support staff are important social supports in navigating college, as are fellow students. In these togetherness sections, the goal is to suggest ways that students can support one another in navigating college. Akin to a reality television show, the students are interacting with each other in ways that build their relationships around some of the challenges and opportunities these students described in their stories. Given the challenges already expressed within the case studies, the goal in these situations is to focus on the positive ways that students can support one another. Inevitably social interactions can also be fraught with negative experiences, and we do not mean to suggest that all social interactions occur positively. Rather, we offer some possible ways to support one another, which students can and will modify to add their own authentic approach. To review student stories alongside these togetherness sections, readers can refer to the table of case studies that precedes chapter 1 and the brief synopsis of student stories included within that table.

*Troy and Aaron.* Troy and Aaron have never met before, but both attended the welcome meeting for a student organization focused on environmental awareness on campus. During an icebreaker activity at the beginning of the meeting, Troy and Aaron are paired up and expected to introduce themselves. They share with each other that, coincidentally, they both chose to attend this meeting because they are determined to try out new interests and experiences during their first year. They joke about how it seemed kind of silly to be doing that, but now they feel better that someone else is doing the same thing!

As the meeting goes on, they continue to talk about their experiences so far. Troy mentions that he felt like a fraud at the very beginning of the year because he left an entire friend group back in his home state and began a new life here at college. He talked to one of his instructors about it, and the instructor helped him see that this was a normal, positive process of "letting go." Aaron immediately relates, and he shares his experiences of transitioning from a Baptist, working-class high school to a more affluent Catholic high school. He went to his advisor, who, like Troy's instructor, encouraged him to engage fully in the college experience. They both say that they are starting to feel more balanced, and they comment to each other about the energy and good vibes that come from going home to see old friends—and how, after going, they look forward to returning to their new friends.

Troy admits that he can identify more with the affluent private school from which Aaron graduated, but he also talks about how he is happier now that he is in college where it is more diverse. Aaron agrees, and he says he is happy to be at a place that is not full of just one kind of people. Both find it reassuring to talk with someone who has experienced the stress of leaving one community and having to find their place in a new one. Their joking and positive energy continue, and the two of them decide to attend an art exhibit on campus—something neither of them would have considered doing in high school. Here's to new experiences!

*Derrick and Michalyn.* Derrick and Michalyn have not met before, but they become lab partners in Chemistry 101. During class, they enjoy having some good-humored conversation, and they tend to do well on their assignments. Much to their surprise, they end up running into each other at a "Healthy Relationships" seminar offered by the campus wellness center. They begin chatting. Derrick mentions the girlfriend whom he followed to college only to have her break up with him. Michalyn reveals that she was in an abusive relationship. They are both shocked and, most importantly, *relieved* to know that someone else who seems to "have it all together" in class has also dealt with some difficult relationship issues. They decide to go for coffee after the event.

Derrick "fesses up" to Michalyn, letting her know that at the beginning of the semester he was miserable and struggling academically. He tells her that he actually failed the first chemistry exam. After that, he relays, he explained to his instructor why he was doing so poorly. The instructor told Derrick that it was very common for students to fight through heartbreak, and that he would eventually learn to better compartmentalize so he could maintain his grades. The instructor also suggested that he go to a seminar about healthy relationships. He is in a much better frame of mind now and has made an A on the last two exams.

Michalyn, fascinated by Derrick's story, says that she was in absolute despair at first. She opened up to an RA during an event at her residence hall, and that is who suggested she begin attending this seminar. She says that she too feels better now, but both of them complain about how several people minimized their experience. People told Derrick to just get over it, that he would have many more girlfriends. Michalyn got similar advice from a few people who didn't understand her full story. But once each had talked with some more supportive people on campus, they realized that their struggles were valid. Thankfully, they also realized they had the power to control their own life experience, especially while in college. They agree to keep each other honest and help one another make their own choices and not let others affect them as much. In the spirit of taking charge, they decide to be spontaneous and attend a comedy show on campus, because they see a flyer for it at the coffee shop. And why not?

*Bryce and Chen.* Both Bryce and Chen needed a one-hour elective, and both ended up taking "Finding your Voice," a discussion seminar focused on assertiveness. Bryce chose the course because some older friends told him to (they said it would be easy). Chen chose it because her advisor thought it would be a good experience for her and recommended that she take it. Early in the semester, Bryce and Chen are paired with each other as part of a role-playing assertiveness exercise. The instructions involve choosing a role for your partner to play, and then conducting a respectful but assertive conversation with that person on a particular issue. Both Chen and Bryce end up choosing their parents, and that coincidence gets them talking.

Chen talks about growing up in a world of strict parental expectations, and Bryce immediately responds with stories about his own experience of never-ending expectations to live up to. They find the activity to be very worthwhile, and both admit that the course is turning out to be a great experience. They commiserate about how hard it can be to speak up to your parents, but how great it is to be in college, where they can really become who they want to be. They make plans to have some respectful but assertive conversations with their parents the next time they go home. To their surprise, they realize that they both secretly love Japanese anime.

As a symbol of their new assertiveness, they make plans to attend a comic exhibit on campus that same evening.

## FURTHER READING ONLINE

- To learn more about the concept of resiliency, we suggest reading this article: Henderson, Nan, November 2, 2012, "What Is Resiliency and Why Is It So Important?" Resiliency in Action, retrieved from https://www.resiliency.com/what-is-resiliency/.
- There are also several quizzes available online to test one's level of resiliency, such as this one that can be completed automatically: Siebert, Al, "Resiliency Quiz—How Resilient Are You?" Resiliency Center, retrieved from http://resiliencyquiz.com/index.shtml; or another that can be tabulated manually: Henderson, Nan, November 2, 2012, "The Resiliency Quiz" Resiliency in Action, retrieved from https://www.resiliency.com/free-articles-resources/the-resiliency-quiz/.
- A related concept, called "grit," has gained recent attention. To read more about grit, visit Angela Duckworth's website for her book, *Grit: The Power of Passion and Perseverance*: https://angeladuckworth.com/grit-book/.
- In addition, visit the research tab on Angela Duckworth's website to learn more about how the scale was developed and what it helps to explain. A grit scale quiz can be completed and tabulated automatically here: "Grit Scale," retrieved from https://angeladuckworth.com/grit-scale/.

## NOTES

1. Lopata, Helena Z., and Judith A. Levy (eds.). 2003. *Social Problems across the Life Course*. New York: Roman and Littlefield.
2. Elder, Glen H., Jr. 1974. Children of the Great Depression: Social Change in Life Experience. Chicago: University of Chicago Press. [1] Kane, Emily W. 2013. "'No

Way My Boys Are Going to Be Like That!' Parents' Responses to Children's Gender Nonconformity." In Susan J. Ferguson (Ed.), *Mapping the Social Landscape: Readings in Sociology* (7th ed., pp. 121–133). New York: McGraw-Hill Education.

3.   Horton, Joann. 2015. "Identifying At-Risk Factors That Affect College Student Success." *International Journal of Process Education* 7(1): 83–101.

Sriram, Rishi. 2014. "Rethinking Intelligence: The Role of Mindset in Promoting Success for Academically High-Risk Students." *Journal of College Student Retention: Research, Theory & Practice* 15(4): 515–536.

4.   Cross, Ted M. 2014. "The Gritty: Grit and Non-Traditional Doctoral Student Success." *Journal of Educators Online* 11(3): 1–30.

Duckworth, Angela L., Christopher Peterson, Michael D. Matthews, and Dennis R. Kelly. 2007. "Grit: Perseverance and Passion for Long-Term Goals." *Journal of Personality and Social Psychology* 92(6): 1087–1101.

Eskreis-Winkler, Lauren, Angela Lee Duckworth, Elizabeth P. Shulman, and Scott Beal. 2014. "The Grit Effect: Predicting Retention in the Military, the Workplace, School, and Marriage." *Frontiers in Psychology* 5: 36–48.

Hammond, Drayton A. 2017. "Grit: An Important Characteristic in Learners." *Currents in Pharmacy Teaching and Learning* 9(1): 1–3.

5.   Baer, Judith C. 2011. "Students' Distress Over Grades: Entitlement or a Coping Response?" *Journal of Social Work Education* 47(3): 565–577.

Boswell, Stefanie S. 2012. "'I Deserve Success': Academic Entitlement Attitudes and Their Relationships with Course Self-Efficacy, Social Networking, and Demographic Variables." *Social Psychology of Education* 15(3): 353–365.

Cain, Jeff, Frank Romanelli, and Kelly M. Smith. 2012. "Academic Entitlement in Pharmacy Education." *American Journal of Pharmaceutical Education* 76(10): 189.

Dweck, Carol. 2009. "The Perils and Promises of Praise." In Kevin Ryan and James M. Cooper (Eds.), *Kaleidoscope: Contemporary and Classic Readings in Education* (pp. 57–61). Mason, OH: Cengage Learning.

Goldman, Zachary W., and Matthew M. Martin. 2016. "Millennial Students in the College Classroom: Adjusting to Academic Entitlement." *Communication Education* 65(3): 365–367.

Holmes, Linda E., and Lois J. Smith. 2003. "Student Evaluations of Faculty Grading Methods." *Journal of Education for Business* 78(6): 318–323.

Jackson, Dennis L., Jill A. Singleton-Jackson, and Marc P. Frey. 2011. "Report of a Measure of Academic Entitlement." *American International Journal of Contemporary Research* 1(3): 53–65.

Jeffres, Meghan N., Sean M. Barclay, and Scott K. Stolte. 2014. "Academic Entitlement and Academic Performance in Graduating Pharmacy Students." *American Journal of Pharmaceutical Education* 78(6).

Kopp, Jason P., Tracy E. Zinn, Sara J. Finney, and Daniel P. Jurich. 2011. "The Development and Evaluation of the Academic Entitlement Questionnaire." *Measurement and Evaluation in Counseling and Development* 44(2): 105–129.

Lippmann, Stephen, Ronald E. Bulanda, and Theodore C. Wagenaar. 2009. "Student Entitlement: Issues and Strategies for Confronting Entitlement in the Classroom and Beyond." *College Teaching* 57(4): 197–204.

Monaco, Michele, and Malissa Martin. 2007. "The Millennial Student: A New Generation of Learners." *Athletic Training Education Journal* 2(2): 42–46.

Sohr-Preston, Sara, and Stefanie S. Boswell. 2015. "Predicting Academic Entitlement in Undergraduates." *International Journal of Teaching and Learning in Higher Education* (November): 183–193.

Vallade, Jessalyn I., Matthew M. Martin, and Keith Weber. 2014. "Academic Entitlement, Grade Orientation, and Classroom Justice as Predictors of Instructional Beliefs and Learning Outcomes." *Communication Quarterly* 62(5): 497–517.

Wasieleski, David T., Mark Whatley, Deborah S. Briihl, and Jennifer M. Branscome. 2014. "Academic Entitlement Scale: Development and Preliminary Validation." *Psychology Research* 4 (June): 441–450.

6. Burke, Lisa A., and Monica K. Cummins. 2002. "Using Undergraduate Student-Faculty Collaborative Research Projects to Personalize Teaching." *College Teaching* 50(4): 129–133.

Carini, Robert M., George D. Kuh, and Stephen P. Klein. 2006. "Student Engagement and Student Learning: Testing the Linkages." *Research in Higher Education* 47(1): 1–32.

Chowning, Karolyn, and Nicole Judice Campbell. 2009. "Development and Validation of a Measure of Academic Entitlement: Individual Differences in Students' Externalized Responsibility and Entitled Expectations." *Journal of Educational Psychology* 101(4): 982–997.

Fitzgerald, Carlton. 2016. "Helping Students Enhance Their Grit and Growth Mindsets." *Educaţia Plus* 14(3): 52–67.

Hochanadel, Aaron, and Dora Finamore. 2015. "Fixed and Growth Mindset in Education and How Grit Helps Students Persist in the Face of Adversity." *Journal of International Education Research* 11(1): 47–50.

Mullen, Carol A. 2011. "Facilitating Self-Regulated Learning Using Mentoring Approaches with Doctoral Students." In Dale H. Schunk and Barry Zimmerman (Eds.), *Handbook of Self-Regulation of Learning and Performance*. New York: Routledge.

Perera, Jennifer, Nagarajah Lee, Khin Win, Joachim Perera, and Lionel Wijesuriya. 2008. "Formative Feedback to Students: The Mismatch between Faculty Perceptions and Student Expectations." *Medical Teacher* 30(4): 395–399.

Tantleff-Dunn, Stacey, Michael E. Dunn, and Jessica L. Gokee. 2002. "Understanding Faculty–Student Conflict: Student Perceptions of Precipitating Events and Faculty Responses." *Teaching of Psychology* 29(3): 197–202.

Wilder, Esther Isabelle. 2010. "A Qualitative Assessment of Efforts to Integrate Data Analysis throughout the Sociology Curriculum: Feedback from Students, Faculty, and Alumni." *Teaching Sociology* 38(3): 226–246.

7. Kane, Emily W. 2013. "'No Way My Boys Are Going to Be Like That!' Parents' Responses to Children's Gender Nonconformity." In Susan J. Ferguson (Ed.), *Mapping the Social Landscape: Readings in Sociology* (7th ed., pp. 121–133). New York: McGraw-Hill Education.

8. Gaines, Donna. 2013. "Teenage Wasteland: Suburbia's Dead-End Kids." In Susan J. Ferguson (Ed.), *Mapping the Social Landscape: Readings in Sociology* (7th ed., pp. 7–18). New York: McGraw-Hill Education.

9. Stuber, Jenny M. 2011. "Inside the College Gates: Education as a Social and Cultural Process." *Inside the College Gates: How Class and Culture Matter in Higher Education.* New York: Lexington Books.

10. Mirowsky, John, and Catherine E. Ross. 2007. "Life Course Trajectories of Perceived Control and Their Relationship to Education." *American Journal of Sociology* 112(5): 1339–1382.

11. Arnett, Jeffrey Jensen. 2015. *Emerging Adulthood: The Winding Road from the Late Teens Through the Twenties* (2nd ed.). New York: Oxford University Press.

# Harnessing Uniqueness and Finding Similar People

Chapter 6 addresses race, ethnicity, gender, sexuality, religion, and other aspects of diversity that shape individual students' expectations and experiences of college life. Some students find the university to have greater diversity than their smaller hometowns, while others came from more diverse urban settings. Many students struggle to understand how they fit in and how to make sense of others' attitudes. Students reflect on experiences with inclusion and exclusion during college, and many come to understand these experiences as part of larger social structures. Readers learn how to harness their identities as a personal strength, while also finding others who are similar enough to understand and support their perspective, values, or interests.

*The Science of College*. Patricia S. Herzog, Casey T. Harris, Shauna A. Morimoto, Shane W. Barker, Jill G. Wheeler, A. Justin Barnum, and Terrance L. Boyd, Oxford University Press (2020) © Oxford University Press.
DOI: 10.1093/oso/9780190934507.001.0001

This chapter focuses on *diversity and identity*, which are key areas of growth for most college students. The goal is to encourage students to reflect on and understand their own identities and view diversity on campus as an opportunity to develop "soft skills." Soft skills refer to engaging with others in emotionally mature, respectful, and empathic ways. Talking with other students about their differences and similarities builds these skills, and college campuses often provide new opportunities to engage with people from different backgrounds.

## STUDENT STORIES: WHAT WE EXPERIENCE

In the following stories, Jacob discusses feeling like a "fish out of water" on campus because it is more diverse than his hometown. Andrea and Cody, on the other hand, report that the same university is *less* diverse than their hometowns. Cameron shares about experiencing racism for the first time, and Eduardo and Marco discuss being bicultural. Linda relates her family's reaction to her dating someone from a different culture, while Landon describes his family's reaction to his desire to learn more about Muslims. Nikolaus describes being categorized as white to boost his chances of getting adopted, and William talks about the pressures of conforming to white ideals. Hayden, who reflects on what it is like to be bisexual, engages the issue of sexuality. Erin and Braden discuss religiosity, the former turning away from it and the latter engaging it more actively. Together, these students are diverse in terms of race and ethnicity, country of origin, culture, gender, sexuality, family status, and religiosity.

---

**#fishoutofwater or #dontbelong**: Do you feel like a fish out of water? Sometimes I do. In class, my prof called this "culture shock." All I know is it's so different here than back home.

**Jacob** describes what it is like to move from a small town where all his classmates were similar to him to a large university with greater diversity:

---

My elementary school years were spent in a mostly white public school. I did very well on all my homework and tests, and I was very interested in school at a young age. I had always gone to school, come home, went right to my homework, and then played outside until dark. I had no cares in the world, and I was privileged to live in a safe neighborhood with tons of other kids to socialize with. These were all kids just like me. I was situated in a neighborhood where my race and class identities were solid, and I had the advantages of being zoned for a great school system. Since my parents were able to afford to live in a place with access to such a school system, I started off with a huge advantage at a very young age . . . Once it was time to consider middle school, I had started to stand out as an academic student. Because my parents were well off, I had the opportunity to attend a private, Christian prep school. . . . There were only about 80 students in my class there, and I still did not encounter people who were much different than me. I did not understand any of the world outside of my little bubble. . . . I was so surrounded by driven people at such a young age that it was all I knew. Every student was required year-round to be in an athletic activity, play an instrument or be in the choir, and participate in fine arts. All of this was to be done while maintaining perfect grades and taking bible classes. We were able to go on amazing retreats, and even a Florida beach trip in eighth grade. In my mind, life was perfect, and I had no idea what the real world was like . . . Things became different when I came all the way to this campus to compete on the track and field team and pursue my undergraduate degree. Even though I had competed in track all throughout my middle school and high school years, everyone on the team was so different than I was used to. It is almost safe to say that no one was alike at all. We had athletes on the team from everywhere in the world, not just across America.

Conversely, **Andrea** describes nearly the opposite experience when she came to campus, as it was less diverse than the urban context she was accustomed to:

When I first came to this campus, one of the things that struck me was the lack of diversity. In my classes back home, we were very mixed, both in race and economic status. There were of course a few students from the upper class, but most were lower to middle income. Our classes also had a lot of minorities, unlike here. In all of my last semester's classes in college, I counted only 10 non-white students. People also regularly make racist comments to me. One instance [of this that I encountered was], my roommate's friend commented on my boots by saying, "are those your ni\*\*\*\* stomping boots?" No one had ever said anything like that to me before and it made me realize just how racist America still is. This is not the only instance of racist comments I have heard since being in the South. Recently, we played a game against a southern university. While I was warming up in the outfield, one of the fans yelled out to one of the umpires, that was black, "Are you blind? Come on dark-faced blue!" I was immediately taken back at the fact that he just screamed this across the field for the whole stadium to hear. He was so unashamed of his racism. One of our outfielders who is Latino also said that he had been yelling nasty comments to her all game. Based on her phenotype, or physical appearance, the man felt that he was superior to my teammate and the umpire and felt the need to assert his superiority in front of a large group.

Similarly, Cody describes experiencing less diversity in college than in his hometown:

I observed this [less diversity] to be true coming from a racially diverse high school, to the more homogeneous context here on campus . . . Because of this, [in high school] I was often learning about, and getting to know people that looked different than me and had different backgrounds. This environment allowed me to be more open and accepting of differences in society and encouraged me to think about social problems in a more encompassing manner, as I could still feel empathy for people that I did not identify with. However, my experience shifted in college. It was clear to me that the lack of minority students represented a racial disparity in our society. As I walk into my classes for the first time each semester, especially honors courses, I notice that many of the students seem to reflect my race and class.

**#diversity #racism**: Had a great conversation today in class about racism, and it made me think back to the first time I ever witnessed racism, in high school. What about you—when was the first time you ever saw or heard something racist happen?

**Cameron** describes his first encounters with racism:

One of the most dramatic contrasts between my two high schools presented itself in the racial makeup of the school. At my first high school, I was never in class with more than two people who were not white, though in my second high school nearly 30% of the students identified as a minority race. My Spanish class had a 4:3 ratio of native to non-native Spanish speakers. In Kansas, I was never exposed to people who were different than me, in a meaningful way. My family, church, school, and community were made up of people that looked just like me: white and upper middle class . . . With this increase of diversity came an increase of issues among people who were different. The first time I heard the word "n******" yelled down the hallway, I gasped. My mouth flung open in disbelief that someone would say that word, much less so loud. Even more shocking was the lack of reaction by everyone else, which helped me see that this was normal there.

Cameron then recounted that people at the second school thought that it was acceptable to say this word if it was used as a term of endearment among non-white students. Though this may have been the norm in that setting, it may not be the case in college. These formative interactions, however, are likely to continue to affect Cameron in college, even though the norms around him have changed. It is thus important to reflect on the expectations of each new social environment.

**#frommexico #opportunity**: Look for the #opportunity in each obstacle. Have sympathy for those who have less than you do. That's what life has taught me anyway.

**Eduardo** explains how growing up as an immigrant has shaped his experience of being bicultural in college:

I spent the first few years of my life in Mexico. When I first arrived in this country, I couldn't communicate. My grades displayed me as being far behind the rest academically . . . My teachers didn't know how much I could truly do because of the language barrier. I had to learn English before I was able to demonstrate to my teachers that I was a bright student with the will to learn despite my disadvantages . . . I also learned that some children need more help than others. My experience encouraged me to pursue a career in which I would help other disadvantaged kids . . . My experience of being an immigrant child, unable to understand, allows me to have sympathy for other kids who need a little extra help to succeed.

**Marco** reflects on being bicultural:

Two days ago, I recovered a repressed childhood memory while watching a George Lopez stand-up special. The comedian and I share a cultural background; we are both first-generation Mexicans in the United States, with two languages and two cuisines . . . For me and George Lopez, there are American ways of doing things and Mexican ways; our culture is having two cultures. So when Lopez brought up the old Spanish phrase, 'Sana sana, colita de rana,' a soothing rhyme used by mothers when their children are in pain [translation: "heal, heal, little frog tail"], I laughed the hardest I had that day, out of pure realization that (a) my 'White-American' self had allowed me to forget how often my own mother used the phrase throughout my upbringing, and (b) that the use of culture to explain how people act collectively worked—George Lopez's audience howled with me, and we all howled together because we had a mutual understanding that 'Sana sana, colita de rana' is how we Mexicans deal with things, things like the scraped little knees of our children.

#interracialdating #interracialfamily: Brought my boyfriend home to meet the family. Turns out my 'rents are actually excited about possibly having a "biracial marriage." Well, we'll see . . .

From a different point of view, **Linda** reflects on dating some-one from another country and reports her family's reaction to the relationship:

Second year of college, I began dating a man named Marco, he was born in the U.S., but his parents moved to this city from Mexico. We began talking because I was minoring in Spanish, and he told me he was impressed that I "knew" another language. Surprised that he felt that way, I responded saying "but you speak both English, and Spanish, because of your family?" and he said "yes but I live in the United States, of course I speak English." What I found interesting is that his life as a child was more integrated with different languages than mine would ever be studying a language, yet I received more praise for my knowledge and effort of learning another language than he did . . . I was privileged to be able to learn a language, whereas anyone raised in a family of a different culture . . . was expected to know English, yet most

Americans don't know another language . . . Because of their race and language barrier, they are excluded from praise for knowing multiple languages.

Moreover, when I told my parents about dating Marco . . . they said maybe we will finally have a "biracial marriage" in the family, almost as though it was a badge to show that we were different from "other whites," and wouldn't be carded off as racist. Then they asked if he was Catholic, and I said yes (I was also raised Catholic), and that reassured them that he wasn't "such a bad guy." However, I question what their views would have been if he would have been Muslim, or Buddhist . . . Their happiness towards the relationship based on Marco's religion, demonstrates the idea that they liked the familiarity of the culture he was brought up in . . . To them, he demonstrated diversity by not being Hispanic versus white [even when at the same time he ironically] "wooed" them with his generic, culturally popular religion.

**#adopted #becomingwhite**: One of my profs talked about "white privilege" today, and I can't help but yet again be confused about whether I am white or privileged. Definitely confusing since I was born to Asian parents, abandoned in Russia, and adopted by a white family.

**Nikolaus** describes race and adoption:

The journey of my life begins in a distant country where I was born and immediately put into an orphanage. In Russia, I was born to parents who were both teenagers, and I was the third child. From an early age, social factors began to forge how my life would play out. The first of these is through labeling . . . This labeling was portrayed in my life through the designation of my race as Caucasian on my birth certificate, even though I could have been simply labeled as Asian. I was most likely labeled this way because it gave me a higher chance of being adopted . . . By being as close to white as possible I could then be more desirable. Passing as white comes through many different forms. I have darker skin because of the location in Russia I am from and am often confused for being Mexican. Just a couple of weeks ago in the dining hall, one of the workers started speaking to me in Spanish, and I had to tell them I didn't understand, and she said, "sorry you just look Mexican." . . . To further fit this white American standard, when I came over to the United States my name was changed from Nikolaus to a name sounding much more American and which passed with a greater degree of acceptance: Nick. [By being labeled white, my adoption fees were most likely higher.] While having a higher price tag may seem silly, it meant that I could be considered white and was advertised that way to attract American families.

**#whitemale #pressure**: Some say that pressure creates diamonds, but I'm not so sure.

**William** discusses a different aspect of diversity:

The structure of the American society is one conducive to the success of white, heterosexual, upper-middle class, Christian males. . . . As a white, heterosexual, upper-middle class, Christian male, I can say that . . . in the midst of all of my privilege, the fact is often overlooked that I still have to work hard to achieve my goals, and furthermore it is often forgotten that because success is supposedly granted to me ahead of others in similar positions to myself, outsiders who know nothing of my life have higher expectations for my success in the modern world. Consequently, if I do not succeed, I as a white, heterosexual, upper-middle class, Christian male will be a social outcast among my friends and family. While it is harder for underprivileged groups to succeed, white, heterosexual, upper-middle class, Christian males are burdened by an anticipation of success at a higher frequency than any other group, because it is perceived as markedly easier. Being a white, heterosexual, upper-middle class, Christian male is both a blessing and a curse in today's society, in that it comes with an expectation of success that not every privileged male can or will reach.

**#bipride #notjustaphase**: happy #bipride. where's the fun in choosing sides??

**Hayden** discusses another aspect of diversity, sexuality:

I am bisexual. This is a phrase I have always struggled to say because although society's attitude toward the LGBT community is changing for the positive, overall, many individuals' attitudes are still hateful and unaccepting . . . As a bisexual individual, I can pass for straight, which gives me a strange sort of privilege, for through this "passing" I can be accepted as a "normal" (read: straight) member of society. Even though heterosexual people can see me as being a member of their group . . . once members of the straight community are aware of my status, full acceptance is rarely entirely given . . . My identity is belittled. I, like many other bisexuals, am told that it is "just a phase" or that I "will figure out what I really am once I find the right person."

**#notcatholic #agnostic**: Just learned what the word "agnostic" means today. I think that is what I am now. Sorry grandma:/

Touching on another form of diversity, **Erin** describes having grown up religious but moving away from religiosity now as an emerging adult:

I considered myself to be Catholic until around my junior year of high school. This was probably because my immediate family was Catholic, and that is how I was raised. Then in high school many of my friends did not have Catholic beliefs, and so I was not exposed to Catholicism through them. Additionally, my school was not afraid to address some controversial beliefs of the Catholic

Church. Through these experiences I concluded that I no longer believe in the Catholic Church.

**#christian**: I'm a Christian. I am not perfect, but I do think Christianity gives me strength.

**Braden** describes how growing up Christian affected his values:

Christianity gave me a unique view on life that allowed me to constantly move between social groups . . . [Within certain denominations,] Christianity views sexual relations before marriage as wrong, including those in the mind brought on by pornography, while the society that exists around us is extremely centered on exploring sexuality and the pursuit of sexual partners outside of the covenant of marriage . . . The human race is innately sexual, due to sex being the way for reproduction, but the sexual desires are for more than just reproduction. Humans have an obsession with sex that occurred throughout the ages and will still occur in the future. These sexual influences were pushed on me and societal influences connected sexuality to masculinity . . . Christianity, however, is meant to be concerned with what is godly and right, not what is masculine or feminine. Through its stance on masculinity and sexuality, Christianity is, in essence, a powerful source of socialization . . . The beauty of society is that there are others who have had similar experiences to mine, but still others who did not . . . [and whose] views on my life and their own experiences could be vastly different from my own.

**#islamophobia:** stop the hate.

**Landon** discusses how he is affected by the anti-Muslim sentiment in his family:

With my continuation and interest in language, I asked my parents (for Christmas) for a book on learning Arabic (for example, a dictionary, or Rosetta Stone type software, etc.). Their first question was if I was going to convert to become a Muslim. I stated no, but I wanted to learn more about their religion. I told them "Arabic is a wide-spread language, and not everyone who speaks Arabic is Muslim." They replied "Well you better not convert!" Instead for Christmas, I got a book against Muslims from the perspective of an African woman being kidnapped.

## SCIENCE: WHAT WE KNOW

As these student stories illustrate, questions about diversity and identity make up an integral part of college life. These questions often arise during emerging adulthood when young people are figuring out who they are and what it means to be an adult. Issues of race, gender, religion, sexuality, and language can surface in college, while emerging adults explore their own attitudes about the privileges and constrictions that come with their identities, as well as learn to navigate the ways these facets of diversity structure university life. Often college presents a time to reflect on what is normal and on the culture of one's upbringing. For example, Becker (2013)[1] finds that social institutions—such as education, family, economic, and political institutions—establish social norms. The shared culture these norms create provides people in the same social groups with similar understandings. Many of the student stories illuminate the ways that race can shape young people's identities, often by conveying a sense that conforming to the dominant culture is required to "make it" (Zweigenhaft and Domhoff 2013)[2] and forms the structure of the university. Jacob recounts how being in college allows him to see being white as coming with certain privileges and expectations. Eduardo, Marco, and Nikolaus all wrestle with what it means to be an American, a category tied up with race, language, and culture. All three of these students experience the feeling of being in-between identities.

Beyond identity issues, it is also important to learn from research that race is related to socioeconomic status. For instance, Thomas Shapiro (2013)[3] has shown how racial differences in rates of homeownership contribute to differences in wealth, a measure which reveals a greater gap between races than does income. **Eduardo** provides an example of this:

> My parents are from Hidalgo, Mexico. They left everyone and everything they loved in pursuit of a job in a foreign nation where I would have more opportunity. Our socioeconomic standing is of the lower class. Growing up, my father worked in construction and my mother had a job cleaning homes, hotels, and rehabilitation homes. The racial wealth gap was prevalent in our family . . . Immigrant families do not have any previous accumulation of wealth or property in a new country. They also simply do not have the documentation to build a mortgage and have credit.

In this way, race and ethnicity are structural issues, meaning they are built into the institutions and processes that form the economy. Matthew Desmond and Mustafa Emirbayer (2013),[4] in a book entitled *What is Racial Domination?*, explain that race is also symbolic, meaning it is something people actively create and recreate as they formulate ideas and meaning-making processes. This is especially true for international students. The authors explain: "We misrecognize race as natural when we begin to think that racial cleavages and inequalities can be explained by pointing to attributes somehow inherent in the race itself (as if they were biological) instead of understanding how social powers, economic forces, political institutions, and cultural practices have brought about these divisions" (2013: 342). For example, in *More Than Just Black*, William Julius Wilson (2010)[5] explains how his race is perceived differently based on the circumstances surrounding his appearance, such as his clothes:

> I am an internationally known Harvard professor, yet a number of unforgettable experiences remind me that, as a black male in America looking considerably younger than my age, I am also

feared. For example, several times over the years I have stepped into the elevator of my condominium dressed in casual clothes and could immediately tell from the body language of the other residents in the elevator that I made them feel uncomfortable. Were they thinking, "What is this black man doing in this expensive condominium? Are we in any danger?" I once sarcastically said to a nervous elderly couple who hesitated to exit the elevator because we were all getting off on the same floor, "Not to worry, I am a Harvard professor and I have lived in this building for nine years." When I am dressed casually, I am always a little relieved to step into an empty elevator, but I am not apprehensive if I am wearing a tie (pp. 1–2).

These symbolic dimensions of race come across in the experiences of many students. Students from racially homogenous social environments may recognize the importance of these dimensions of race for the first time in college, once they are interacting with more diverse student bodies. Whether in a more diverse environment, or a less diverse environment, or because they are suddenly confronted with racism, their experiences illustrate how race affects their college experiences and social interactions in the world at large.

Granted, ideas and issues related to race arise long before young people enter college. Debra Van Ausdale and Joe Feagin (2013)[6] study young children and find that even at three and five years of age, kids grasp racial and ethnic concepts and use them as meaningful categories for interpreting social interactions. They explain: "The complex nature of children's group interactions and their solo behaviors demonstrates that race and ethnicity are salient, substantial aspects of their lives" (p. 140). Despite the ongoing difficulties of navigating race and racism, we are mindful of a book entitled *Cosmopolitan Canopies*, in which Elijah Anderson (2013)[7] engages in what he calls "hopeful sociology" by identifying places within cities in which people change racial stereotypes. These city locations allow people to put their "urban guard" down a bit, eavesdrop on each other, and in other ways engage in what Anderson calls folk ethnography: assessing information about each other through thoughtful observation. We believe that college can likewise provide a context in which people can change their preconceived notions about those in other racial and ethnic groups. As Cody of this chapter explains, "Urban areas, being more diverse, tend to facilitate more empathetic, positive race relations (Anderson 2013). My high school was large and extremely diverse; therefore, it could be compared to an urban area that consists of many different races and cultures."

In addition to race and ethnicity, many other forms of diversity and identity emerge in campus life, and often intersect to affect students' identity. By way of illustration, Marco of this chapter says, "Even 'doing gender' (West & Zimmerman 1987, as cited in Risman 2013) played a role in identifying with either group [White or Hispanic]. Across racial lines, similar performances can result in different, gendered meanings, as well as meanings that intersect with race itself." This highlights the role of gender and sexuality in individuals' identities and behaviors. C. J. Pascoe (2013)[8] studied talk of sexuality and found that negative stereotypes of gendered behavior, especially regarding masculinity, are often used to reify gender categories. In day-to-day forms of speaking and interacting, and whether intentionally or not, people may ostracize other groups that do not look or act the same as their reference groups do. This in effect polices the boundaries between in-groups and out-groups, or those like "us" and those that are different.

Georg Simmel discusses this in an essay called "The Stranger" (1908),[9] in which he describes strangers as being outside of a group and yet still helping to define the group by confronting it with the difference that makes it distinct from other people and groups. If nearly all of one's experiences are in being an outsider, the result is *social isolation*: disconnection, often evidenced through having few close friends, a concept distinct from loneliness, which is the subjective experience of being alone regardless of the number of connections (Parigi and Henson 2014).[10] The obvious downsides are that disconnection can lead to feelings of loneliness and a loss of community over time. Yet there are potential advantages to experiencing isolation. First, being an outsider creates a detachment that allows for rational analysis of a group's dynamics, without biases wrought from emotional connection to members of the group. Plus, a degree of detachment from groups may be necessary in order to have difficult conversations, as defined by Stone and Heen (2010)[11]: discussions of what matters most, the subjects we simultaneously desire and struggle to discuss and that arouse strong emotions.

One of the best examples of a matter that many Americans find it difficult to discuss is religion. As Erin of this chapter summarizes, "Similarly to class and race, religion is an extremely complex, but also extremely important part of our society. It provides people with a social group that has similar beliefs and values as themselves (Dandaneau 2013) ⋯ Socialization, or interacting with others to form our personal beliefs and values, makes up a large part of what religion a person identifies with, believes in, and belongs to (Dandaneau 2013)." Steven Dandaneau (2013)[12] describes religion as a universal cultural phenomenon that consists of institutionalized social practices, having to do with rituals that are deemed sacred, and which often fosters bonds of social solidarity among those sharing the same beliefs or partaking of the same rituals. Erin adds, "This [the importance of religion] has become more and more evident to me as I have grown older . . . Our individual religious beliefs are important when looking at society because they make up such large social institutions for people to be involved." William of this chapter also reflects on the ways that Christianity forms an important aspect of his identity, which can both connect and divide.

In recent decades in the United States, the religion that tends to stir the highest emotional response and is likely the least understood of major religions is Islam. This is well illustrated in Landan's story about his family's apprehension toward Muslims. By Landan's account, their apprehension seems to stem from negative and inaccurate preconceptions. As Jen'nan Read (2013)[13] explains, American Muslims actually represent a diverse group who are generally "highly educated, politically conscious, and fluent in English" (p. 520). Their religious beliefs and practices are not uniform. Read adds: "In a country marked by a declining salience of religious boundaries and increasing acceptance of religious difference, Muslim Americans have largely been excluded from this ecumenical trend . . . we need to move past the fear that Muslim Americans are un-American so we can bring them into the national dialogue" (2013: 526). What Landan is encountering are erroneous beliefs in society about who and what Muslims are. In fact, many Americans overestimate the size of most minority groups in society, whether it be Muslims, members of the LGBTQ community, immigrants, or other racial and ethnic minorities. It seems that although many Americans want to embrace diversity, most overestimate how much diversity there actually is. At the same time, most white Americans do not interact with anyone who is not also white, leaving colleges and universities to be one of the few places where people from different backgrounds have the opportunity to interact and learn from each other.

## ADVICE: WHAT WE (CAN) PROVIDE

**#fishoutofwater #sodifferent #diversity** Both **Jacob** and **Andrea** feel disconnected in ways that are normal among emerging adults. Although administrators and advisors often stress exploring different career paths and skill sets, transitioning into adulthood can also entail trying out different kinds of places, getting used to different kinds of people, and learning how best to engage within one's given social context. The safety net of emerging adulthood means that one can explore and experiment with fewer consequences. For Jacob, this may mean stepping outside of his comfort zone and embracing the diversity of campus while carving out a smaller group of friends with whom he shares interests and a similar background. Likewise, Andrea may decide that now is the time to explore the unique things a smaller place has to offer, as well as find a way to connect with her interests back home (for example, art, music, cinema, sports, food). We recommend that students like Jacob and Andrea find supportive adults on campus who can help explain that becoming an adult will occasionally mean working in unfamiliar settings and with different groups of people. College is the time to explore how to fit in within unfamiliar circumstances and how to make connections in those settings. It is an important life skill, and one which students can—at least from time to time—enjoy learning along the way!

Both Jacob's and Andrea's feelings of disconnectedness come not only from the size of their classes or university, but also from the broader social environments into which they've been plunged. As Stuber (2011) [14] notes, colleges and universities are not neutral settings; rather, they operate with cultural norms and expectations that some students may find difficult to grasp and practice. Whereas some students at Jacob's university come from larger cities and social settings and thus "have a leg up," Jacob is not the only one from a less diverse background. And although Andrea has found campus less diverse than her hometown, her situation is similar to Jacob's in that she must also work to integrate herself into her university's social life by "socially and psychologically [separating] from life prior to college" (Stuber 2011: 11, as both inspired by and adapting Tinto 2012[15]).

There are several things students like Jacob and Andrea can do to become more connected to their institutions. Perhaps most importantly, they should look for opportunities to build additional cultural and social capital by getting involved with extracurricular activities, such as student groups, clubs, community service, Greek life, and internships. Doing so will not only help them along their academic and career paths in the long run, but it will also benefit them personally in the short term by providing them with the opportunity to make new friends and feel less isolated. For Andrea in particular, it might be helpful to become involved in groups that advocate for or work toward specific diversity goals. Many of these groups can be found easily online. This would allow her to cultivate a more diverse network of friends and help her respond to the racism that understandably unsettles her in her college environment.

To students like Jacob, we recommend finding activities outside of their comfort zone in order to make friends with students from different backgrounds, perhaps checking them out online first. Knowing everyone back home is comforting is great, but it is also important to recognize that college is the time to hone the social skills involved in interacting with all kinds of people. These skills may prove crucial when Jacob graduates and begins his career—potentially in a big city or even another country. Andrea, too, should see her new environment as an opportunity to gain skills. Finding activities she enjoys and engaging with her fellow students (many of whom are already friends with each other) can help her find her

own place and build relationships that will reduce her feelings of disconnectedness over the next few years. Especially given the variety of ways
her life may play out, it is good for her to know that college is the time
to build up skills—including social and cultural ones—that will help her
thrive in different kinds of social environments later in life.

**#diversity #racism** Like Andrea and Jacob, **Cody** and **Cameron** notice
how different campus is from their pre-college life. Each of these students
has their own experiences and sense of what is familiar. When they begin
college, they are challenged to think about their prior lifestyles. We recommend that these students embrace the opportunity to rethink things
and seek out resources on campus to aid them in doing so. For example, if
a student is from a homogeneous background and wants to see other cultures, he or she can visit a multicultural center on campus or find an activity (sports, theater, student groups), or an online site that brings together
students from different backgrounds. It is also crucial that these students
begin to think about how they can use their own lifestyles and experiences to advocate for someone else on campus. Sometimes it is easiest to
begin this sort of advocacy online, by supporting diverse groups of people
with likes on social media apps, or reposting their content. Additionally,
students can find a registered student organization of the group of people
with whom they want to work. Important in all these examples is that students seize the opportunity that college provides to encounter, converse,
and navigate relationships with a diverse array of people.

Cameron relayed how he first heard the "N" word when someone
called it loudly down the hallway. This is an intense experience, and we
recommend that students like Cameron think about how they can use
that experience. For example, Cameron could talk with Jacob, Cody, or
Andrea about what happened, to ask questions about what kind of environment they grew up in and how they learned to be respectful (or not)
of other cultures. Students can talk with each other about how to talk
with someone who did not have the same exposure as they did, as well as
how to learn from others when they engage them about new experiences.
Sometimes these challenging conversations are best had online, where
students can respectfully vocalize social problems and offer anonymous

readers tips for improving. Even if their friends are not initiating these conversations with them, students can take it upon themselves to become leaders and to model to their friends how to have those difficult, necessary, and meaningful conversations. This is part of developing "soft skills" that bridge divides across racial, ethnic, and cultural lines.

**#frommexico #opportunity and #interracialdating #interracialfamily** The stories of **Eduardo, Marco,** and **Linda** also highlight how students learn key social skills during college. For Eduardo, we recommend reflecting on having empathy for someone. Empathy is a soft skill that cannot be learned from a book. Being able to empathize with other people will enable Eduardo to listen and offer feedback in a constructive, respectful way in the workplace. For both Eduardo and Linda, who know both Spanish and English, we encourage them to think about the value these language skills can have in a workplace. Speaking Spanish builds cultural competence to work with the Latino community, or if they pick up another language, with that community as well. In addition, we advise these students to harness their ability to communicate with people from diverse cultures. Gaining experiences speaking with people from different cultures will help the students engage their language abilities in an empathetic way.

Eduardo and Marco could also consider getting involved with the international student populations on campus. Perhaps they could work with a student group to reach out through social media to local high schools or immigrant communities in order to help new students transition into college. In this way, they can employ their own experiences in the service of others. This will also bolster their college credentials and provide them with further social support on campus related to their cultural experiences. Being able to follow their own path through college and share their sense of biculturalism with others will undergird their resiliency and promote their unique stories. We advise these students to embrace their cultural background and to connect with the Latin American Studies Department to learn more about their heritage and how their backgrounds can be a strength in their academic background.

**#adopted #becomingwhite #whitemale #pressure** With **Nikolaus** and **William,** two distinct sides of white male privilege are engaged. Nikolaus describes how his classification as white promoted his chances of adoption, even though his ethnic background and appearance are not typical of white Americans. William lists the advantages of his undoubtedly white and male status, but also feels pressure to live up to the high expectations he thinks others have for him. What these two students share is that they are highly aware of the advantages that can come with being labeled white and male. These background social statuses affect them in college because they believe they have what they need to perform well. In light of the intense pressure that William describes, we advise him to seek out ways to prevent that pressure from overcoming him and from becoming a source of resentment against people who are underrepresented. For example, he could start a blog to share his experiences. Otherwise, he is at risk of relying on his background as a crutch, and he may end up diminishing what he is capable of accomplishing.

We recommend that students like Nikolaus and William let their work in college speak for itself, and caring adults on campus would do well to reiterate this point (especially because such students may need to hear it often). It is helpful to recognize that some doors may be open to them because they are white and male, or (in cases like William's) because they come from a well-resourced background. However, they should also think about how to own their pathway and construct the education plan they want, keeping in mind what resources they have and how their backgrounds affect their college experiences. In addition, as with the previous set of students, we recommend that William and Nikolaus think about ways they can leverage their statuses, advantages, disadvantages, and experiences to serve others. For instance, they might work with both similarly and less privileged groups on campus and in high schools by sharing their own insights into college, starting or engaging in dialogues across racial and cultural lines, and connecting on social media. Indeed, one great way to confront the pressure to live up to certain standards is to reach out to those who have less, instead of comparing oneself to those who are similarly or better situated. These are ways to harness the good and the bad aspects of students' backgrounds to shape personal strengths.

**#bipride #notjustaphase #notcatholic #agnostic #christian** For **Hayden**, **Erin**, and **Braden**, we have some simple pieces of advice. Braden

is a devout Christian, and thus we recommend that he visit campus minis-
tries or find a place of worship off campus. This will provide him a place to
exercise his faith and find like-minded individuals. Hayden is secure in his
sexuality and sounds well-poised to help others to understand bisexuality.
We encourage him to build on the experience of people misunderstand-
ing his sexuality by advocating for himself and others, including through
existing student groups and organizations. Erin is squarely in the life stage
of emerging adulthood and does not want to constrain herself. We recommend, however, that instead of completely writing off her religion at this
early point in her life, she should reach out to her mom. We advise her
to take the time to explore, moving beyond her own personal reasons, in
order to seek out information from other people.

   #islamophobia For the final student featured in this chapter, **Landon**, we
recommend that he consider how learning more about Arabic and Muslim
communities could affect his career. Considering the ways his passion for
religious diversity challenges his parents, we advise him to find other social
support and alternative perspectives on this interest. To gain the cultural
competency he desires, he would need to utilize the resources on his college campus. For example, Landon could investigate whether the university
offers Arabic as a major or minor, and whether there are professors who
are Muslim. If so, he can reach out to these professors to learn more about
Arabic and Muslim culture. There may be jobs in which Arabic language
proficiency is especially desired, and talking with faculty or advisors about
those positions could help Landon carve out his own career path. In addition, Landon can seek out students on campus whose first language is Arabic
and students who are just learning the language. In these pursuits, we advise
Landon to be mindful of his family background. If his parents are unaccepting, he can still pursue his goals and dreams, but he will need to find ways
to explain to them why he is so passionate about this. Seeking out campus
resources will help him to be resilient in this process and to teach him how
his career path can benefit from the cultural sensitivity he seeks to build.

   In summary, there are some similarities in the advice we offer to different students. This is because all students should be mindful of their
individual realities, how their context and backgrounds shape who they

are and how they can work with others. We advise students to consider how openness to other people, as well as learning the ways their lives are both similar and different, can develop their soft skills. Taking the time in college to reflect (see appendix A), have constructive conversations, and seek out opportunities to discuss differences will serve them well. At the same time, we recognize that joining clubs and reaching out across racial, religious, and identity lines does not solve the structural problems related to race, gender, sexuality, and religious differences. Moreover, at this particular moment in the United States, college campuses are environments where discussions of rights, privilege, advantage, and disadvantage can quickly become heated and emotional. We strongly support students' right to organize and make themselves heard when they are advocating for themselves and others. We also implore students to engage in difficult conversations as a way to learn about and find ways to work across differences in race, sexuality, religion, and other identities and belief systems.

## TOGETHERNESS: WHAT WE (CAN) SHARE

Next, we offer a possible dialog between several of our case studies.*

*Regan and Abby.* During the second week of classes, a sociology class is in the middle of a group activity entitled "Crossing the Line" (see appendix C for a description of this activity). Two participants in the activity, Regan and Abby, begin chatting because they noticed each other's "Go Greek" T-shirts.

---

* As described with the first togetherness section in chapter 5, faculty and support staff are important social supports in navigating college, as are fellow students. In these togetherness sections, the goal is to suggest ways that students can support one another in navigating college. Akin to a reality television show, the students are interacting with each other in ways that build their relationships around some of the challenges and opportunities these students described in their case studies. Given the challenges already expressed within the case studies, the goal in these situations is to focus on the positive ways that students can support one another. Inevitably social interactions can also be fraught with negative experiences, and we do not mean to suggest that all social interactions occur positively. Rather, we offer some possible ways to support one another, which students can and will modify to add their own authentic approach. To review student stories alongside these togetherness sections, readers can refer to the table of case studies preceding chapter 1 and the brief synopsis of student stories included within that table.

Regan tells Abby that questions about owning your own car and traveling to a different country made her realize that she may be more "privileged" (to use her instructor's word) than most of her class, which is something she did not expect. Abby completely agrees. Both of them become immediately self-conscious about how that might affect the new friendships they hope to make on campus, and both pledge to never let that be a factor. Abby mentions a new friend of hers, Austin, who went through rush but ultimately decided not to join a fraternity because he simply could not afford it. Abby had promised herself that she would not lose touch with Austin just because she was Greek and he was not. Regan thinks that is a great story. They promise each other that they will step outside their comfort zone, and use these four years to make friends who are different than them.

*Riberto and Austin.* Also during the "Crossing the Line" activity, Riberto and Austin strike up a side conversation. They had a slightly different experience from Regan and Abby—they have become aware of their lack of privilege. They began chatting because on several questions related to working-class backgrounds, they were the only two individuals in the class who crossed the line. They bonded by cracking a few jokes about some of the other questions, especially the one about owning your own car. Riberto says that the idea of owning your own car as a college student is plain crazy, and that he was just glad that the university had a public transit system that was included in his student fees. His hometown did not have a public transit system, which made it very difficult to get around. Austin shares his story about how he invested so much time in rushing, only to realize there was no way he could afford to join a fraternity. He worries that this will affect his social life, and, more importantly, his ability to meet people that might help him down the road. Ultimately, they agree that college is a great opportunity that provides them with many things they did not have back home, but also that this experience does not change who they are as individuals. They both share their insight about how college is a way to create a more financially stable future while maintaining the core values instilled in them by their working-class families. They are very proud of where they come from and cannot wait to see what the next four years will bring.

*Chikako and Erin.* As the "Crossing the Line" activity progressed, Chikako and Erin began to converse because they sat next to each other. Chikako noticed that they both hesitated to stand up in response to a few of the same questions, but he felt much better to see someone had similar feelings on those issues. They begin to talk about their parents. They share one slightly sarcastic story after another about how their parents stifle them, even though they mean well. Chikako loves his parents but they tend to suppress his secretly bold personality. He is tired of being stifled, and he is so ready to let it all out! Erin can totally relate. She grew up with devout Catholic parents—something she respects them for. She grew up scared of being different because it made her feel guilty about being a bad person. But after talking to people like Chikako, and really engaging in courses like this one, she is beginning to realize that she is not a bad person just because she is curious. She wants to check out some of the other religious student organizations on campus, and is excited about her new freedom. Both feel newfound relief that they are not the only ones on campus dealing with this type of guilt.

## FURTHER READING ONLINE

- For further reading on this topic, see this description of how Photoshop was used to "doctor diversity" into a university's promotional materials: Wade, Lisa, September 2, 2009, "Doctoring Diversity: Race and Photoshop," The Society Pages, retrieved from https://thesocietypages.org/socimages/2009/09/02/doctoring-diversity-race-and-photoshop/.
- Alternatively, here is an example of an advertisement that challenges the compartmentalization of status by adeptly combining race, class, and gender in interesting ways: Wade, Lisa, March 12, 2013, "Managing Stigma: Doing Race, Class, and Gender" The Society Pages, retrieved from https://thesocietypages.org/socimages/2013/03/12/race-class-and-gender/.

Additional ideas for activities on this topic can be found at the following Web pages:

- Gorski, Paul C., "Circles of My Multicultural Self," Ed Exchange, retrieved from http://www.edchange.org/multicultural/activities/circlesofself.html.
- "Cultural Artifacts," On Course, retrieved from http://oncourseworkshop.com/self-awareness/cultural-artifacts/.
- "Diversity Continuum," Eastern Illinois University, retrieved from http://castle.eiu.edu/eiu1111/DiversityContinuum.doc.
- Fishbowl Listening Exercise: Lakey, George, "Fishbowl, Panel and Speak-Outs : Three Listening Exercises, retrieved from https://www.trainingforchange.org/tools/fishbowl-panel-and-speak-outs-three-listening-exercises.
- What's the Difference, within the Defining Diversity section of these 101 Games for Trainers: Pike, Bob, "101 Games for Trainers," O'Reilly, retrieved from https://www.safaribooksonline.com/library/view/101-games-for/9780943210384/.
- "Flip Side—Human Awareness," Elizabethtown College, retrieved from http://www.etown.edu/offices/diversity/files/diversity-binder.pdf.
- "The Depth and Breadth of 'Multicultural,'" Cada, retrieved from https://secure.cada1.org/i4a/doclibrary/getfile.cfm?doc_id=23.

## NOTES

1. Becker, Howard S. 2013. "Culture: A Sociological View." In Susan J. Ferguson (Ed.), *Mapping the Social Landscape: Readings in Sociology* (7th ed., pp. 95–104). New York: McGraw-Hill Education.
2. Zweigenhaft, Richard L., and G. William Domhoff. 2013. "The Ironies of Diversity." In Susan J. Ferguson (Ed.), *Mapping the Social Landscape: Readings in Sociology* (7th ed., pp. 398–412). New York: McGraw-Hill Education.

3. Shapiro, Thomas M. 2013. "Race, Homeownership, and Wealth." In Susan J. Ferguson (Ed.), *Mapping the Social Landscape: Readings in Sociology* (7th ed., pp. 266–277). New York: McGraw-Hill Education.

4. Desmond, Matthew, and Mustafa Emirbayer. 2013. "What Is Racial Domination?" In Susan J. Ferguson (Ed.), *Mapping the Social Landscape: Readings in Sociology* (7th ed., pp. 338–353). New York: McGraw-Hill Education.

5. Wilson, William Julius. 2010. *More Than Just Race: Being Black and Poor in the Inner City.* New York: W. W. Norton & Company.

6. Van Ausdale, Debra, and Joe R. Feagin. 2013. "Using Racial and Ethnic Concepts: The Critical Case of Very Young Children." In Susan J. Ferguson (Ed.), *Mapping the Social Landscape: Readings in Sociology* (7th ed., pp. 134–144). New York: McGraw-Hill Education.

7. Anderson, Elijah. 2013. "The Cosmopolitan Canopy." In Susan J. Ferguson (Ed.), *Mapping the Social Landscape: Readings in Sociology* (7th ed., pp. 631–643). New York: McGraw-Hill Education.

8. Pascoe, C. J. 2013. "Dude, You're a Fag?" In Susan J. Ferguson (Ed.), *Mapping the Social Landscape: Readings in Sociology* (7th ed., pp. 315–323). New York: McGraw-Hill Education.

9. Simmel, Georg. 1908. "The Stranger." In David P. Frisby and Mike Featherstone [1998], *Simmel on Culture: Selected Writings.* Thousand Oaks, CA: Sage Publications.

10. Parigi, Paolo, and Warner Henson. 2014. "Social Isolation in America." *Annual Review of Sociology* 40(1): 153–171.

11. Stone, Douglas, and Sheila Heen. 2010. *Difficult Conversations: How to Discuss What Matters Most.* London: Penguin.

12. Dandaneau, Steven P. 2013. "Religion and Society: Of Gods and Demons." In Susan J. Ferguson (Ed.), *Mapping the Social Landscape: Readings in Sociology* (7th ed., pp. 509–518). New York: McGraw-Hill Education.

13. Read, Jen'nan Ghazal. 2013. "Muslims in America." In Susan J. Ferguson (Ed.), *Mapping the Social Landscape: Readings in Sociology* (7th ed., pp. 519-526). New York: McGraw-Hill Education.

14. Stuber, Jenny M. 2011. Inside the College Gates: How Class and Culture Matter in Higher. 2012. *Inside the College Gates: How Class and Culture Matter in Higher Education.* Lanham, MA: Lexington Books.

15. Tinto, Vincent. 2012. *Completing College: Rethinking Institutional Action.* Chicago: University of Chicago Press.

# Becoming a Leader and Giving to Others

This seventh chapter examines how learning from personal experiences and structural challenges can put students on a path to leadership. Chapter 7 shows students that another important aspect of college is figuring out how to become a leader. Being a leader requires recognizing one's personal strengths and learning how to engage those strengths on campus, which builds skills and experiences for broader civic engagement. The goal in this chapter is to alert students to the ways that college provides an opportunity to construct future paths. Moreover, this chapter presents several student stories that suggest the wide array of options for finding a niche group or activity on campus, which can help students feel integrated and develop valuable leadership skills.

*The Science of College*. Patricia S. Herzog, Casey T. Harris, Shauna A. Morimoto, Shane W. Barker, Jill G. Wheeler, A. Justin Barnum, and Terrance L. Boyd, Oxford University Press (2020) © Oxford University Press.
DOI: 10.1093/oso/9780190934507.001.0001

This chapter focuses on *campus engagement* as an important step toward civic engagement generally. We view every college student as capable of being a leader and discuss the many ways that people can find "their thing" on campus. Whether it be getting involved in Greek life, band, athletics, campus ministry, student organizations, or simply finding groups of friends who share similar interests, there is something for everyone on most college campuses. While students are in one sense more connected than ever before, thanks to social media, most entering college students still have a great deal to learn about how to engage respectfully and meaningfully with others, especially groups of people they may not have encountered much prior to college. This chapter shares student stories on this topic and then summarizes research on the importance of practicing generosity and civic engagement during college. Later in the chapter, we also offer advice to help students figure out how to harness their particular set of strengths in becoming social leaders.

## STUDENT STORIES: WHAT WE EXPERIENCE

In the following stories, Shawn discusses how technology use can lead to social isolation. Alternatively, Felicia views technology as enabling connection across space and time. Many students talk about finding the groups on campus where they feel a sense of belonging, such as Norah in marching band, Omar as a student athlete, Desiree in a sorority, and Phillip in both campus ministry and theater.

> **#ihatetechnology #isolation**: Walked around campus today, and every person I passed was on their cell phone, not looking up, not talking to each other. Technology is ruining us.
>
> **Shawn** says this about social isolation:
>
> Throughout the years, I have seen a shift in the social lives and interactions that has been caused by the increase in technology.

Rather than go outside and play with the neighborhood children, many stay inside and watch television or play on their tablet. As a child, I played outside with the neighbor kids, but I still stayed inside and watched television sometimes. For my parents staying inside was never an option; therefore, between my parents' childhood and my childhood, there was an increase in both isolation and technology. Not only has there been an increase in isolation between an individual and the outside world, but there has also been an increase in isolation between an individual and their family. As I got older, my family ate together less and less because me and my sister started having other things to do like homework. As my sister got older, she started staying in her room and watching television rather than socializing with the entire family.

**#ilovetechnology #connection:** Had a great video chat with my folks today. Just love how technology makes us feel so connected across the miles.

**Felicia** holds a very different view of technology, which she praises for facilitating long-distance connection:

Technology . . . allows people to maintain relationships over long distances . . . Growing up with a cellphone, the internet and a TV has allowed me to interact with the rest of society at any given time from virtually anywhere . . . We are a more mobile society and can keep in contact with people easily over great distances . . . I am characterized by a lot of statuses: female, student, Honor's College student, Texan, Christian, sorority member, and more. I am unique in this combination of identities, and the modern world of technology has allowed me to maintain all my statuses at once. Technology allows each of my identities to continue to shape who I am, even over distance. Being able to speak with my family in a different state allows them to offer me advice and guidance, continuing familial ties over a long distance.

**#marchingband #ilovemusic**: Marching band season is back, and it's time to remind everyone how much commitment this takes. We practice longer than the football players. We sweat more than the cheerleaders. We hype the crowd. Marching band *is* a sport.

**Norah** describes getting involved on campus, through the marching band, which functions as a near total institution:

> The splitting of friends meant that I would have to start over when I came to college. I did this by joining different groups, most notably the marching band . . . Three days a week we would rehearse for two and a half hours, then Saturdays would go from 7 hours before kick off, through a 3 to 4 hour game, then up to 2 hours after for clean up; we also have to come 2 weeks before classes start to begin freshman orientation for band and summer rehearsals, which are 8am to 8pm. To join the band, just like many other social groups there are certain ways of doing that . . . The marching band has certain standards of playing and so we do not let everyone in . . . The marching band has provided a melting pot for such different backgrounds and serves to provide entertainment as well as a social vehicle through college.

**#collegesports #studentathletes**: Happy Monday you guys! Getting ready for the big meet this weekend. Aiming for a new personal best and want to thank everyone in advance for coming out to support the team. As one we are nothing, as many we are strong.

Another student, **Omar**, describes a similar kind of involvement in athletics:

> We have all been re-socialized into more similar people and athletes. Our coaches . . . like us to all be in uniform and act in a certain way that represents the university well. We have several responsibilities, programs, and advisors who have shaped us into [university mascot] athletes. Everyone dresses very similarly in the athletic gear we are given, and we even have a separate dining

hall from regular students. No one has much free time to do what they want, since we are all stretched so thin among athletic responsibilities. Even our team academic advisors want to make sure we are able to make it to practice, first and foremost, and will not allow us to take courses that are offered during practice times. Athletic performance is a huge priority among the coaches, and if they are giving scholarship money, they pretty much have control over what we can and cannot do. There are rules about going out on the weekends, what we can eat, and who we can socialize with. We are all required to participate in the community service project that our teams are a part of . . . I have been changed and socialized into this new life.

**#sistersforlife #volunteering:** Every day we choose happiness, love, and giving. Proud of my sisters for working hard today to give back to others. So inspiring!

**Desiree** talks about how her involvement in volunteering in high school is one reason she now feels at home in a sorority:

When I began high school, I prepared myself for college and life beyond with the help of my parents . . . One aspect of this was showing volunteerism. They enrolled me in two programs . . . that involved volunteering and community outreach through local healthcare institutions. Both of these programs were for girls of a certain age and led by family-oriented, working women . . . As a participant in these programs, I was required to complete a certain number of volunteer hours and attend meetings that included activities such as making cards for patients and touring hospitals. The culmination of both these programs was a ball where each girl wore a long dress and was presented for their accomplishments . . . When I moved out of my house and went to college, I continued to perpetuate the upper-class traditions by joining a sorority. Similar to the volunteer programs I participated in in high school, the foundation of a sorority is philanthropy . . . My sorority again is filled with girls with similar backgrounds and cultures as me. They too participated in debutante balls and volunteer training programs. In this way, we have formed a new culture in college . . . College, unlike high school, is run by a power hierarchy centered around the fraternities . . . Before going to college, my parents gave me the talk about always staying with a buddy, being cautious, and never walking alone. This is a consequence of being female. Women are thought of as vulnerable and weaker than men . . . For this reason, we have stuck together. My friends and I took our shared understanding, and now act collectively to have the most successful outcome. This manifests in supporting each other academically, socially, emotionally, and physically through the obstacles that come with a whole, different college culture and being away from home. In this environment, it is nice to have a group that mirrors the values that I was raised with . . . Being a member of a sorority on campus has been a great way to meet people and get involved, but I know that it is changing who I am and what I place value on . . . Before joining a sorority, I never noticed when other people wore Greek letters, but now that is the first thing I notice . . . because of the push within Greek Life for "Greek Unity" and for making friends inside the Greek circle.

**#friendgroups #campusministry #theatre:** A big shout of thanks to all who helped make the show possible tonight. Also want to thank my campus ministry peeps for coming to support me. Was nice to finally introduce my two #friendgroups to each other!

**Phillip** discusses navigating distinct friend groups with different values and norms:

Currently I have two major groups of friends on campus, which I became a part of in two drastically different ways. The first was the community at campus ministry, which I started going to during welcome week, at the suggestion of my mother. Immediately when I first walked in I was warmly welcomed by the staff and I became fully integrated . . . as soon as my third visit because some older students brought me into the fold based on our common interests. It was extremely affirming to have what felt like a kind, strong support system so early on in my first semester here. I didn't feel like a friendless freshman anymore . . . As a student with next to zero existing ties at the university, who was raised in a Methodist church back home, I was probably the ideal recruit. I was open to the attention however, and the tactic worked like a charm.

On the other hand, my first encounters with my fellow theatre students were interactions based almost entirely on gossiping and speaking ill of other people in the department. Shared disdain was the strongest factor in forging friendships among groups of people . . . That is not to say that there is any overt hostility present between people in the department; on the contrary, everyone is perfectly pleasant to each other during day-to-day interactions. Instead we choose to release our feelings of animosity to trusted confidants (who come in the form of casual friends, at best) . . . The high contrast in style between my social groups makes for a little extra work for me, with having to straddle between them [the two groups and their very different norms of behavior]. But the fact that I get to choose and curate my social interactions in college is important to my sense of personal identity in society.

## SCIENCE: WHAT WE KNOW

Does technology increase social isolation? That is a central question for many scientists in sociology, political science, and communication today. D. Stanley Eitzen (2013) summarizes major findings on this topic by stating, "the bonds of civic cement are disintegrating as we become increasingly separate from each other, from our communities, and from society" (p. 623).[1] In contemporary society, people are highly mobile—moving an average of every five years, switching jobs regularly, divorcing, living alone in rising numbers, and spending more and more time indoors to enjoy the benefits of technology: air conditioning, television, video games. However, a drawback is that people can be more isolated from each other. In short, "paradoxically, the current communications revolution increases interaction while reducing intimacy" (p. 625).

A student in this chapter, Shawn, describes this by saying: "The increase in technology has increased isolation . . . This increase in isolation will cause the nation to be filled with lonely, bitter, alienated, and depressed people (Eitzen 2013)." His point is that there is a danger that people can hide behind their screens, not truly connecting even when in each other's presence. Plus they can be heavily influenced by the kind of media they engage, and the extent to which it conveys the truth about the events and people involved (Lindner 2013).[2] For example, Felicia of this chapter, who overall has a positive view on the role of technology, concurs with Shawn in saying, "This [the widespread availability of social media] means that socialization is even more far-reaching than ever before. The media controls what is shown on TV and in the news, so it controls people's feelings towards an event (Lindner 2013). This means that the media can socialize people on a large scale using technology and can control people's understanding of an event." Social media can support social engagement, or disconnection, depending on how it is used.

On a college campus, it is not difficult to combat the potentially isolating effects of technology. Campus life provides ample opportunities to find a group to join. In fact, university campuses are one of the most socially dense contexts encountered during emerging adulthood. Most students experience a greater degree of choice and flexibility in selecting their friend groups in college than in high school, which is dominated by cliques. Yet the "joiner" culture on college campuses also has drawbacks. For example, some social groups, such as "high-risk fraternities"[3] (as referred to by **Desiree**) promote norms that make people act against their own better judgment and inhibit others from protesting activities that promote a "rape culture" (e.g., #metoo). As the student describes, this can result from gender expectations that turn women into "objectified victims"[4] of sexualized social contexts, which college campuses can be. Along with this intense example, there are also numerous other everyday examples of group norms producing negative effects, such as downplaying academics by promoting absenteeism or stigmatizing academic accomplishment. Whatever groups they are a part of, however, students can still be intentional actors, both within their own life stories and within the roles they play in other people's lives. Part of navigating college is assuming the adult roles of figuring out how to be a good citizen to others, on campus and in community generally.

Acting in the interests of others is something social scientists commonly refer to as *altruism*. However, contemporary scholarship on other-oriented behaviors questions the assumption that altruistic actions are performed to benefit others. It turns out that many altruistic acts are entirely beneficial to the giver or cooperator (Simpson & Willer 2015; Fischer 2010).[5] This is why some scholars have turned to the term *generosity* to describe activities that are intended to promote collective well-being, regardless of whether they also help out the giver (Herzog & Price 2016).[6] In any case, a necessary precondition for being involved in voluntary associations and charitable giving is trusting other people (Glanville 2016).[7] College is a key time to build that social trust by participating in a wide range of social groups, because emerging adulthood is the life stage during which most people form enduring patterns of participation (Núñez & Flanagan 2016).[8]

Involvement in social and civic groups is changing as technology evolves. Scholars disagree over whether younger generations are increasingly individualized in the ways they participate in civic life (Settersten & Ray 2010),[9] or whether the change is only in methods of organization, from the face-to-face interactions that predominated in the past to online interactions that are more common today (Winograd & Hais 2011).[10] Whether or not young people are more individualized online, scholars find an overall trend toward increasing isolation (King, Harding, & King 2010).[11] Thus, it is important for students to overcome their hesitation to join social groups, and especially community activities. One must engage multiple forms of intelligence and leadership styles (Riggio et al. 2013)[12] to find one's unique voice and offer it in shared spaces, online and in person. College provides an excellent social context in which to "try on" different ways of relating and to practice civic articulation—indeed, trying on different ways of relating is a hallmark of emerging adulthood: forming personal and social identities.

Becoming a leader requires social engagement. Leaders must step up to get involved in changing circumstances they do not like, rather than shirking away from them or blaming them on other people. Leadership today can take a wide variety of forms. Sometimes leaders hold positional power within organizations, but increasingly social media enables leadership through being a social influencer. Leaders transform their social contexts to encourage and compel greater ethical attention to inclusion and equity.[13] Leadership entails a focus on the welfare of others, and college engagement can build life-long practices of engaging justly and generously.

## ADVICE: WHAT WE (CAN) PROVIDE

**#ihatetechnology #isolation** It is clear that **Shawn** desires to disconnect from technology. It sounds like he had a lot of experience growing up with technology, but perhaps it was forced on him. Shawn's critical eye on technology can give him some strengths that other students may not have. Thus, we recommend that he check out organizations or classes that focus on technology, whether it be gaming or some other topic. This will enable Shawn to connect and socialize with others who enjoy critiquing technology.

That Shawn sees some drawbacks of technology could be an opportunity for him to get involved in technology industries: instead of merely assuming technology is destructive, he could help companies and organizations to think creatively about how to foster social ties through technology. We also advise Shawn to recognize that it can be okay to disconnect. Being aware of the drawbacks of connecting online can push him to find human interaction in-person, by joining clubs and organizations with other people who enjoy disconnecting from technology. Some of the best advice for Shawn comes from the reading he cites (Eitzen 2013: 630):

- Engage in public activities;
- Have meaningful face-to-face conversations with friends on a regular basis;
- Get to know your neighbors, co-workers, and the people who provide services for you;
- Join with others who share a common interest;
- Work to improve your community;
- Become an activist, joining with others to bring about social change;
- And, most of all, we need to moderate our celebration of individualism [and our tendency toward self-absorption] and [to] develop instead a moral obligation to others, to our neighbors (broadly defined) and their children, to those unlike us as well as those similar to us, and to future generations. [brackets added for clarification]

**#ilovetechnology #connection** For **Felicia**, someone who loves technology and sees the benefits more than Shawn does, technology is a symbol of developing her own social capital, allowing her to stay in contact with her friends and family. It is a way of maintaining those social relations, no matter how far away. We advise students like Felicia to embrace this love of technology and to consider ways that it can pay off later. For example, being able to use Snapchat and Twitter could translate into a useful skill in workplaces that engage social media. The ability to keep up those relationships from back home is likewise a skill that helps Felicia juggle connections with a variety of people.

At the same time, our advice for Felicia is similar to Shawn in that she too needs to get connected on campus. Being able to use technology to keep in touch with her family and friends from back home can translate to new ways of building friendships with people on campus. Technology can provide a wonderful outlet, but it is also beneficial to have face-to-face conversations and to make time to unplug, to put down mobile devices and have personal human interactions. College campuses are filled with opportunities to meet other people in person, and we advise Felicia to try to meet new people on campus who share similar interests to her friends back home, in order to build that in-person network too.

**#marchingband #ilovemusic** While **Norah** is in the marching band and refers to this as a dominant part of her identity, she also mentions having a "band self" and a "non-band self." Considering that band demands so much of her time and commitment, we would encourage her to ponder ways to develop other aspects of herself outside of band. Even as she attends to these other aspects, however, she needs to also remain in good standing in the band to retain her band scholarship. To help her successfully resolve those tensions, we recommend that Norah visit with an advisor. An advisor could help her to see the valuable soft skills she is gaining, such as managing her time well as she works from morning until night, and balancing the demands of practice with that of her coursework. Her advisor could underscore how well those skills translate to a variety of careers. This may help Norah relax and recognize that she can devote space and time to band without allowing other aspects of herself to wither.

**#collegesports #studentathletes** As **Omar** described, college athletics can be viewed as a total institution because participants must follow an extensive set of rules to stay in good standing. Because athletics plays a large role in Omar's identity, we recommend that he, like Norah, seek ways of branching out. Supporting other aspects of himself would be beneficial during his college years and beyond. There is always a chance that an injury could occur and hinder his athletic ability, and the best protection against this possibility is investing in more than just athletic pursuits. Like military members who retire from service or are no longer connected with a certain branch of military, many athletes experience a loss of self when their collegiate or professional careers end. We thus encourage Omar to find ways to participate in other meaningful activities, perhaps off-campus. For example, if Omar is religious, he could go to a religious function. Or if he wants to cultivate his own generosity, he could consider reaching out to volunteer in an after-school program with local kids.

Although Omar already feels busy, he may feel enriched if he can squeeze in some involvement with other social groups on the weekends or after practice.

He could ask: Who am I, besides a student athlete? When it comes time to transition into a career, this will be an important question to answer in order to maintain a sense of self. We want to be clear that the structure that athletic programs provide, in high school and in college, can be highly beneficial. At the same time, athletes should also be aware of the drawbacks of that structure. It is best to prepare for the day when students leave that structured atmosphere and no longer have people telling them when and how to accomplish it all. We advise Omar to remember that his life will not be this way indefinitely. College provides student athletes with a chance to plan for life after athletics, to take ownership of the decisions they will need to make, and to be confident in their ability to transition into a career of their choosing.

#sistersforlife #volunteering In her story, **Desiree** provides an interesting reflection on how volunteerism has been part of her college pathway. It helped build her resume for college, and as she recognizes, it is bolstering her capacity to talk confidently with women in charge. She sees that volunteering is not only about giving back but a way of building connections. It helped her get into a sorority, which was instrumental in her making new friends. While volunteering may have begun as a desirable credential, it became a process that changed her and is shaping who she is becoming. We advise students to learn from Desiree by reflecting on what path they are carving out and why. This is an excellent opportunity for Desiree to recognize that college is not simply about the degree. Also important, as she is beginning to recognize, is the process. Embracing the reasons she is in a sorority, why she wants to volunteer, what she wants to gain out of that volunteering, all of these reflections will remind Desiree that college is an experience. We encourage Desiree to take ownership of the connections she is making and recall the ways that social capital will continue to support her beyond the walls of that institution.

#friendgroups #campusministry #theatre As some other students have mentioned, **Phillip** describes how part of the college experience is learning how to handle different friend groups. In his case, he has quite distinct groups of friends, and he recognizes that these groups have divergent norms for fitting in and forming connections. He feels he was somewhat pushed into one group (campus ministry) by his mom, but they seem welcoming. The other group (theater) he gravitated to because of his major, and they seem more splintered. Moving between these groups gives Phillip a unique perspective. From the latter circle, he can learn how to fit in with a small group, and from the former he can learn how to broaden his circles, to be more inclusive of others. Keeping up with two very different groups can be tricky, however, and it sounds like it may be wearing on Phillip.

We thus recommend that Phillip talk with some more senior classmates, perhaps ones who participate in campus ministry or theater. He can seek out someone who he notices also navigates different friend groups, perhaps even the same combination. From these classmates Phillip might learn some strategies that others use for belonging to multiple groups of friends, and conversations on the subject will also make him feel more integrated. The key is finding a sense of connection with people in the group that is meaningful and authentic, not based on keeping part of oneself hidden. It is hard for students to find their way in two contrasting contexts. Talking with friends can help to normalize that feeling and make Phillip realize that he is not as different as he thought; instead, he is experiencing a common aspect of college.

In addition, we advise Phillip not to think of the norms of the theater group as predetermined and set in stone. He is a member of this group and has the ability to influence its norms. It is great that he is aware of the ways the group socializes him and connects with new members. Yet he should also think about what characteristics of his religious friends he enjoys and how to bring more of that welcoming atmosphere into the theater group. A common and relevant phrase is: "Be the change you wish to see." In this case, when someone in the theater group begins badmouthing others, Phillip could be the one to speak up. He could say something like this: "I fully understand where you are coming from, and at the same time I have noticed that sometimes our connections seem to revolve around picking on other people. Maybe let's shake things up for a change and talk about what we enjoyed." Figuring out how to change a group dynamic, without pushing people away, is an important leadership skill. Plus, it can help Phillip to integrate the different aspects of himself across groups, creating a greater sense of stability within both circles.

Returning to the central themes of this chapter, we advise students to consider how to integrate their various connections and experiences into an authentic sense of self. This will ward against feeling like an imposter and build an identity as a leader who can rise above petty group dynamics to create meaningful action. Authenticity does not have to mean acting the same in every situation, but it does mean having enough of a coherent sense of self to know how to be true to one's values across social situations. One of the lessons that college teaches is that what may be considered appropriate in one group is not appropriate with another. Learning how to read those social cues enables students to live up to the expectations of new situations. Another key lesson of college is learning how to become an engaged citizen, to be generous to classmates and community members. Emerging adulthood is a key life stage for building the lifelong habit of service, and that begins with having an integrated self from which to give to others. Feeling torn across different groups can be exhausting, making students feel limited in their capacity to give to others. Reflecting on ways to achieve greater coherence across different groups can lessen that mental drain and free up more energy for generosity.

## TOGETHERNESS: WHAT WE (CAN) SHARE

Next, we offer a possible dialog between several of our case studies.* Written by the youngest among our authorship team, this section is meant

* As described with the first togetherness section in chapter 5, faculty and support staff are important social supports in navigating college, as are fellow students. In these togetherness sections, the goal is to suggest ways that students can support one another in navigating college. Akin to a reality television show, the students are interacting with each other in ways that build their relationships around some of the challenges and opportunities these students

to capture the energy with which students converse with one another and noticeably changes in tone from prior sections.

*Devon, Austin, Abby, Charlie, and Jacob.* Devon and Austin are chatting with each other at a midsemester Homecoming party. Austin shares his story about going through Greek recruitment only to find out that he could not afford to join a fraternity. Devon completely understands. He does share some advice, however. He says that networking is all about looking for things that you genuinely enjoy that will also allow you to connect with other people. He says, "You do not have to do something as expensive as going Greek if you do not want to." He has been learning golf, something he never thought he would do. But already, it has allowed him to spend some quality time with many new people. Austin and Devon talk about how they might meet people at this party who they can stay connected with for a long time.

Not long after, Abby notices that Austin is at the party and immediately runs over to say "hi." She is there with another new friend, Charlie. After some introductions, they swap stories about how crazy and busy the first two months of college have been. Charlie tells a funny story about a wild experience she had at a party a few weeks ago, and everyone shares a good laugh. She says she loves telling that story, but she admits she has been pretty stressed out lately because she cannot find the time to do her homework. They can all relate. Abby jumps in to suggest some advice. She says that people think it looks cool to "party hard," but that there are ways to keep up going out without overdoing it. Her sorority sisters have showed her a few. She always has a "buddy" with her to keep each other out of trouble, and she always shows up to a party or function as early as she can so she can have plenty of fun but still get back to her room in time to study

described in their case studies. Given the challenges already expressed within the case studies, the goal in these situations is to focus on the positive ways that students can support one another. Inevitably social interactions can also be fraught with negative experiences, and we do not mean to suggest that all social interactions occur positively. Rather, we offer some possible ways to support one another, which students can and will modify to add their own authentic approach. To review student stories alongside these togetherness sections, readers can refer to the table of case studies preceding chapter 1 and the brief synopsis of student stories included within that table.

if she needs to. Charlie now feels so excited! Austin chimes in too, saying that Abby always gives such great advice.

Jacob, who is standing nearby, cannot help but overhear their conversation. He jumps in and agrees wholeheartedly. He says, "College is so different from high school in almost every way!" It took him awhile to get the hang of it. He and Charlie begin talking about all the ways they have learned to adjust in such a short time, both feeling reassured that someone else felt as overwhelmed as they did in the beginning. They agree that it has been challenging, but also very fun. The five students make plans to hang out together after the football game this weekend.

The next week, Devon, Austin, Abby, Charlie, and Jacob discover they are actually in the same class. The class meets in a large lecture hall, and they used to sit dispersed throughout the room. Now that they met outside of class, they gravitate to each other. The instructor hands out a worksheet and asks the class to complete the Leadership Compass activity. They are told that they will need to work together to create a group project. In the past, they would have hated working on a group project, especially because it makes them nervous about receiving a good grade. But since they have shared their perspectives with each other outside of class, they are more open to figuring this out together. They fill out the leadership activity and tabulate their results. It turns out that Devon is a Nurturer, Austin is a Mobilizer, Jacob and Charlie are both Teachers, and Abby is a Visionary. Reflecting on how this jazzes with their own experience of each other so far, they talk readily about how they have already started to notice the different strengths they all bring.

The group decides to work together on a video for their class presentation. Since Charlie is funny and organized, the group decides that she should plan out what each of them will say. Abby chimes in to say that she can help Charlie brainstorm, since she thinks she has a good sense of the big picture for the assignment but needs some help making it happen. Jacob offers to take notes on their discussion each time they meet and to set them up with a group on a popular app so that they can be in touch with each other. Austin gets a bit impatient with how long it takes everyone to decide on the details, but after a few weeks, he begins to see how cool the idea is that they are developing. He then helps the group get excited each time they come together and reminds everyone about the energy they had flowing the last time they met. Devon misses a few of the group meetings because he had to help out some family members, but whenever he makes it to the meetings, he helps facilitate the discussion and validates others' multiple perspectives. They wind up getting an A on the assignment, but more importantly, when they discuss their experience of the group, in preparation for their individual reflection assignments that they have to submit along with the group video, they realize they learned a lot from this experience.

## FURTHER READING ONLINE

Other ways to reflect on strengths in becoming a social leader include the following:

- Anderson, Edward, "Strengths Quest: Curriculum Outline and Learning Activities," Azusa Pacific University, retrieved from http://www.weber.edu/WSUImages/leadership/docs/sq/curriculum.pdf.
- "How Good Are Your Leadership Skills," Mind Tools, retrieved from https://www.mindtools.com/pages/article/newLDR_50.htm.
- "Quiz: What's Your Leadership Style," Leadership IQ, retrieved from https://www.leadershipiq.com/blogs/leadershipiq/36533569-quiz-whats-your-leadership-style.
- Zenger, Jack, and Joseph Folkman, August 12, 2013, "The Eight-Minute Test That Can Reveal Your Effectiveness as a Leader," *Harvard Business Review*, https://hbr.org/2013/08/how-effective-a-leader-are-you.
- Serafin, Tatiana, August 15, 2011, "How to Assess Your Leadership Skills," Inc., retrieved from https://www.inc.com/guides/201108/how-to-assess-your-leadership-skills.html.

- Along with leadership, another important strength to build during college is academic integrity. Here is a resource for reflecting on what it means to take personal responsibility for individual and group work: "Chapter Seven—Academic Integrity," Stony Brook University, retrieved from https://you.stonybrook.edu/firstyear/chapter-seven-academic-integrity/.

## NOTES

1. Eitzen, D. Stanley. 2013. "The Atrophy of Social Life." In Susan J. Ferguson (Ed.), *Mapping the Social Landscape: Readings in Sociology* (7th ed., pp. 623–630). New York: McGraw-Hill Education.
2. Lindner, Andrew M. 2013. "Controlling the Media in Iraq." In Susan J. Ferguson (Ed.), *Mapping the Social Landscape: Readings in Sociology* (7th ed., pp. 453–463). New York: McGraw-Hill Education.
3. Boswell, A. Ayres, and Joan Z. Spade. 2013. "Fraternities and Collegiate Rape Culture." In Susan J. Ferguson (Ed.), *Mapping the Social Landscape: Readings in Sociology* (7th ed., pp. 216–228). New York: McGraw-Hill Education.
4. Loe, Meika. 2013. "Working at Bazzoms: The Intersection of Power, Gender, and Sexuality." In Susan J. Ferguson (Ed.), *Mapping the Social Landscape: Readings in Sociology* (7th ed., pp. 79–94). New York: McGraw-Hill Education.
5. Simpson, Brent, and Robb Willer. 2015. "Beyond Altruism: Sociological Foundations of Cooperation and Prosocial Behavior." *Annual Review of Sociology* 41(1): 43–63.
   Fischer, Claude S. 2010. *Made in America: A Social History of American Culture and Character.* Chicago: University of Chicago Press.
6. Herzog, Patricia Snell, and Heather Price. 2016. *American Generosity: Who Gives and Why.* New York: Oxford University Press.
7. Glanville, Jennifer. 2016. "Why Does Involvement in Voluntary Associations Promote Trust? Examining the Role of Network Diversity." *Sociological Inquiry* 86(1): 29–50.
8. Núñez, Jennifer, and Constance Flanagan. 2016. "Political Beliefs and Civic Engagement in Emerging Adulthood." In Jeffrey J. Arnett (Ed.), *The Oxford Handbook of Emerging Adulthood.* New York: Oxford University Press.
9. Settersten, Richard, and Barbara E. Ray. 2010. *Not Quite Adults: Why 20-Somethings Are Choosing a Slower Path to Adulthood, and Why It's Good for Everyone.* New York: Bantam.
   Trimble, Nicole. "Leadership Compass." n.d. Corporation for National & Community Service. Retrieved from https://www.nationalservice.gov/sites/default/files/resource/leadershipcompass.pdf.

10. Winograd, Morley, and Michael D. Hais. 2011. *Millennial Momentum: How a New Generation Is Remaking America.* New Brunswick, NJ: Rutgers University Press.

11. King, Martin Luther, Vincent Harding, and Coretta Scott King. 2010. *Where Do We Go from Here: Chaos or Community?* Boston: Beacon Press.

12. Riggio, Ronald E., Susan E. Murphy, and Francis J. Pirozzolo. 2013. *Multiple Intelligences and Leadership.* Milton Park, UK: Psychology Press.

13. Caldwell, Cam, Rolf D. Dixon, Larry A. Floyd, Joe Chaudoin, Jonathan Post, and Gaynor Cheokas. 2011. "Transformative Leadership: Achieving Unparalleled Excellence." *Journal of Business Ethics* 109(2): 175–187.

# Making Informed Choices, for Now and Later

This concluding chapter explains that college provides a safe place to explore different career options. Students learn that switching majors, interning, working as a research assistant, and talking with professors are all excellent ways to test out majors and assess whether a career in that field is a good fit. The chapter addresses tips for changing majors, talking with parents about desired careers, finding a vocation or career path, and shaping professional identity. The book culminates with a section about how to navigate college, and life generally, with research-based decisions. Following these recommendations will ensure that students continue their journey as learners, informed citizens, and social leaders long after they finish reading this book.

*The Science of College*. Patricia S. Herzog, Casey T. Harris, Shauna A. Morimoto, Shane W. Barker, Jill G. Wheeler, A. Justin Barnum, and Terrance L. Boyd, Oxford University Press (2020) © Oxford University Press.
DOI: 10.1093/oso/9780190934507.001.0001

In this concluding chapter, we summarize the central points of this book. First, college is a *process*, not a destination. It is important to allow the process to change students significantly, and for students to know that they should not expect to leave college with the same expectations they had upon entering. Second, college has a hidden curriculum. The explicit curriculum of college courses represents half or less of what students really need to learn during college. In addition to mastering the content of their classes, college students must also discover how to navigate choices for their adult life. That entails learning how to deal with being bored, tolerating frustration, working through what can at times feel pointless, even interacting with people that students dislike. Additionally key is learning how to have fun in safe and responsible ways, a.d balancing the greatest personal responsibilities and freedom that life has yet offered. College life is complicated, and it can be wonderful. College should be and often is life-altering.

## STUDENT STORIES: WHAT WE EXPERIENCE

**#drivingwithoutdirection**: "Why am I here?" Everyone else seems excited and cruising along with what they are up to. All I know is that my parents said "go to college," so here I am.

Since middle school, **Ellie's** dad has emphasized the importance of going to college. "Get an education," he'd say, "that's the one thing no one can ever take away from you." While in high school—where classes were mundane, and the teachers assigned busy work—Ellie dreamed of college as a magical place where things would be more interesting. Now that she is finally there, college seems like it's just a continuation of high school. She is living at home to save money and doesn't feel that she is really a part of the campus community. At this point, she just does not want to let her father down. Though she received some scholarships, she does not see the point in continuing to spend money on college if she does not know how to make it worth it.

**#tooeasy #notchallenged**: College is so easy! In my AP classes in high school I had to study so much more than I do now in college.

**Tyrone** went to a high school that was pretty challenging (he'll never forget that one English teacher who gave him a B because his essay references were not perfect!). He took many AP classes, had calculus, did lots of writing. Now in college, he finds that his classes are a breeze and feels under-challenged. He wonders if he picked the wrong college and is thinking about transferring. But he is not sure if he wants to start all over again at a new place.

**#parallelplan #changingmajors**: I made a big life-altering decision today and haven't felt this excited about school for awhile, tho it's also kind of scary moving away from what I know.

**Kiersten** explains her decision to change majors, walking away from her original plan: When I first came to this university, I had grand plans of becoming an investigative reporter, exposing corrupt governments and corporations. Now, I am more focused on creating financial security for myself, something that my parents didn't have. . . I am lining myself up with internships and positions that will hopefully mean a more financially stable future. That also means not working for the Associated Press like I had originally intended, although I still believe in pure, unbiased journalism.

**#americandream #proudimmigrant**: Living the dream—here in my first day as a college student and aiming to make my family proud.

In contrast, **Isabella** describes sticking with her original plan and explains her plan's origins:

Starting out as an immigrant here, my grandmother, along with my dad, aunt, and uncle, were very poor. She worked to provide for her children, which echoes me and my mother's situation. She selflessly worked as a seamstress here and a housekeeper there for families in the wealthy suburbs of Houston. Making what she was making, it was impossible for her to accumulate any wealth as she could not purchase a home and she had no car . . . [Then she established her own business.] She was able to really take off in a career that she loved. My father, aunt, and uncle were able to catapult themselves as well. The dry-cleaning business owned by my grandmother was divided between my dad and my uncle. They were able to grow their businesses and accumulate wealth for themselves. My aunt took the academic approach. She was the only one who went to college and earned her bachelor's degree. She then went on to medical school and earned her Doctor of Medicine. All of my family has assimilated into the upper–middle-class culture, yet we are always mindful of our humble beginnings . . . My desire to become a doctor stems from [my aunt's] success despite the odds. I look at how she carries herself and I see the lifestyle she has, and I want that for myself.

**#vocation #publichealth**: God, help me to continue to throw myself into your capable hands and follow my #vocation to increase #publichealth.

**Abram** explains how his religious beliefs fed into his career choice:

I feel that God has called me to go into the medical field . . . My passion for nutrition and health is much of the reason why I have decided to pursue a career in the medical field. I am sickened by the scourge of chronic illness that so many people deal with in the United States . . . A few of my favorite verses that speak about the need of moderation in our lives lie in the book of Proverbs. Chapter 23 verse two speaks about the drastic need of people to exercise moderation in their eating habits. Self-control is demonstratively important for anyone who wants to have good health, regardless of the influencing factors around them . . . If people would choose to live responsible lives and say no to many of their appetites and desires and not expect doctors they pay to give them fixes for the problems in their lives, I believe that patients' overall health would improve drastically.

**#genderinstem #findingyourownway**: Sometimes you just know where your destination is. "I am not afraid of storms for I am learning how to sail my ship." —Louisa May Alcott

Showing yet another way that career goals can be established, **Sierra** explains how experiencing paternalism fueled her passion for pursuing a career in STEM:

When I was ten years old, I told my father I wanted to be a doctor. He told me that I would be in school until I am thirty and would never settle down and get married as a result. A similar situation occurred when I was in kindergarten. I enjoyed drawing and painting and told my parents I wanted to be an artist. Instead of entertaining the idea as a normal response, my dad told me "there's no money in that." I understood that I was expected to have a high-paying job, but nothing that would interfere with my future duties of being a wife and mother . . . I was upset by the idea that I could not have a professional occupation such as a doctor, because it would conflict with expectations of domesticity, and instead chose to rebel against such ideas . . . I was not meant to be in school for too long and miss my prime to have children.

I never identified as a feminist and still do not, however, the control my father tried to exhibit over me gave me an understanding of it [feminism] . . . Being aware that I live in a patriarchal society further helped me to understand what my parents expected of me as a daughter . . . I had always thrived in math and science courses, therefore when I discovered engineering, I took an interest. When I walked into my first engineering class, I was the only female in a class of twenty . . .

I was viewed by my male peers as a weak link. I was not meeting the gender role assigned to me. I wore make-up and dressed to my gender, and this somehow made me look dumb. I was forced to work twice as hard to prove myself. I built better bridges, designed faster circuits, and got better grades.

## SCIENCE: WHAT WE KNOW

What many of these student stories describe is a process called career decision-making. Jessie Carduner and colleagues (2011)[1] studied the process of choosing a major and a career and found that settling on a major and career prior to or early in college is not always a good thing. This is particularly the case when students make decisions about their major before they have acquired enough information. In addition, deciding on a career is not a one-point-in-time deal. Revisiting and revising decisions about majors and intended career paths during college equips students to navigate later changes to career plans. Conversely, in what Carduner and colleagues refer to as "multipotentiality," many students have a variety of career options available to them. Sometimes they get stuck, paralyzed in the face of all the paths they could choose. Students need to avoid both extremes: that of making decisions too soon and being too wedded to them to learn from new information, and that of getting stuck in the overwhelming amount of possibilities and delaying decisions indefinitely. From the perspective of our navigation analogy, you do not have to have your final destination picked from the start, and you can be open to changing exactly where you end up, but you do not want to stay stuck in one place, either. You have to start by selecting a general direction to travel.

As Daniel Chambliss (2014)[2] states, one of the most important activities that college students need to engage in, after acclimating to the campus social world, is to begin making academic choices. Students should work on mastering academic learning only after they declare their majors, figure out which professors they wish to continue to study with and learn from, and determine whom they should turn to for career advice. Before this process begins, however, students should prioritize exposure. The first semesters of college provide an excellent opportunity to take courses that are different from any topics that students have been exposed to before college. Learn what is available first, and do not feel obligated to choose an academic path too quickly.

As they set out to choose majors and careers, students should recognize that not all learning takes places in the classroom or on campus. In a book called *Making the Most of College*, Richard Light (2004)[3] finds that learning outside the classroom (e.g., through extracurricular activities and social events) helps college students to make better, more informed career decisions. He also offers insights on which kinds of classes are most effective for student learning. Many students, he reports, learn better from highly structured classes, with many quizzes and short assignments that give students relatively quick feedback from the professor on their progress. Likewise, students benefit greatly from courses that let them make changes to assignments before receiving a final grade, learning the art of revision. This means that students might want to seek out courses with these traits, which are not always present in the large introductory sections of highly popular majors (e.g., pre-med classes such as introductory biology). While those classes are vital prerequisites, many courses in other departments can provide different types of structure and feedback that students need to make more informed decisions about their academic careers, especially early in college.

"The transition from education to work is a key developmental task of emerging adulthood," wrote Julia Dietrich and Katariina Salmela-Aro (2016: 334).[4] Interpersonal contexts of work and preparation for work have changed in recent decades, and the burden is squarely on students' shoulders to seek work preparation accordingly. As students navigate college, they often need to revise their career goals, and such a change can be considered a positive sign that students are allowing college to change them. Likewise, success can entail leaving behind career goals that were not suited to a student's strengths, or that are unobtainable in today's job market or given the student's social and economic resources. Most importantly, college provides the context in which students can practice handling inevitable setbacks, gaining skills that will aid them when they encounter barriers later in life.

## ADVICE: WHAT WE (CAN) PROVIDE

**#drivingwithoutdirection #whyamihere** Actually, **Ellie's** uncertainty about her life path is not that surprising. According to Jeffrey Arnett (2015)[5] and other life-course researchers, Ellie is experiencing at least two characteristics of emerging adulthood: instability and feeling in-between. Arnett states that some emerging adults are clearly not ready for college, but due to pressure from parents or society, they find themselves enrolled. Emerging adults can often flounder as a result, and in order to be successful they must find a connection. Ellie mulls over her current situation. She understands she is supposed to have a plan for her life, but her plan ended after "attend college." She knows she needs to update "The Plan," but she is unsure how.

If Ellie were to reach out to a caring adult in her life about this—be it a college advisor, professor, parent, or anyone she trusted to help her make changes—one of the best research-based pieces of advice she could receive would be to enroll in a smaller course. Even at large public institutions, such classes are often more available than most students know. A smaller class would help her be better engaged and facilitate making connections with other students and with the course instructor, with whom she's more likely to interact face-to-face, given the class size. While Ellie is enrolled in college and enjoys more academic freedom than she has ever had before, living at home finds her still under the same rules and expectations of adolescence. Instead of moving forward as she thought college would enable her to do, she feels stuck in place. She is ready to become an adult, but she does not know how to get started. Most importantly, Ellie can still make this transition during college, if she finds the right people to help her navigate it.

Ellie was the first in her family to attempt any schooling beyond a high school diploma. After her mother's death, her family was just her and her father. Ellie watched her father work extremely hard to provide for the two of them and is proud to claim a "working-class" background when questions about what her family does for a living arise. Ellie's father has expressed his desire for her to earn a college degree for as long as she can remember. He wants her to be financially secure so she will be able to provide for her own family someday. Ellie has her father's unwavering support for her education, but she does not have adequate social support at college. Getting connected outside the classroom and becoming invested socially, as well as academically, in her future will give Ellie the connections she desires even if she has not vocalized them. These connections will certainly aid her in discovering what motivates her and boost her chances of finding a major that sparks her interest. The most crucial thing for Ellie is to take charge of her education, to make her college experience her own. Ellie should find other students who share similar interests, academic or otherwise, and talk to them or to faculty and staff in the classes she does enjoy in order to identify some areas of study she might have overlooked. She could benefit from enrolling in courses that present different types of feedback and learning as we described earlier. Just listening to others as they talk about the value of college, or a particular major, or trying a new type of class may excite her in ways she may not have seen on her own.

**#tooeasy #notchallenged** In certain ways, **Tyrone** is one of the classic "overachievers" who, in high school, "labor over homework until 2:30am, after spending their afternoons and early evenings participating in a roster of activities" (Stuber 2011: 3).[6] Since researchers find that this pattern prepares students most for elite universities, it is understandable that Tyrone is struggling over how his expectations are mismatched with the approach of the public university he attends. However, if he recognizes the importance of extracurricular involvement in facilitating the returns of college, Tyrone may not need to switch schools to find fulfillment.

Whether he eventually transfers or ultimately finds the intellectual engagement he desires at his current university, we encourage students like Tyrone to try to more fully engage with their current campus. At the very least, this will help Tyrone to broaden his horizons, and prepare him to work in a variety of organizational settings and with people who come from backgrounds less advantaged than his own, even if he does transfer. But in the process, he may find that carving out his professional path within his current public university develops skills he does not yet possess, and that graduate school could fulfill some of his academic aspirations.

For example, if Tyrone is a pre-med student interested in serving patients, then the experiences he is gaining at his public college may bolster his ability to communicate with patients from a range of socioeconomic backgrounds. For instance, patients from less affluent backgrounds may be less verbose in explaining their physical symptoms, requiring Tyrone to ask more probing follow-up questions to ensure he can provide the correct medical advice. Though highly selective universities may provide the kind of cultural status that is perceived to lead immediately to high-paying positions, public and other kinds of university settings often involve exposure to a greater range of people, with different kinds of economic, social, and cultural capitals. In all but the rarest of circumstances, professionals in any field can gain from such exposure in college.

More than offering academic credentials and a stamp of approval into high society, college also provides ways of escaping the "bubble" students found themselves in prior to college. Tyrone can rise to this challenge by stepping out of his comfort zone. He can get to know people who may not have been able to take calculus in high school, or who attended high schools that did not offer the course at all. The goal is to learn more than just what gets said in class. Maybe someday he will still decide to transfer, but for now Tyrone should take full advantage of all his university has to offer. He may like the person he becomes, and at the very least he will feel better knowing he did not waste his time experiencing new things.

**#parallelplan #changingmajors** Modeling some of the changes that college students need to make to their career plans as they gain new information is **Kiersten**. Students need to continually re-evaluate: Are their intended career plans the best way to accomplish their goals? In the process of interrogating their goals, students need to talk to people and do research. Kiersten likely did this, got some advice, and fine-tuned her original goals. That is something that she should be proud of and other students can aspire to do. At the same time, in light of Kiersten's emphasis on financial security, it is important to underline that students can find financial well-being in most career paths, if they work hard and make strategic choices based on what excites them about that job. They should not change their goals simply for the sake of money. It is better to match pictures of success to passions and interests. It sounds as though Kiersten is on the right track to figuring this out.

**#americandream #proudimmigrant** While **Isabella** appreciates her cultural background and her family's status, she wants to improve her position, and that is an excellent dream. In fact, it is *the* American dream. It is also important, however, for Isabella to ask herself whether she is pursuing a career in medicine for the right reasons. Her socioeconomic background will shape her college experience to some degree, yet her own choices also help determine how she will end up. How truly fascinated is Isabella in a career in medicine? Does she simply want to become like her aunt or is she really excited about being a doctor herself? She should consider what a physician does day-to-day and whether that lines up with what she is interested in doing. Perhaps it does, or perhaps it is the lifestyle that attracts her. If that is the case, then Isabella would do well to consider a wide array of other options that provide similar lifestyles and socioeconomic status while fitting her specific interests more closely. Becoming a doctor is not the only route to financial security; it is merely one of the best-known.

**#vocation #publichealth** Like Isabella, **Abram** aspires to be a doctor, but for quite distinct reasons. Abram seems to have a strong passion for health, one related to his religious faith. The fact that he talks specifically about his public health concerns, something that attracts less attention than the general dream of becoming a doctor, is a good indicator that he is going into a field that fits his interests. At the same time, during college Abram should seek to develop an ability to relate to his future patients. He seems to attribute health issues to lack of responsibility and perhaps some deficiencies in those who struggle with poor health. Exposing himself to a wide range of students during college may broaden his empathy for people who come from different circumstances than his own and whose health problems are not exclusively the result of poor choices. Likewise, getting to know other students who are interested in health but do not share his religious beliefs and motivations could be useful later when working in a diverse group of health professionals.

**#genderinstem #findingyourownway** In her story, **Sierra** also demonstrates awareness of how her background contributes to—but does not determine—her career plan. The constraints enforced on her by her family compel her to seek her own sense of self apart from these restrictions. While she describes her gender as setting her apart from others in her major, and perhaps also in her future career, her personal empowerment and her understanding of the valuable role she plays are likely to continually motivate her to succeed in the field of engineering. That is a good sign. At the same time, it would be helpful for Sierra to find others who share in her minority status. It is likely that a student group of females in STEM fields exists on campus. If it does not, she could establish such a group. Then, instead of feeling isolated in her classes, Sierra and other young women could fuel their shared passions together.

More generally, all these students need to ask whether they are fully engaging in the process of college. Selecting a major and a career path are perhaps the most important decisions they will make in college. This is the time to reevaluate preconceived notions of what to be and do, and to take ownership of where their lives are headed. The awareness these students have of how their backgrounds influence their plans is valiant and can make for excellent material to share in applications for scholarships and awards. However, young people must not feel that college and life plans are *determined* by these backgrounds. Where students come from and what they have experienced before college can inform their decisions about the right path to take in college, but students should not feel any less free to make their own choices.

Wrapped up in finding the best path for oneself is understanding that there is no one-size-fits-all answer. Someone like Sierra, who is a STEM major, would do well to pay particular attention to filling out her electives and fully engaging in other general education classes to round out her education. This will help her to gain skills in decision-making, communication, and other "soft" skills that all careers require. On the other hand, someone like Kiersten, who has a liberal arts major, would benefit from seeking out internships and job-shadowing opportunities. Her liberal arts major may already stress soft skills, and she can round out her experience through internships—getting out in the real world, participating in specific career development opportunities, and gaining particular hard skills. In summary, students should seek to balance the two sides of the equation, reflecting on the strengths of their intended major and on what limitations they can supplement through other activities.

## TOGETHERNESS: WHAT WE (CAN) SHARE

*Chikako and Sierra.* A student organization on campus is hosting a fall carnival event for local kids, and Chikako and Sierra are both assigned to the face-painting booth. They begin to chat while they paint. Sierra is the first to speak, asking Chikako what her major is. Chikako responds by saying "well, do you want to know my official major—the one my parents chose for me—or do you want to know my real major, the one I truly love?" Sierra says simply "you too?!" and they both laugh in front of the kids. Chikako explains that she is listed as a pre-law political science major because that is what her parents want her to do. They are both attorneys. But Chikako loves kids and wants to be an education major. That is why she volunteered for this event! Sierra knows the feeling. She is a STEM major at the moment, but deep down she really loves art, which is why she was so excited to help with face painting. Sierra also mentions that she felt better after discussing things with a career counselor, who gave her some ways to explain that a career in art can still be very practical. Chikako says that she had a similar experience when she spoke with a trusted faculty member during her office hours. They share with each other some tips on articulating their desires and plans to their parents, even though that seems like a very scary thing to do.

*Camille and Kristen.* At the same fall carnival, Camille and Kristen are volunteering at a booth that has giant foam building blocks for children to play with. To pass the time, and to attract more people to the booth, they start planning how to build the tallest possible structure out of the blocks. This gives way to a conversation about how they have both been doing a lot of real-life planning as well—plans that involve careers, majors, and courses. Camille says that she feels stressed because she loves so many different fields but she cannot put together a concrete plan. Kristen mentions that she felt the same way, but after going to a career fair and talking with her academic advisor, she has learned some new strategies for narrowing down her options and incorporating them into one flexible plan. She is still exploring for sure, but she feels much more in control of it all and is even having a little fun now that she can relax (because she knows she has several good career options to choose from!). Camille is very intrigued, and after chatting for quite awhile, Kristen gives Camille the contact information for that advisor.

*Connor and Tyrone.* Connor and Tyrone are working at the dunking booth at the carnival. They chose to volunteer together because they have become friends during the semester. Connor talks about how much he has benefited from having Tyrone tutor him. He is now getting to the point where no more tutoring is needed, and they have begun to just hang out as friends. Tyrone says that he has benefited even more, and he is grateful for the experience. He did not even think about tutoring until a faculty member mentioned it after seeing how bored Tyrone was in class. It all seems so crazy now because Tyrone wants to be a professor, which is something he may have never even considered if he had not started tutoring Connor.

## TIPS: WHAT WE (CAN) DO

In this final section of the chapter, we highlight ten tips for all college students. Although these have been covered in one way or another throughout the book, it helps to restate them explicitly. We encourage students to revisit these tips in the years ahead.

1. Find yourself, know yourself, trust yourself, create
   yourself, become yourself

The stereotypes out there in pop culture about the college experience are plentiful. Popular movies give you a wide variety, from *Animal House* to *Pitch Perfect*, from *Legally Blonde* to *Drumline*, and from *The Social Network* to *Monsters University*. And you know what? They are all true. But they do not even come close to representing the infinite number of ways to experience college. Here is the truest of all stereotypes about college: it is a time to find out who you really are. As we learned in chapter 1, most of your classmates are discovering what it means to be an independent adult, and they are all doing it in their own way. Furthermore, as chapters 5 and 6 highlight, everyone is affected by their own unique background, and we all differ from each other in many significant ways. Everyone is experiencing college in their own way—there is no such thing as "fitting the mold," no matter how hard you try. There is no mold into which all students fit. At the same time, everyone is facing similar challenges. This is a time to reflect on what you already know about yourself, and what might be left for you to discover. It may even feel like you are creating a new "self" at times, one that is different from how you felt before college. Your hobbies and friends may be a lot different from those you had just a few short years ago. And that is ok! Just as you might have realized as you read chapters 2 and 4, you gain confidence, over time, from understanding where you come from, where you are now, and where you might go next.

2. Explore: Embrace the experience . . .

The first thing you learned from reading chapter 1 is the concept of *emerging adulthood*. Whether you feel ready or not, you are probably faced with the challenge of figuring out your own path to adulthood. We discussed a bit more about this in chapter 4 and here in chapter 8. A necessary prerequisite to finding a path is *exploration*. Or, said differently, it is time for you to wander around a bit and see what you like and what you do not. Is this wasted time? Absolutely not. It may feel like you are under a lot of pressure to decide *right now* what kind of adult you will be. That is indeed a daunting task. But you have time to explore your options first. In fact, your happiness as an adult may depend on whether you explore your options before committing to a path. In chapter 3, you read that college is both a credential and a process. Embrace that process to see what benefits may emerge. Step outside your box a little bit. Chapters 5 and 6 described how college can be an incredibly diverse place, full of individuals with a myriad of different backgrounds, beliefs, values, and interests. Interact with individuals who are different than you; try out experiences you would not normally try; and, hopefully, learn some things that you did not think you would ever find interesting. This process of exploration will make your college degree truly valuable—both to you and to your future employers. Just as you read in chapter 7, engaging in the campus community is key to becoming a leader. Exploration with an open mind is the first step. Embrace the experience!

## 3. . . . and Decide: Have some "long-term right-nows"

As you might have guessed, after genuine exploration comes soulful decision-making. Simultaneous with the exploration we just discussed is the process of making decisions, both big and small. Chapter 1 also mentioned that one of the primary outcomes of emerging adulthood is independent decision-making. College is both exhilarating and terrifying largely because it is full of decisions. All of a sudden you have the ability to choose your major, your bedtime, your relationships, your study habits, your class attendance, your leisure activities, your diet, and so on. This can absolutely feel overwhelming at first. But, over time, you may discover how wonderful this new autonomy can be. In chapter 4 we learned how important it is to develop a sense of ownership over your learning process. In chapter 7 we noted that this is also a fundamental part of becoming a true leader. Treat your decision-making with care. From books like this, and from faculty, staff, and friends, you already have a wealth of trustworthy research, real-life experiences, and practical advice. Make sure that your short-term decisions—even things as small as whether you go to the gym, the library, or the party tonight—line up with the much bigger long-term decisions you have made, such as academic and career goals. Make good choices, learn to prioritize, and know what is important to you.

## 4. Experience learning

In chapter 2, we described the major role that *soft skills* will play in your future, and in chapter 3 we showed that college is, in part, a developmental process. We also described how college offers opportunities to develop more human, cultural, and social capital. Finally, in chapters 7 and 8, we reflected on how engaging in various parts of the campus community is vital to becoming a leader. What do all of these lessons tell us? That learning is important, and it happens both inside and outside of the classroom. When you began college, you may have been focused mostly on classroom learning, which is to be expected. But hopefully by now you realize that college can mean so much more. There are countless ways to develop abilities such as interpersonal skills, teamwork, leadership, multimodal communication, and multicultural awareness, just to name a few. Think big and small. Perhaps you can seek out a once-in-a-lifetime study abroad or internship experience. Perhaps you can start today with a one-time volunteer experience or by joining a student organization. These opportunities exist on every college campus and oftentimes go underutilized. Such experiential learning will increase both your long-term career opportunities and your enjoyment of the college experience.

## 5. Take a social science or humanities class

Perhaps one of the longest-standing objectives of most colleges is to instill the ability to ask one seemingly simple question: Why? Your professors probably want you to demonstrate this ability in the form of raw intellectual curiosity about topics they discuss in class. Likewise, the ability to ask yourself "why?" as you examine your study skills and time management will lead to better academic performance, as you may have already learned. A much more refined version of this ability to ask "why?" will manifest as *critical thinking*, one of the most valued personal skills across the board, and one that social science and humanities classes help to develop. Both professors and employers alike covet critical thinking. Lucky for you, college is a virtually endless playground to develop that skill, as much of this book demonstrates.

Chapter 4 talks about a personal sense of ownership over the learning experience. Chapters 5 and 6 teach that college is full of unique individuals and groups who can deepen your understanding of various perspectives and worldviews. Chapter 7 illustrates that this environment provides an opportunity for civic engagement and leadership development. To make college your own personal experience, you must be intentional. Whether you become a scientist or an artist, a business owner or a politician, your journey should allow you to examine why the world is the way it is, why our society is what it seems to be, what changes you desire, and where you fit in to this big equation.

## 6. Make your own luck

Chapter 4 delivered one of the key takeaways from this book. Your story is *your* story. Learn to take charge of your own experience. We know from chapters 3, 5, and 6 that we do not all start from the same place or with the same resources—not by a long shot. But we all have the ability to make decisions, take action, and control where we go from here. There is no one way to be successful in college. Know yourself, and know what works for you. Remember where you come from and then focus on the opportunities in front of you. From choosing majors to refining study habits to selecting extra-curricular activities—there is no one-size-fits-all. Develop your own method of organization and planning. Study your way. Pay attention to what works and adjust when needed.

## 7. Make friends IRL

Social networking is great. The process of crafting a personal profile and feed and connecting with people despite geographical limitations is now part of our everyday life. But college offers something different and rare: the chance to make a bunch of new connections *in real life*. The concept of "networking" is nothing new. A common piece of advice is to connect with people, both academically and socially, who may be able to help you be successful in the future. Chapters 1 and 2 mention the process of resocialization, of learning a new culture. Chapter 3 introduces the notion of social and cultural capital, while chapters 5 and 6 explain just how diverse a college campus can be. Chapters 4 and 7 explain the importance of actively interacting with that environment. Expanding your network may seem super complicated, but it does not have to be. One bit of common-sense advice can take you a long way: Make real friends. Sometimes lost in the pressure to "network" is a fruitful understanding of what that means. Simply introducing yourself to someone probably will not mean much in the future. But if you make authentic connections with other students, faculty, and staff, these meaningful relationships may provide the foundation for what you do after college and how you get there. Sometimes a seemingly trivial interaction, like a conversation about shared interests, can lead to a long-lasting, mutually beneficial connection. Do not treat friendships as transactions. As with the first tip in this section regarding the need for exploration, you may initially feel like there is no practical purpose behind some of your social activities. But let your interests guide you. You might make a lifelong friend from joining a club, or you might meet a lifelong faculty mentor at a campus event. If you seek out new experiences and develop authentic relationships, you may be surprised by how these goals can enhance your journey both in college and the world beyond.

It is impossible to discuss social interaction among young people without mentioning how smartphones and social media are transforming it. When danah boyd (2014)[7] conducted a study with youth, she discovered that while many interactions on social media generally mirror long-existing social interactions, there are also key differences. As boyd describes, there are four differences that social media and technology make for social interaction, namely (1) the persistence and durability of online social expressions (meaning that comments online often remain long after a private comment to a friend), (2) the visibility of social media and the broad audience of who can view interactions that may not have been intended for them, (3) the spreadability of content, referring to the ease and speed with which interactions online can be shared, and (4) the searchability, referring to how easy it can be to find content online.

With these facts in mind, contemporary college students must manage their online presence with not only their current concerns but also their future careers in mind. Positive steps can range from "whitewalling" social media content[8] that could be damaging to students' reputations to beginning to build a professional identity and presence in online spaces that will be highly visible by the time students apply for jobs. In short, preparing for a career means not only gaining exposure to different topics and determining which major is right for you, but managing the way you present yourself to the outside world—and prospective employers.

## 8. Work hard, play hard, sleep hard

Make sure to align all your seemingly small daily behaviors with the college experience you want. Prioritize what is important to you and act accordingly. Listen to some of the tried and true maxims about successful college students and take them to heart. Go to class. Write down everything. Take care of your own health and wellness. If you are a procrastinator (aren't we all?), then plan your procrastination: if an assignment should take an hour to complete, then allot at least two hours to do it to allow for distraction. Break big assignments into much smaller parts. If you like learning with peers, form a study group. If you like to study in absolute silence, find a good study place other than your residence hall. If you make time to study and take care of business first, there will still be time to have fun.

## 9. Go fail at something

Implicit in all of the advice we give in this book is that it is OK to fail some-times. In fact, it is necessary! You cannot explore without stumbling upon experiences you do not like or succeed in. You cannot truly learn without making mistakes (and receiving some bad grades) to learn from. Knowing this can save you a lot of stress. Expect to make mistakes or fall short, and expect to forgive yourself. Equally important is to expect others to fail, and to forgive them just the same. The cruelest phenomenon on college campuses is the pressure to appear as though you "have it all figured out" or "have a plan and stick to it." What a myth! One of the most common interview questions from both employers and grad schools involves peo-ple's ability to handle adversity and failure. The last thing either of those groups would want is someone who pretends to never have made a mis-take. Learn to fail gracefully, and learn to turn your failures into assets. This may help you approach college with passion instead of fear.

## 10. "There is always help at Hogwarts for those that ask for it"

Harry Potter references may be cliché, but none rings truer than the one quoted here. The characters in this popular book and movie series can always find someone at their school to help them as long as they ask. The same is true on college campuses. In so many ways, the college experience can feel difficult, isolating, overwhelming, or even impossible. Please rest assured that you are not the only one that feels this way. If there is only one lesson learned from this entire book, let it be this: you are not alone. You are surrounded by caring faculty members, advisors, and fellow students. It may not be immediately obvious amid the swirl of activity and informa-tion on a college campus, especially during your first year. But that is OK.

All you have to do is ask for help. Ask your instructors before class or during office hours (usually posted in your class syllabus). Also, you have an advisor—a staff or faculty member, depending on your campus—responsible for giving you guidance. Find out who your advisor is and pay them a visit, even if you do not have an obvious reason. And do not forget that you are surrounded by students who face the same challenges as you. It may not come naturally to ask other students for advice, but give it a shot. You may even be able to do this online through the software used to manage your courses (look for discussion boards or direct message functions). If things get serious, know that your campus most likely has a counseling center or health clinic to go to. Also, the offices of student affairs or the dean of students can always help if you are in the middle of a crisis. Asking for help is the first step to success. All "success stories" begin with someone helping someone else. And do not forget that this works both ways. You may have the opportunity to help others yourself, so be ready!

## CONCLUSION

This book addresses many key issues that emerging adults encounter during the first year of college and beyond. Chapter 1 began by illustrating how emerging adults—in a relatively new life stage—are different from entering college students of the past, and, as a result, may have different experiences than the parents or grandparents who often provide social support and advice to them. Chapter 2 put into context emerging adulthood amidst larger economic, social, and cultural trends, all while highlighting the struggles emerging adults may experience while moving, changing identities, romantic partnering and breaking up. Beginning with chapter 1, the student vignettes provided real-world examples of these experiences. Chapter 3 laid out why it is important to earn a college degree, including the gain of specific skills, knowledge, and cultural capital that remain central for navigating other life changes upon graduation. Importantly, this chapter acknowledged that where students come from—their social class background—affects the difficulty or challenges they are likely to face as they start their college careers. In turn, chapter 4 emphasized the importance of taking ownership of learning and remaining flexible to the unique experiences that different courses and majors offer as students decide what fits them best.

Subsequently, chapter 5 described the importance of resiliency in the face of challenges, especially by considering the life course as a social construction. Students, on the one hand, have the freedom to shape their experiences in college, but cannot completely control nor accept total responsibility for the social contexts that they encounter or the inequalities embedded within those contexts. On the other hand, viewing students as having no control over their social contexts takes away from the importance of students owning their own learning and of developing resiliency in the face of inevitable setbacks. This culminated in chapters 6 and 7, where the student stories highlighted struggles with race, ethnicity, gender, sexuality, biculturalism, and religion, as well as uncertainty in how to become a leader and engage their wider communities. Where chapter 6 encouraged readers to harness their identity to find others like themselves and to understand diversity as another critical "soft skill" for use upon graduation, chapter 7 stressed that students should recognize their personal strengths as they look to build civic engagement and hone their leadership abilities.

In sum, the primary aim of this book is to address challenges and opportunities faced by many first-year college students. At the same time, more advanced college students may also find the book helpful. Indeed, students are encouraged to revisit this book as they continue to navigate college. The themes of the book also raise questions that are relevant to the college experience in general, including ways to balance personal agency and awareness of social influences on behavior in an ongoing way. This book aims to aid students in forming a helpful middle ground between two extremes: viewing themselves as 100% in control, or alternatively not accepting any personal accountability for college and life outcomes. Students need to be aware of the ways they are shaped by their social contexts, and the potential for negative influences there. Yet, students also need to embrace their personal abilities to navigate past issues they encounter, remove those inevitable roadblocks along the way, and perservere in their relentless pursuit of successful pathways through college and beyond.

## LETTER TO ENTERING FIRST-YEARS STUDENTS
## (FROM A REAL COLLEGE FIRST-YEAR STUDENT)

Halfway through my first semester of college I now realize there are a few things I would have done differently. Both academically and socially. All of these things would make my life exponentially easier now.

I would have read my syllabus and made myself reminders to do assignments. I knew professors didn't remind you to do things in college, but it never really occurred to me that I should remind myself regularly to do things. Because of this failure, I've missed several assignments over the weeks and am seriously playing catch-up.

Socially I would have not gone out with the cute guy downstairs. While it seems like a good idea at the time, trust me, you do not want to be involved with anyone in your dorm romantically. It makes for awkward laundry room moments and ruins social circles.

That being said, make friends with people in your dorm. I can't stress that enough. I love my neighbors and we have a great relationship. Every week we have "family dinners" and half our floor goes downstairs and cooks big meals.

Also, learn when to say no. Know when it's a good idea to go out and when it's an excellent idea to stay in and study. Both are important.

Additionally, cultivating a good relationship with your roommate is an excellent idea. Everything from what temperature your room should be set to, to rules on having people over should be discussed and agreed on. And be friends with them. Sleeping with a stranger for any amount of time is just weird.

—FROM, A College Student

## FURTHER READING ONLINE

- Many leaders around the world majored in the social sciences or humanities and they emphasize the soft skills that higher education develops: "Educational Pathways of Leaders," British Council, retrieved from https://www.britishcouncil.org/sites/default/files/1.6_educational-pathways-of-leaders-infographic.pdf.

- In this article, sociologists advise new college students to collect mentors and friends: Wade, Lisa, and Gwen Sharp, June 14, 2017, "Collect Mentors and Make True Friends: Advice for New College Students from Sociologists," Pacific Standard, retrieved from https://psmag.com/education/collect-mentors-make-true-friends-advice-new-college-students-couple-sociologists-66914.

## NOTES

1.  Carduner, Jessie, Gary M. Pakah, and Jamie Reynolds. 2011. "Exploratory Honors Students: Academic Major and Career Decision Making." NACADA Journal 31(1): 14–28.
2.  Chambliss, Daniel F. 2014. *How College Works*. Cambridge, MA: Harvard University Press.
3.  Light, Richard J. 2004. *Making the Most of College: Students Speak Their Minds*. Cambridge, MA: Harvard University Press.
4.  Dietrich, Julia, and Katariina Salmela-Aro. 2016. "Emerging Adults and Work: A Model of Phase-Adequate Engagement." In Jeffrey J. Arnett (Ed.), *The Oxford Handbook of Emerging Adulthood* (pp. 334–345). New York: Oxford University Press.
5.  Arnett, Jeffrey Jensen. 2015. *Emerging Adulthood: The Winding Road from the Late Teens through the Twenties* (2nd ed.). New York: Oxford University Press.
6.  Stuber, Jenny M. 2011. "Inside the College Gates: Education as a Social and Cultural Process." *Inside the College Gates: How Class and Culture Matter in Higher Education*. New York: Lexington Books.
7.  boyd, danah. 2014. *It's Complicated: The Social Lives of Networked Teens*. New Haven, CT: Yale University Press.

8. boyd, danah. November 8, 2010. "Risk Reduction Strategies on Facebook."
Apophenia. Retrieved from http://www.zephoria.org/thoughts/archives/2010/11/
08/risk-reduction-strategies-on-facebook.html.

   Populate Digital. November 25, 2010. "Whitewalling: The New Trend in
Facebook Identity Management." Retrieved from http://www.populatedigital.com/
online-privacy/whitewalling-the-new-trend-in-facebook-identity-management/.

Despite the challenges and stresses they can present, classrooms can be places of exponential learning, and social science classes in particular expose students to ideas that enable them to reflect on themselves. Self-reflection is an essential tool in finding your way through college, and so for each chapter we offer activities that can promote such reflection. Most of these activities can also be implemented in group settings, so consider gathering a group of friends to complete some of them—especially if they are also reading this book. For each activity, we draw upon our own best practices (in classrooms, advising, and as former participants in student groups) to suggest ways to address the challenges we describe throughout the book. In linking the previous sections, our aim with the activities for each chapter is to engage you in the problem-naming and problem-solving processes that are most crucial for success in college. These activities reflect the experiences, roles, and diversity of our author team and should work well in raising your own awareness of the issues this book addresses.

## CHAPTER 1—DISCUSSING EMERGING ADULTHOOD AND GENERATIONAL LABELING

To get started with an activity related to the content of this book, we recommend reading the background on emerging adulthood in chapter 1. Read over the case studies and the advice we provide at the end of the chapter. Reflect upon and then jot down your answers to the following questions:

1. Do you think of yourself as an adult?
2. What do you think it takes to be an adult? When will you know you are an adult?
3. How might becoming an adult be more complicated than just having a job?
4. What barriers do you think young people encounter on the way to becoming an adult?
5. Do you think it is more challenging to become an adult today than it was for your parents, or for your grandparents; or do you think it is just different?

If you have the opportunity, ask these same questions of some of your classmates. How are their answers similar to yours? What are the primary differences? We find knowing more about emerging adulthood generally enables you to become a better advocate for yourself with parents and other adults, including employers. Consider whether you have ever encountered adults who have a negative impression of today's young people, as a whole or in reference to particular generations of young people. If so, do you think their impressions may have been missing information about emerging adulthood and the changing life course? Specifically, it is helpful to think about how negative impressions of young people could change if older adults knew more about how it takes young people today longer to complete their schooling and find stable jobs than in the past. To conclude this activity, take a few minutes to write down what you could say to these adults to advocate for yourself and other emerging adults.

## CHAPTER 2 — UNDERSTANDING HIGHER EDUCATION
## AND DEVELOPING ACADEMIC SKILLS

To work through developmental tasks of emerging adulthood, while also challenging your own preconceived notions about college, we recommend that you give the following activities a try. For the first activity, start by reading the student stories at the beginning of the chapter. With which do you most identify: multiple moves, big transition from high school, or recent breakup? Think beyond the specifics of each particular student story. Perhaps you have experienced other kinds of disillusionment when you encountered the reality of college and how it may be different from what you had imagined. Take a few minutes to write down what in your own story resonates with or is similar to the student story you chose, as well as how it is different. Discuss this topic with other students, especially other students who are reading this book. Write down any common themes you notice after speaking with other students.

A second activity, one that can orient you to the higher education system, is to examine the "About" section of your university website. Find that section (or one similar) and read every link. Who does what on your campus? Can you determine what each individual's title means? Is it clear what each office does for you institution? What is the mission of your institution? What traditions are associated with your institution? Do you know of any famous or influential individuals that graduated from your institution? Chat with one of your instructors or a staff member on campus about some of these topics. Ask them to clarify anything you are unsure about. Finally, if you have the opportunity, try to explain this material to a friend or family member that is not affiliated with your institution.

As a third activity, take some time to reflect on these topics: study skills, the ability to take quality notes, strategies for increasing reading comprehension and improving your test-taking capacities, and advice on taking initiative with your professors. How competent do you feel in each of these areas? Based on the science section of the chapter, which introduces you to the value of a college education beyond boosting your income by describing the kinds of skills that employers desire, we invite you to take ownership of your learning by employing strategies that work for these skills. As several student stories in this chapter illustrate, university study habits need to be more elaborate than the approaches used in high school. Do you find yourself asking, "What do I need to do to get an A?" or "What are the steps for getting into medical school?" These questions indicate that you may be thinking about college as a destination rather than a process, an end rather than a means to adulthood decisions.

- Visit our online website supplements to find additional resources.
- We also included a number of relevant resources in the chapter 2 online reading section, with tips for success in college, ways to improve test-taking, reading comprehension, study habits, and how to survive finals.
- Finally, one of the most important actions you can take is to connect with the academic support offices that exist on your campus. Is there a tutoring center on campus? How about a writing center or a math-specific tutoring center? Ask an advisor, an instructor, a friend—anyone you can think of to make sure you know about all the support resources on your campus.

A fourth and final activity involves a very simple task: go talk with one of your instructors. Determine the office hours of at least one of them, and plan to visit with the instructor during these office hours. Rather than approaching professors to ask questions such as "What do I need to do to get an A?" or "What are the steps for getting into medical school?", we recommend that you engage professors as a resource for developing your own plan. This will help you confront any apprehension you may have regarding what happens during office hours. You should know that there is no cookie-cutter process for success in college. At first, it may be frustrating when instructors do not provide you with rubrics that spell out step-by-step the process for success. This may be what you were used to, but college tends to be very different. Let your instructors help you adjust to this change. Use your first visit to your instructor to think about your expectations for college and the ways you intend to navigate it.

## CHAPTER 3—MONEY MANAGEMENT AND FINANCIAL LITERACY

Because the focus in the third chapter includes the economic aspects of college, we urge you to spend some time investigating the rising costs of student loans and college education more generally (see online reading section for more information). On the one hand, viewing information about the amount of money that students are paying to attend college can be overwhelming, and is something we should take care to avoid as much as possible. On the other hand, it would be irresponsible not to address the financial aspects of the college experience. We have sat with numerous emerging adults who did not know about or really understand the financial implications of the loans they had during college. Many of these emerging adults later regretted not becoming more informed about finances earlier on when their budget was more within their control—before they had committed to a certain housing situation, and so on. As uncomfortable or confusing as this topic can be, we think it deserves your attention.

The top takeaway of this chapter is that social class helps shape individual lives and experiences during college. Sometimes Americans are uncomfortable talking about social class. It rubs against the grain. But most folks in the United States can readily recount money stories that, in their way, reveal the contours of social class. We encourage you to ask yourself, "What is my money story?" Talk with people about money. Discussing your financial background with other students is also one of the great opportunities of college—meeting people who come from a range of socioeconomic backgrounds. Hear each other's stories, and try to wear each other's metaphorical shoes for a while. Then spend some time thinking about financial goals, expected income, and how budgeting as early as possible in emerging adulthood can help people build a comfortable life.

Student debt, financial goals, estimating income, budgeting, financial literacy—these aren't topics that most college students enjoy discussing, but they still stand to benefit greatly from the discussion. In addition to the links at the end of chapter 3 (in the online reading section), here are other financial literacy activities.

*Identifying Your Financial Goals.* Here is an excellent quote from John Ricchini and Terry Arndt[1] on budgeting:

> When people think of budgeting, they usually envision hours spent pouring over piles of bills, accounting for every penny, and depriving themselves of certain pleasures. However, the budgeting process does not have to be like this at all. Developing a budget simply requires creating a plan—a plan that will allow you to pay for life's necessities, as well as some luxuries. The secret to making it work, however, is creating one and sticking to it. By evaluating your financial goals, determining how you make and spend money and occasionally reviewing your overall plan, you will be able to better manage your time, your money, and meet your financial goals. What are your financial goals? Your goals can be anything that is important to you, like buying new clothes or CDs, paying off a credit card bill, purchasing an airline ticket home for the holidays, saving money for a spring-break trip, or even just saving a few dollars a month in case of an emergency. By establishing your financial goals you give yourself an incentive to stay focused on developing and maintaining your budget.

*Exercises.* Make a budget using the following worksheet, estimating as well as possible current income and expenses, both fixed and flexible. Read over the online resource on the difference between fixed and flexible costs (the link is in the online reading section at the end of chapter 3). Then fill out the worksheet on the next page.

# A Budget for College Spending

---

**INCOME**

| | |
|---|---|
| Money from home | $_____ |
| Money from savings | $_____ |
| Part-time work | $_____ |
| Scholarship, grant, or student loan | $_____ |
| Other | $_____ |
| TOTAL INCOME | $_____ |

**EXPENSES**

FIXED EXPENSES

| | |
|---|---|
| College room and board or rent | $_____ |
| Car payment and insurance | $_____ |
| Credit card payment | $_____ |
| Health insurance | $_____ |
| Emergency fund | $_____ |
| Savings | $_____ |
| Other | $_____ |
| TOTAL FIXED EXPENSES | $_____ |

FLEXIBLE EXPENSES

| | |
|---|---|
| Tuition | $_____ |
| Books | $_____ |
| Meals and snacks | $_____ |
| Telephone bill and utilities | $_____ |
| Social and recreation | $_____ |
| Transportation | $_____ |
| Personal | $_____ |
| Clothing allowance | $_____ |
| Health care | $_____ |
| Other | $_____ |
| TOTAL FLEXIBLE | $_____ |
| TOTAL FIXED AND FLEXIBLE EXPENSES | $_____ |
| TOTAL INCOME | $_____ |
| Minus TOTAL EXPENSES | $_____ |
| BALANCE | $_____ |

---

*Evaluating your Results.* After you complete your budget worksheet, evaluate your results: How did your budget turn out? Was it what you were expecting, or were you surprised? What changes do you think you can make to your finances to improve it in light of both short- and long-term financial goals? How likely is it that you will make those changes? Reflect on the statements that follow.

*Living beyond Your Means.* To quote Ricchini and Arndt,

> If the Remaining Income amount in your income statement is a negative number, you are living beyond your means. In other words, you are spending more money than you take in. If earning more money is not an option, you need to reduce your expenses. Look first at your variable expenses to determine what expenses might be reduced. Check your fixed expenses next. If changes can be made, implement them and reevaluate your budget. Continue reducing or removing items until your budget balances. If you are still unable to balance your budget, consider seeking professional assistance. Living above your means even for just a few months can have serious long-term consequences, affecting your class performance and/or plans for degree completion.

*Living within Your Means*

> If the Remaining Income amount in your income statement is a positive number, you are living within your means. In other words, you are spending less money than you take in. Living within your means is a great accomplishment, and you should be proud of yourself. However, just because you are living within your means does not necessarily mean that you are meeting your financial goals. If those goals require your setting aside a little extra money every month, be sure to budget for that as well. (Ricchini & Arndt 2004)

## *Preparing for Unexpected Expenses*

No matter how diligent you are at budgeting, it is impossible to imagine every potential expense . . . Although you can't anticipate every possible expense, what you can do is plan for them. For example, you can develop a category in your fixed expenses for an emergency fund. Each month, simply set aside a few dollars to be saved. (Ricchini & Arndt 2004)

## CHAPTER 4—OWNERSHIP OF LEARNING AND TIME MANAGEMENT

For activities related to the topics of chapter 4, we encourage you to engage in the numerous resources that exist on managing time, goal-setting, prioritizing, and scheduling. However, beware that many of the available worksheets on these issues are simplistic. Some students may benefit from them, but we have heard a number of students moan over the busywork that seemingly mindless worksheets entail, sometimes even feeling the presence of the worksheets insults their intelligence. We think the most essential skill that you can gain is developing a *framework* for navigating your way through college. This orienting framework needs to spring from your values, what you desire and aim to be and do. These are not necessarily values with theological weight. We mean values in a broader, sociological sense, as anything you desire that gives you meaning. Without some degree of clarity about what your values are, worksheets on time management and priorities will prove futile. Even the best strategies can become busywork without some deeper understanding of what orients your actions. As an emerging adult, it is critical that you reflect upon what measuring stick you use to guide your own decisions.

*Time Budget.* Similar to the income-expense spreadsheet in the previous section, you can make something called a "time budget." The time budget works on the same principle as the expense worksheet. You can enter your fixed and flexible expenses, in terms of time. Having outlined where you spend your time, you can think about what time goals you want to set for spending your time in ways that help you to get the most out of college. Then consider whether you want to reprioritize where you invest most of your time. To do this, start with 120 hours for each five-day schoolwork week. Then create lines for each of the following time categories: class/seminar, work/job, study time, sleep, eating/meals, commuting/travel, personal business/chores, relationships (including intimate, friends, and family), leisure/entertainment, other (and write out what other types of time are). After listing your current time investments, ask yourself whether any of these are moveable. Consider whether there are ways to put some of these time investments together, to be more efficient in how much time it takes to accomplish certain tasks, or whether there are ways to expand tasks that you want to further prioritize. Talk this over with your friends and family, especially how this time budget is consistent with your values and goals for college.

*College Pathways.* We recommend discussing the topics of this chapter with other students. You can informally discuss (inside or outside of class) which of the college pathways described by Armstrong and Hamilton (2013)[2] you see yourself as being on: the professional pathway, the party pathway, or the social mobility pathway. In addition to chatting with other students, take some time to reflect individually by writing down answers to these questions:

1. Which pathway do you think you are on as you navigate college?
2. What aspects of your personal and social biography help you align with this pathway?
3. In what ways do you think you could improve your alignment with the pathway you are, or hope to be, on?

It is important to remember that all three pathways are acceptable routes to traverse through college. The problem is not being on one versus another pathway; rather, the goal is to avoid misalignment with a pathway that is not the best fit.

*Personal Values.* Some people think that younger generations, such as Millennials, are becoming more selfish. For example, an article in *Time* magazine garnered a great deal of attention in 2013 under the headline "The Me, Me, Me Generation: Millennials Are Lazy, Entitled Narcissists Who Still Live With Their Parents."[3] Conversely, others suggest that generosity is rising among millennials, asking as a *USA Today* article did: "Millennials: The Giving Generation?"[4] Take a moments to peruse both articles. With these divergent views about young people in mind, decide which of the following categories most accurately describes you: (a) individualist, (b) collectivist, or (c) voluntarist.[5] An individualist is some-one who is primarily self-oriented, whose actions are focused on self-gain. Individualists are happiest in groups that clearly provide more benefit than cost to them; they like it when they get more out of participating in a group than they have to put into it. Collectivists are at the opposite end of the spectrum; they are primarily other-oriented, with actions focused on benefiting others, often accompanied by self-sacrifice. A collectivist is happiest in groups that have a strong sense of group identity, in which it is clear that each individual is part of something that is bigger than themselves and which satisfies their urge to put the good of others above their own. A voluntarist stands, in a sense, in the middle ground between these, with inclinations to do good for others that are understood as ulti-mately self-benefiting. Someone who is a voluntarist may participate in social groups and want to contribute to them, but voluntarists also value their independence and would be inclined to leave a group if it demanded higher conformity than they desired.

So, which of these categories describes you? Give it some thought and then write down your explanation. Discuss it with someone that knows you very well to see if they agree. These outlines simplify a great deal of nuanced scholarship. At the same time, they offer a great starting point for thinking about your personal values to categorize yourself as belonging to one of these groups. It is important to think about how each of your values come together into a coherent whole. Nearly everyone would agree that making decisions alone is important, that helping others is good, that sometimes competition can be motivating, and that quality teamwork can be motivating too. It can be helpful to complete value inventories (see the online reading section for examples) to gain a better understanding of what each of your values looks like independently.

*Work Values.* Taking the value assessment process a step further, we also encourage you to evaluate your work values (see online reading section for a suggested worksheet on work values). Figuring out what kind of work setting will best fit your value orientation can help students choose majors, jobs, and workplaces. After gaining a clearer sense of your own value orientation (through the previous activity), you should now consider what kind of career and organization would be the best fit for you.

Most people entering college today have seen how work alignment did not go well for some in previous generations. The rise in job turnover, layoffs, and divorce rates (often related to work burnout or financial worries) means that the typical college student has seen their parents or others around them struggle with how to balance careers, families, fun, and contributing to communities. We encourage you to give some thought to how you will make sure that does not happen to you, which means critically evaluating which careers will best sustain your personal, family, and community values. This kind of reflection may not only promote a deeper sense of self, it also may boost your performance in job interviews by enabling you to demonstrate an authentic sense of self and work that does not overly simplify either.

*Time Management.* Along with assessing values, it is helpful to process the "nitty gritty" of using time wisely. There are many resources on time management, and we suggest a few in the online reading section of chapter 4. We also think that time management resources often "lose the forest for the trees," so to speak. In this case, the forest is people's general value orientations, the ideals that they want to carry out. Then, with that guiding compass to orient the map, the next step is to evaluate what barriers may get in the way of a person achieving their values. We offer this adapted table of time-wasters and time-savers to aid this process.[6]

| Time Wasters | Time Savers |
|---|---|
| 1. Indecision<br>2. Inefficiency<br>3. Interruptions (unanticipated or not; for example, spending time on social media is an anticipated interruption)<br>4. Procrastination<br>5. Rumination<br>6. Disorganization<br>7. Accumulation<br>8. Burnout, sickness, or emotional drain | 1. Develop a sense of value orientation and make decisions that align with values.<br>2. Create an organizing system that helps to carry out value orientations and does not invite avoidance.<br>3. Consider what kind of interruptions are meaningful and important, and which are not; then accept the former and ward off the latter.<br>4. Analyze the root cause: is it because of anxiety, or is it because the task is undesirable? If it is the former, see the online reading section for a link to a wellness assessment, and/or visit a campus health center. If it is the latter, consider whether this indicates a need to reconsider one's major or class selections.<br>5. Reflect on the important aspects of college and life, and do not "over-think" mundane matters (for example, consider what the most important content of a chapter is; don't memorize).<br>6. Make to-do lists, keep schedules, organize time.<br>7. Every so often, remove items from to-do lists, turn down invitations, and otherwise avoid clutter.<br>8. Set aside time to care for oneself and to care for others |

If you want to move toward a deeper exploration of time management, here is another activity. This is an individual activity, but it would be even better if you include a few friends. For starters, brainstorm the types of goals that you or anyone else could have, such as getting good grades, buying a car, or getting more sleep. The goal is not to evaluate each of your responses, but merely to assemble a variety of goals you may have. At the same time, this activity works best if you offer realistic goals and do not seek, as comedic as it may be, to offer goals no one would reasonably consider at this moment in time (for instance, make $10 million).

You will need some index cards for the next part of the activity. After generating a variety of ideas and writing out a list, select one of the goals from the list, and then write on each index card a different reason or excuse that someone may have for not reaching this goal. Again, think creatively and also reasonably (for instance, "because they do not have internet access" would not cut it). Once you have filled up your index cards, put the reasons/excuses in order based on the extent to which people can control them. The bottom of the ranking is reserved for "parking lot" issues, which are reasons that require an enormous amount of effort or several people to change (for example, "college costs too much" or "politicians never support ___").

Moving up from parking lot issues, you should put next those items that a person could do solo, but which may take considerable time or energy (for example, "change my parents' mind about a major"). Toward the top, then, are those reasons that could be most readily altered (for example, "does not know how many more credits would be needed to switch majors" or "work does not allow enough time for studying"). Now come up with strategies for ways to address the top three reasons within the next month. To conclude this activity, ask yourself the following: What types of factors went into deciding that something was a parking lot issue? What factors made an issue seem movable? How might knowing the difference help you not get stuck ruminating on parking lot issues?

*Health and Well-being.* Most universities provide orientations on alcohol use, sexual assault, and other campus issues. We advise you to pay serious attention to those orientations and trainings, as there are many intense issues that you can confront, whether due to your own actions or not. It is easy to think the worst situations only happen to other people while in truth they could happen to anyone. Best to be prepared. That being said, we recommend that you turn to sources on campus for the most up-to-date information on these issues. Rather than address specifics that may change as new information becomes available, we offer a few global statements on these subjects. Alcohol and drug abuse, eating disorders, and other forms of physiological and psychological distress are real issues that deserve attention. Many of these emerge for the first time or worsen during college, and students should consider whether they need help now for something that seemed minor or controllable before. We also want to add a social perspective to the readily available messages, which typically concentrate on how the body and brain contribute to these issues. There are multiple ways to treat problems; some have to do with intrinsic aspects to a person (what is on the inside) and some deal with extrinsic factors (what is outside a person), and neither should be ignored. In attending to extrinsic factors, you should consider whether you need to make changes to friend groups, to relationships, or within your family to enhance your ability to deal with a problem.

*Academic Integrity.* Many campuses also address academic integrity in orientation sessions. We will defer to general orientations on this subject and urge you to attend to the "gray" areas, the acts that may not seem like outright cheating to them. Some students want to cheat, but many other students wind up in trouble over issues that they did not understand to be wrong at the time.[7] For example, it is increasingly easy for instructors to detect that a student has submitted the same term paper to multiple classes, which is generally considered to be an integrity violation, unless permission was granted by all instructors involved. Submitting materials in papers or presentations that were developed by someone else without citing those materials is also a problem. Many times students know that it is wrong to plagiarize an original source, but they may not realize that taking material from a blog or study guide about an original text without citation likewise violates academic integrity. Whether students are allowed to consult with others when completing quizzes or exams, especially when taken online, varies across courses. You should consult your instructors for their policies on this matter, as there is no universal guideline, but not knowing that an instructor's policy was for non-collaboration can still result in a violation. More generally, you should consider whether you want to be the kind of person who relies on the work of others to succeed. Do we want to be operated on by a doctor who cheated through medical school? Do we want a pilot who cheated on a flight exam? No. Be the kind of professional who acts with integrity, who will not cross moral lines even if blurry, and who can be relied upon to produce their own work. Form that lifelong practice now.

## CHAPTER 5—CAMPUS SUPPORT AND RESOURCE SCENARIOS

One of the chief ways that you can bolster your resiliency in college is to make campus resources part of your social support system. You may have already encountered the laundry lists of available offices and their contact information provided by instructors or staff members trying to help you. You may have also already realized that these lists are not always that helpful. You can probably find geographic locations of these resources using map apps or your university's website, but do you know if the specific problems you may encounter are addressed by a resource on this list? With or without a list, do you know the best keywords to use in order to find particular information on university websites (or websites generally)? The activities associated with chapter 5 (described next) seek to increase these skills, especially to ensure that you understand how best to access the basic tools for navigating college.

A big part of bouncing back in the face of adversity is knowing where to start and actually getting started, rather than letting challenges pile up and become overwhelming. At the risk of stating what may be obvious to you, one of the best ways to tackle adversity and learn more about available resources is to ask Google. We suggest narrowing the keyword search to include only websites of the university. For example, we are at the University of Arkansas, whose website is uark.edu. To restrict searches to university Web pages, you can open Google Chrome and type this into the URL field: "counseling services uark.edu." Only counseling services available at the University of Arkansas will be returned in the results. (Students can often accomplish the same thing by using a search field within the campus website, but this approach saves a couple steps.) Here are some examples of information you should practice finding online, perhaps bookmark the pages most relevant to you:

1. What is the name and location of the campus medical facility or health center? Are walk-ins allowed, or do students need to make appointments first?

2. Where can students receive counseling? Is it available in the same facility as the health center or at a separate facility? Is both individual and group counseling available?

3. Does the university have a Dean of Students or an Office of Undergraduate Studies? If so, where is it located, and how can students meet with a representative of this office?

4. Where is the writing center located, and what are its hours? Does it offer walk-in times, or is it open by appointment only?

5. Is there a tutoring facility on campus, or can campus offices help to connect students with tutors available on particular topics?

6. Where is the Registrar's office located?

7. Where is the Financial Aid Office located? Is there a location where students can pay their college bills in person? What are the Web addresses for setting up automatic payments for tuition or meal plans?

8. What are the hours of the library? Are there multiple library locations? What is the website for interlibrary loans (often called ILLIAD) through which students can request access to books and articles from any library affiliated with the campus?

9. Where are the computer lab locations, and what are their hours? Are students able to print at all locations, or are there particular locations with printers, or with color printers? How do students refill their printing quotas or cards?

10. If students have declared a major, what is the location of the department for that major? What is the department website? Who is the chairperson for the department? What are the names of some of the faculty in the department?

The point of this activity is for you to gain experience in finding the answers to these questions. Even if you were given handouts answering all these questions at orientation, it is critical that you still learn the process for finding this information for yourself.

Now it is time for a second activity in which you apply these skills to some real-life problems that you may face as a college student. For the potential problems listed next, take time to research relevant campus information and resources, and then write down the actions you would take to address the problem:

- You need to add or drop a class.
- You need to pay a bill.
- It's flu season, and you know you get sick easily.
- You want to know what scholarships are available for current students.
- You want to know how to apply for an RA position.
- You need to find a work-study position to help out with finances.
- You don't know why you received a parking ticket.
- You have been sexually assaulted.
- It's late at night and you need a walking escort across campus.
- You don't understand how to finish your math homework.
- You're finding it difficult to keep up with assignments in your English Comp class.
- Your professor assigned you to a group to complete a project. Each person in your group is responsible for writing a portion of the group paper. You're concerned that one member of your group has a looser definition of plagiarism than you.
- You always wanted to study abroad, but you aren't sure how you could afford it.
- You enjoy meeting people from other cultures, and you want to get involved with some international students.

- You have an outstanding account balance that needs to be resolved.
- You aren't sure what major you want to study.
- You don't understand how to complete an assignment your professor gave you.
- Your computer has begun acting erratically.
- You don't feel safe in your residence hall.
- You and your roommate aren't getting along at all, and you think it's time for a change.
- You've heard of assessments for finding majors or career interests, and want to take one.
- You know your budget will be tight next semester, and you're hoping to find a way to avoid paying big bucks for textbooks.
- There are three weeks left in the semester, but you're quickly running out of swipes on your meal plan.
- You want to form a new student organization.
- You want to sign up for an intramural sport.
- You are looking for things to do on the weekends.

Finally, it is time to put your new skills to the test in a very comprehensive way. You will find many different scenarios in what follows that real college students have experienced. The first step in this activity is for you to put yourself in the middle of these scenarios. Assume that it is you who is experiencing what is described. How should you respond to each scenario? Which campus resources should you interact with? If possible, this activity would be even more effective if you can include one or more friends. One of you should assume the identity of the main character in the scenario while the other person should pretend to be that student's roommate or good friend. Rotate these roles as you move through the different situations. As you work through these scenarios, also consider this question: Why do you think that some students are reluctant to use social and academic support services, even though they need to access them in order to succeed?

## Advising and Career Development

1. Chelsea has not completed the last five assignments for her biology class, and she failed last week's quiz on cell structure. She doesn't know how to catch up.

2. Recently, Chuck completely lost his motivation to study. He is still getting good grades in his courses, but he does not see the point of what he is doing in life right now. He wonders if he should take a year off from school.

3. Jose appreciates the freedom that college permits him, especially compared to high school. His first Monday-Wednesday-Friday class doesn't start until 10:40 a.m., and he is out by 2:00 p.m. on Tuesdays and Thursdays. With all this free time, he starts delaying homework assignments and test preparation, believing he'll just save them for later in the day or another time. Four weeks into the semester, he already feels behind.

4. In her first year, Vanessa began taking courses with a cohort of students wanting to go to physical therapy school. When asked to describe the cohort and whether it has been helpful to her, Vanessa states: "I'm in the cohort for physical therapy, so we all just take the same science classes. Following their suggestions helps a lot. If it hadn't been for them, I think I would've been lost." Vanessa relies on the cohort for advice about the classes and the path she will take. She sees her cohort as a credible source of information about school and trusts the information given to her.

5. Rachel lives in the Quad, and one of her roommates has a boyfriend over constantly. The roommate's boyfriend eats all their food without asking for it or replacing it. Her roommates are becoming impatient, but they do not want to cause conflict.

6. Salva just received his math midterm, and the grade was much lower than what he expected. He studied extremely hard for this exam and thought he was well-prepared. He doesn't understand why he missed some of the problems or how the final grade was determined.

7. Trevor always attends his physics class, takes notes, and follows along with the lecture as best he can. He joins a study group before the first test but quickly realizes when he meets with his peers that he has not grasped the major concepts. Everyone else seems to have somehow gleaned the most important points of the chapters and lectures and can use the information to solve the problems, but not Trevor. He feels lost and unsure how he could sit in the same class with these students but come away with such a different level of information.

8. Evan founded an after-school acting troupe for at-risk junior high and high school students. He's found his passion, as he can practice a talent that he honed growing up and help people at the same time. He's a pre-med biology major, but his heart is not in his coursework, and his grades reflect his lack of interest. His GPA hovers around a 3.50, though his biology/chemistry/physics GPA is barely a 3.0. Going into his junior year, he has started shadowing at a local surgery clinic and will begin studying for the MCAT in January.

9. Martina is a self-described "master note-taker." She writes down the key points of the lecture, doesn't try to get every word, fills in the gaps after each lecture, and reviews her notes each day. On her midterm exams, however, her highest grade was a B, and she made C's in three other tests. Now, Martina is confused about what to do. She knew her notes forwards and backwards, so why isn't she making A's?

## Study Abroad

1. In many ways, Sam has loved her university experience, but at times she has found the curriculum a little rigid, with the set number of core courses and waiting to take upper-level classes in her majors. She also gets a little tired of people saying, "What are you going to do with that?" when she says that she is a sociology

and German major with a religious studies minor. She likes learning for the sake of learning and finds herself reading about other
cultures and religious beliefs frequently. Learning languages
comes easily to her. Her goal is to be fluent in German, and
already she can make her way through both formal and informal
conversations, but she'd really appreciate the more in-depth learning that studying abroad would allow. Money, however, may be
an obstacle for Sam. She has a small scholarship and her parents
are able to pay the difference, but little is left over after tuition and
fees are paid at the beginning of each semester.

2. Taylor did well in his first semester although he had not felt
sure how he would transition to the university. Though his high
school GPA was solid, he went to a small school in a rural part
of the state and didn't know if that would translate to success in
college. He quickly learned to review his notes each day, read
assignments in advance of class, and start preparing for exams
a week beforehand. Still, he thinks maybe he is motivated more
by a fear of failing than by liking his classes right now. He is
thinking about the possibility of studying abroad. He doesn't
have many friends and is afraid to tell the handful of people he
has met that he has never been out of the country and only once
has been in an airplane. His feelings are jumbled. On the one
hand, he wants to take advantage of all the college offers and
develop friendships, but on the other hand, the thoughts of being
so far from home is not comfortable. It won't be for his mom and
dad either.

3. Gabby's family took vacations every summer for as long as she
can remember, and Europe was a frequent destination, instilling
in Gabby a love of travel and the ability to adapt quickly to new
environments. The emphasis on studying abroad is one of the
main reasons she selected this university. She's an international
studies and anthropology double major, with the ultimate goal
of working for the International Olympic Committee (IOC).

To make herself marketable for a career with the IOC, Gabby is taking two world languages—French and Russian—and she believes that the best way to become proficient is to study in a French- or Russian-speaking country. Gabby is a planner. She likes structure and wants to begin working out the details now, as she selects her study abroad program.

4. Devon is a pre-med biological sciences major. He knows that medical schools will receive hundreds of applications from students majoring in biology and chemistry, so he wants to choose activities that will distinguish him. Studying abroad, he feels, will provide a strong look to his profile. He is interested in learning about cultures, but a longer program may conflict with his MCAT preparation. So much of his academic plan is regimented, and he must complete certain classes—like human physiology and biochemistry—before taking the MCAT at the end of his junior year. Devon loves the idea of experiencing a new culture and taking classes outside the natural sciences to broaden his perspective. On top of staying on track for the MCAT, he is also concerned about shadowing at medical clinics, volunteering, and taking a leadership role in his favorite student organization.

5. Sam recently met with her academic advisor and learned she can graduate in three years, even though she has a major and two minors. Sam has the Arkansas Governor's Distinguished Scholarship and the Chancellor's Scholarship, so finishing early would mean giving up a full year of paid funding. Sam will consider the options she and her advisor discussed. She can graduate early, stay a fourth year and take classes for the joy of learning, stay and add a second major to her degree plan, or study abroad. She's already studied abroad once, in the summer between her first and second year, with the Classics in Rome Program. She's intrigued with the idea of a different kind of international learning experience than she had previously.

## Academic Integrity

1. Bradly, Anna, and Phinneas all have a multiple-user text mes-
   saging service through SupportMe. They use it to stay connected
   with one another through the school day since their class schedules are different. They also use it to chat about course assignments in cell biology. Although they are in different sections,
   they have the same instructor, so they can conveniently ask one
   another for help on a particular problem without having to get
   together. The second cell biology test is on October 28. Bradly
   has it first at 8:00 a.m. Anna's test is at 10:30, and Phinneas's takes
   place at 2:00 that afternoon. When Bradly finishes his test, he uses
   SupportMe to text Anna and Phinneas several of the questions
   that were on his test as a heads-up for the types of questions they
   may see on their tests. Anna reads Bradly's text and uses the questions as a study guide. Phinneas, however, texts Bradly back and
   tells him he shouldn't be sending out test questions, as he could
   get in trouble for sharing exam questions with others who have
   not taken the exam. Bradly is surprised, thinking that he is just
   helping out friends. Anna texts back that she sees nothing wrong
   with what Bradly did, that it wasn't like he sent them the actual
   test. Ask students: Did Bradly violate the academic integrity
   policy by sharing test questions? If someone texted you questions
   that would likely be on your next test in a class, would your view
   be more like Phinneas's or Anna's?

2. Robert's political science professor uses clickers to keep track
   of attendance and assigned readings in a class of over 200
   students. At the beginning of each class, Robert clicks in with an
   answer to a question related to the assignment. If he clicks the
   correct answer, he receives 10 points. If he clicks an incorrect
   answer, he still gets 3 points for being in class. At the end of the
   semester, Robert's accumulated clicker points will account for a
   quarter of his final grade. Robert needs to see his advisor, and
   the only appointment slot he finds open is for the same time as

his political science class. If he doesn't take this appointment, he won't be able to see his advisor for another two weeks, which will delay his registering for classes with the risk that he won't be able to get in the classes he wants. So he cuts a deal with his friend Taylor, who is also in the class: "If you will cover for me today, then I will click in for you whenever you have an appointment that conflicts with this class." Taylor agrees and takes two clickers to class that afternoon. But before he can use them, Professor Greenway notices that Taylor has not one but two clickers on his desk. "Why the extra clicker?" she asks Taylor. Ask students: How should Taylor answer? Should Dr. Greenway turn him in for a violation of the academic integrity policy? How does Dr. Greenway figure out who owns the other clicker? What happens to Robert?

3. Helen is nervous as she walks across campus to take her honors microeconomics midterm. She recites concepts as she walks, hoping to get everything to stay in the front of her brain long enough to do well on the test. She also keeps checking her phone: her dad is in the hospital and Mom was going to text her with an update on his condition. Her dad's health is only adding to her nervousness. Helen takes her regular seat in the classroom, checking her phone one last time for news of her dad. When she sees copies of the test coming down the row toward her, she places her phone on her desk and takes a deep breath. Here goes . . . Helen has just turned to the second page of the test when she feels someone looking down at her desk. "Why do you have your phone on and placed on your desk?" Professor Iglesia asks. Before she can answer, the professor continues, "This is a violation of the academic integrity policy. You may continue, but I will have to turn you in for violating the policy." Ask students: Which part of the university's academic integrity policy does Professor Iglesia believe Helen has violated? Do you agree with the professor? Why or why not? What could Helen have done differently so that she did not end up in this situation?

4. Kelsey submits her first paper as a college first-year student in her Composition I class. The instructor notices a 40% match to online sources, according to SafeAssign. After comparing these sources to her paper, it is apparent that two paragraphs of the five-page paper were copied directly from a website without citation. In her meeting with the instructor, Kelsey claims she didn't understand that she was supposed to include quotation marks and thought including the source in her bibliography was sufficient. She pleads that she was not trying to steal someone else's work and it was just an honest mistake. Ask students: Do you think Kelsey violated the academic integrity policy? Why or why not?

5. For students' third essay in honors world history, Professor Luna asks for an annotated works cited page. Professor Luna reviews her expectations of the assignment: students are required to list at least six sources in MLA format and offer a half-page description of each source, and the source will be incorporated into their final paper—standard information on an annotation, she states. Needing to do well in his final two assignments, Terrance finishes his assignment a week before the deadline but plans to wait and submit it on the due date. Before class one day, Anthony tells Terrance he is confused about what MLA format looks like and what should be included in an annotation. He asks Terrance if he can look at his, and Terrance agrees, emailing Anthony a copy. Rather than search for his own sources, Anthony submits the document as his own, unbeknownst to Terrance. Professor Luna realizes that the students' assignments are identical, gives each student a zero on the assignment, and submits both names to Academic Standards. Ask students: Do you think Terrance violated the academic integrity policy? Why or why not? Is Terrance more culpable than Anthony? How should Terrance justify his actions when meeting with the standards committee? What should be the punishment for Terrance and for Anthony?

Finding the right information is only half the battle. To truly get the support you need, you should be interacting with other human beings. Another valuable activity for incoming college students is to practice asking people on campus for help in employing college resources. Find a few other students on campus and ask them some of the following questions. It may seem intimidating at first but interacting with other people on campus is key to forming the support system you need to succeed.

1. What is the best-kept-secret place to eat on or near campus?
2. What is the best place to meet up with people on campus for fun?
3. Where is the best place on campus to study?
4. Which campus computer lab is most accessible?
5. What is the best place or website to buy books and class materials?
6. Who is a professor that everyone should try to take a class with?
7. Who is the best advisor to meet with to sort out classes and career options?
8. What is the most interesting art piece on campus?
9. What is the best sporting event to see, especially one that not everyone knows about?
10. What is one thing you wish you would have known when you were a first-year student?

## CHAPTER 6—DIVERSITY AND FORMING CONNECTIONS

When considering the topic of diversity, the most important step is to focus on authentic (not generic) ways of grappling with real student differences and similarities. The student stories offered at the beginning of chapter 6 can spark reflections and discussions on race and ethnicity, immigration, sexuality, gender, religiosity, and culture generally. Additionally, the resources listed in the online reading section at the end of chapter 6 aim to promote a welcoming campus community that respects differences and highlights underemphasized commonalities.

Another way to address diversity is to use the activity called "Crossing the Line." It is best implemented as a group activity (even if it is just you and a few friends). The goals are to introduce you to the diversity of others, to expand your definitions of diversity, and to help you connect with similar peers. This activity typically starts with each participant standing on one side of a room. Pretend that there is an imaginary line down the middle of the room. A volunteer will read various prompts with the instruction to cross the line if the statement applies. Alternatively, participants can simply sit in a circle and raise their hands (or otherwise make themselves known) if the statement applies. If you are unable to gather a group of friends for this activity, simply read each prompt, consider whether it applies to you, and then consider the experiences of students that would have an answer opposite from yours. Here are the prompts, and feel free to add some of your own:

- Cross the line if . . .
    1. You are from out of state;
    2. You know what you want to major in;
    3. A school other than this was your first choice;
    4. You have lived in another state;
    5. You graduated from high school with fewer than 50 classmates;
    6. You had over 500 people in your graduating class;
    7. You have been in love;
    8. You are in love;
    9. You have a hero or role model in your life;
    10. You have visited another country;
    11. You own your own car;
    12. You always arrive to meetings, events, and class late;
    13. You want to have children someday;
    14. You plan to get married in the future;
    15. You define marriage as between a man and a woman;
    16. You plan to live in a big city;
    17. You would be happy to live on a farm;

18. You have cried at least once this year;

19. You have laughed at yourself at least once this year;

20. You are the oldest in the family;

21. You are the youngest in the family;

22. You are adopted;

23. You are an only child;

24. You come from a family of four or more children;

25. You have had primary responsibility for raising another member of your family;

26. Your parents are either divorced, separated, or never married;

27. You consider yourself to be a religious person;

28. You are Catholic;

29. You are Protestant;

30. You are Jewish;

31. You are Muslim;

32. You are Hindu;

33. You are some other form of religion or spirituality;

34. You are an atheist or agnostic;

35. You are a person of color;

36. Your parents or grandparents might still have prejudicial thoughts;

37. You did not cross the line in a previous statement when you should have.

In this activity, the goal is to provide you with a mostly nonverbal way of observing differences and similarities within a group. Participants are learning more about who composes their group, and recognizing the diversity within the group and how that contributes to common and distinct experiences. Conclude this activity by writing down answers to the following questions: What made it easy or difficult to participate in this activity? What were the categories that had the greatest degree of similarity, and of difference? Was that surprising? How did it feel when only a few people stepped forward?

During this activity, please remember to establish a safe environment in which it is acceptable for everyone to move or stay still as they are comfortable. No one should feel forced to disclose anything they are uncomfortable sharing. Participants may laugh or in other ways express a degree of discomfort with this situation, and that can become a powerful way to engage with each other. A simple "Why do you think there was laughter when we discussed——?" can be the beginning of an important conversation. In our experience, it works well to write down your reflections independently immediately following the exercise and then share together as a group.

Another activity that can be completed in tandem with this one, or as a follow-up, is called Similarities and Differences. The objectives of this activity are to discover similarities and differences among people; to identify differences that require little effort to discover; and to identify how sometimes unseen similarities exist despite stereotypes to the contrary. As with the first activity, this one is best implemented as a group activity. Participants should begin by forming into groups with others who have visible similarities to them. Once groups are formed, participants should identify one thing that they value about their similarities. Then they can discuss ways that they are different. Once this is completed, participants should disband their groups and instead form groups based on visible differences. Once groups are formed, they should identify one thing they value about their differences. Then they can discuss ways that they are similar. Finally, as one big group, discuss how college students can feel like a "fish out of water" and whether this activity challenges that perception.

## CHAPTER 7—PERSONAL STRENGTHS, LEADERSHIP, INTEGRITY, AND CIVIC ENGAGEMENT

The first step to becoming an active and engaged citizen, on campus and in the community, is recognizing your particular strengths as a social leader. Between the common claim that "no two leaders are the same" and the opposite extreme view that "leaders are all alike" is the reality of the middle ground: leaders exhibit a set of leadership types. There are a variety of ways to classify leader types, which emphasize different aspects of being a leader. The set that we recommend was developed by Paul Schmitz (2011)[8] in a book called *Everyone Leads: Building Leadership from the Community Up.* The leader types are summarized in an excellent handout produced by Everyday Democracy (https://www.everyday-democracy.org/resources/leadership-compass-activity).[9] The compass consists of four leadership types: nurturers, teachers, mobilizers, and visionaries. While individuals can have aspects of any of these leader types, this activity may help you recognize which of your leadership qualities are dominant, and which type best represents the way you are most comfortable leading.

This leadership compass activity can be completed on your own, or in a group. Begin by following the instructions for rating which leadership qualities best describe you, then tabulate the responses to discover which leadership style is your strongest. The handout above describes ways of implementing this in a group setting, but you can certainly complete this activity alone to reflect on what you "bring to the table." It should be underlined that no one style is better than another; rather, each kind of leader is important for a well-balanced team. After tabulating the responses, review the Leadership Compass (https://www.nationalservice.gov/sites/default/files/resource/leadershipcompass.pdf).[10] This handout provides additional descriptions of each leader type's approach to work, and it lists the best ways to work with a leader of each type. You can benefit from learning about your own style, and may gain even greater insight by learning about the leadership styles of others. Considering that most workplaces, across all sectors, need people who can lead personally *and in teams*, it is essential for you to gain exposure to a wide array of others' work and leadership styles during college. Though sometimes students dread group work in class, working together with a team is crucial to the college experience, and we encourage you to embrace it as providing one of the more tangible, real-world skills for life after college. Completing this exercise can deepen your sense of where others in your group are coming from, and spur creative thinking about how to engage different types of leaders by emphasizing their particular strengths.

These topics of leadership and teamwork give you another opportunity to reflect on academic integrity at your institution. Students and faculty often view issues of academic integrity differently (Park 2003)[11] and different instructors hold somewhat different expectations. Many students tend to think of the most extreme, black-and-white form of plagiarism: cheating on an exam. However, more common forms of plagiarism include using material from another source and passing it off as one's own work (Park 2003). This can be done intentionally, from buying papers online to using the work of other students who took the course in the past. It can also include unintentional forms of plagiarism, however, which stem from not knowing how to cite information found online or in other sources, or not understanding what constitutes a paraphrase of material written by others.

To help you think through these issues, try this activity. Read each of the examples of possible academic dishonesty below. For each one, write "yes" or "no" to indicate your opinion on whether it constitutes cheating.

1. Taking an exam in place of another student or having someone take an exam in your place.
2. Rewriting passages for a paper that you are typing for a friend.
3. Having someone write a paper to submit as your own work.
4. Discussing your outline/ideas for a paper with a friend in your class who is writing on the same project.
5. Allowing another student to copy from you during an exam.
6. Changing your lab results to reflect what you know they should have been, rather than what you actually got.
7. Turning in the same paper to two different classes.
8. Studying from old exams.
9. Getting questions or answers from someone who has already taken the same exam.
10. Borrowing an idea for a paper without footnoting the source.
11. Working on homework with other students.
12. Including a few items which you didn't really use on a bibliography.

13. Changing a few answers on a graded exam and resubmitting it for a higher grade.
14. Reading just the abstracts of articles, rather than the entire article, when researching a paper.
15. Asking someone to proofread your draft of a paper.

If possible, now ask at least one friend to do the same, and then compare your lists. Are there any differences? Finally, bring this list to at least one instructor to get their input and guidance.

## CHAPTER 8—ACTIVITIES—CAREER EXPLORATION AND PERSONAL STATEMENTS

The activities for this chapter encourage you to reflect on and discuss your values and purpose and connect those to making decisions about your majors and careers. We also offer strategies for you to draft personal statements and talk with your parents about career choices.

*Values Discussion.* This activity can be completed as a personal reflection or in a small group. As a personal reflection, take plenty of time to write answers for each of the questions that follow. As a small group activity, select a leader/facilitator and follow these instructions: "Have participants find two people who are wearing the same color as them. Have them find a spot where they can talk together. Instruct them they will be talking about some issues, career or personal goals, and you will give them new topics every few minutes. This exercise allows them to get to know each other better, and start thinking about what kind of career or field they are interested in. After 30 to 45 minutes, the instructor will ask everyone to sit down, and have one individual from one group talk about his/her partner. Here are some samples:"[12]

- Talk about the most important thing you have learned this year.
- What are the easiest and hardest emotions for you to express and why?

- What is something that few people know about you?
- What do you value in a friend?
- What do you want to be doing in five years?
- What is one goal you have for next year?
- What is a motto you try to live by?
- What is the greatest challenge you are facing?
- What do you like most about yourself?
- What do you value in a loving relationship?
- What do you value most in life?

*Purpose Discussion.* The purpose of this exercise [13] is to challenge you to assess your personal and professional goals. A forward-thinking mindset and a long-term goal will help you to stay focused academically. Moreover, it will guide your planning of your first year and suggest a path to achieve your short- and long-term goals. First, consider the concepts of vision, mission, purpose, and goal. Imagine that you are the CEO of a large corporation (choose one you are familiar with or make one up). Create a vision, mission, purpose, and goal for this corporation. Now, using that same logic, create your own personal vision, mission, purpose, and goals might be.

**Vision**: You should have a mental picture of what you would like to do in the future. Vision answers the question: Where do you want to go? Vision is the formation of an ideal. Considerations about dream careers and sources of happiness aid the formation of a vision. Some questions for stimulating an understanding of vision follow:
- What is your vision for family life?
- What is your vision for a dream job?
- What is your vision for your business?

**Mission**: Once you identify your career interests, you should consider what career paths will take you there. Have you mapped out the road you need to take to make your vision or dream a reality? A mission is a step-by-step procedure, and it varies based on your career interests. A mission answers the question: How will you get where you want to go?

- Do you have a personal mission statement?
- Do you know what it will take to achieve your dreams?
- Have you explored what career path will lead you toward your ideal job?

**Purpose**: Most actions worth taking must carry a purpose for the one undertaking it. It's the purpose that urges us to move forward with our dreams. Purpose answers the question: What are you about? It describes what makes you tick. Consider these questions:

- Do you feel you have a life purpose or calling?
- Why are you interested in getting a college degree?
- Why do you want to attain a particular job?

**Goal**: Since the purpose is the why, the goal is the what. Goals are the desired results of efforts and answer the question: What do you hope to accomplish? Consider these questions:

- What is an academic goal you hope to accomplish this semester?
- What is a personal goal you hope to accomplish this year?
- What is a professional goal you hope to accomplish in 10 years?

*Selecting a Major.* We encourage you to read "Choosing Your Major" by Mary Lou Taylor (https://www.albright.edu/wp-content/uploads/2019/03/How-to-Choose-Your-Major-Tip-Sheet.pdf).[14] What follows are a number of additional questions to consider, as well as ideas for additional activities to guide you in selecting a major.[15]

An Inside Look at Selecting a Major

Individual Questions

1. Describe how you have attempted to select a major field of study up to this point.
2. What should be the role of parents, friends, and people in your community in the selection of your major?
3. What are the best resources to use as a student in the selection of your field of study?
4. Describe how your major may enhance your career choices.
5. Should your selection of a major be primarily influenced by your potential future income? How important are other factors in your major selection? Please explain.
6. Describe how your interests, talents, and personality should affect your major selection.
7. Describe how electives and a minor are important considerations when selecting a major.

Class or Group Discussion

1. Consider which aspects of previous jobs or activities you have enjoyed thus far.
2. Would you like to continue these interests in a major?
3. Do you enjoy working with people or working alone? What majors or career opportunities should you avoid?
4. Do you know your strengths? How can you build on these?
5. What basic questions can you ask yourself that may help with your decision on a major?
6. How anxious are you to begin working? What are the advantages of a college (or graduate) degree?

Activities

1. Make an appointment for personality and career testing.
2. Speak to individuals who work in fields that are of interest to you.
3. Make a list of careers with which you are familiar.
4. Visit career placement centers and speak with your professors about career opportunities.
5. Read as much as possible about your areas of interest.

Outcomes

1. Discuss guidelines for decision-making about choosing a major.
2. Develop a personal strategy for choosing a major.
3. Name two resources for career guidance and the importance of each.
4. List various majors and their corresponding career possibilities.

Another useful activity to spur reflection on potential careers is to begin drafting your own personal statements. Personal statements are often needed to apply for scholarships, awards, and graduate school. While incoming first-year students may still have a few years before they need to submit a personal statement, it is never too early to begin constructing a draft. At minimum, this asks you to consider where you are headed. Moreover, it serves as an opportunity to consider how your personal biography and background can aid you in asserting your unique contributions.

Multiple issues can deter students from beginning to draft a personal statement: (1) Personal statements are terribly named; they are really *professional* statements with personal biographies interpreted professionally; (2) "Writer's block" can prevent students from combining all the information they have encountered into something that they enjoy writing, that adequately reflects their professional identity, and that makes others want to invest in them, their dreams, and their future trajectory; (3) Many students feel they do not have interesting stories. In our experience, students often think that if they haven't overcome severe hardships (physical, mental, socioeconomic, and so on) or haven't accomplished some extraordinary feat (founding a charity, and the like), then their stories are fundamentally uninteresting. The question "What are my unique contributions?" is a way to help you see that your story is unique and can be a compelling way to discuss your strengths. To lessen these potential barriers, this activity introduces you to *the experience* of beginning to think about and draft a personal statement, to form the foundation of a working document that you can revise as you journey through your undergraduate career.

## TIPS FOR DRAFTING A PERSONAL STATEMENT

1. Break down "writer's block" issues by separately drafting portions that can be synthesized into a personal statement later on.
2. A final draft should never be a first draft, and all quality writing results from multiple rounds of revisions. The goal is merely to craft a first draft, which can be refined and rewritten as your plans inevitably evolve.
3. Exchange your drafted personal statements with other students to gain peer-review feedback. This may be intimidating at first, but it is incredibly helpful to involve peers in this process.
4. Examples of reflection topics to be written on index cards throughout the semester include the following:
   a. What is my background? (forming initial connections exercise)
   b. Who have I been? (reflecting on what prior experiences mean for their professional selves)
   c. What is my [university] identity? (university traditions exercise)
   d. What is my [college or school] identity? (college/school resources and advising exercise)

e. What is my [major] identity? (major -specific study skills, groups, course plans)

f. Who am I now? (reflecting on current undergraduate identity, as evolving from youth)

g. What is my professional identity? (goal-setting and career development exercises)

h. What are my unique contributions? (diversity, family backgrounds, race/ethnicity, gender, sexuality, religion, nationality, and other cultural norms and experiences)

i. What is my generous identity? (civic engagement/ philanthropy/citizen exercise)

j. Who do I aspire to be? (aspirations, career trajectory, desired life, ways to give)

k. What are my limitations? (time management, study skills, financial aid, health)

l. What resources can support my strengths? (university resources, campus community, family, and friends)

m. What will I mobilize? (how students will draw upon resources to mobilize aspirations)

Finally, don't forget to talk with your parents about your evolving career plans. Nearly all students enter college with ambitions and preconceived notions of what they want to do. As they navigate college, however, these plans can and often should change. You need to keep parents informed of those changes.

## FURTHER READING ONLINE

Here are a few resources we have found helpful:

- Here's a handout regarding the Cornell system for taking notes: http://www.riverland.edu/riverland/assets/File/study-tips/ Cornell_System.pdf.

- A handout to explain the forgetting curve is here, by John Wittman of CSU Stanislaus, retrieved from https://www.csustan.edu/sites/default/files/groups/Writing%20Program/forgetting_curve.pdf.
- Some tips for improving study skills, for example, are here, on this Virginia Tech "Study Skills Checklist," retrieved from https://www.ucc.vt.edu/academic_support/study_skills_information/study_skills_checklist.html.
- Here are some resources for discussing memorization and remembering, "Improving Concentration / Memory," Virginia Tech, retrieved from http://ucc.vt.edu/academic_support/online_study_skills_workshops/improving_concentration_memory.html.
- You should also think about finding study environments that are conducive to learning: "Study Environment Analysis," Antelope Valley College, retrieved from https://www.avc.edu/sites/default/files/studentservices/lc/StudyEnvironmentAnalysis.pdf.

## NOTES

1. Ricchini, John, and Terry Arndt. 2004. *Voyage to Success: Your College Adventure Guide.* Alexandria, VA: Life After Graduation, LLC.
2. Armstrong, Elizabeth A., and Laura T. Hamilton. 2013. *Paying for the Party: How College Maintains Inequality.* Cambridge, MA: Harvard University Press.
3. Stein, Joel. 2013. "The Me, Me, Me Generation: Millennials Are Lazy, Entitled Narcissists Who Still Live with Their Parents." *Time.* Retrieved from http://time.com/247/millennials-the-me-me-me-generation/.
4. Newlon, Cara. 2013. "Millennials: The Giving Generation?" *USA Today.* Retrieved from https://www.usatoday.com/story/news/nation/2013/12/11/millennials-most-giving/3962781/.
5. Fischer, Claude. 2011. *Made in America: A Social History of American Culture and Character.* Chicago: University of Chicago Press.
6. We modified (significantly) a time-wasters and time-savers chart that we think originated with Butler, Gillian, and Tony Hope. 1996. *Managing Your Mind: The Mental Fitness Guide.* New York: Oxford University Press. Here is one version of a reproduction of it: "Time Management Activities," http://jstutz.weebly.com/uploads/4/3/8/2/4382964/timemngmtbrochure.pdf.

7. Nuss, Elizabeth M. 1984. "Academic Integrity: Comparing Faculty and Student Attitudes." *Improving College and University Teaching* 32: 140–144.

8. Schmitz, Paul. 2011. *Everyone Leads: Building Leadership from the Community Up.* San Francisco: Jossey-Bass.

9. Everyday Democracy. 2015. *Leadership Compass Activity.* Retrieved from https://www.everyday-democracy.org/resources/leadership-compass-activity.

10. Leadership Compass. 2007. Corporation for National and Community Service. Retrieved from https://www.nationalservice.gov/sites/default/files/resource/leadershipcompass.pdf.

11. Park, Chris. 2003. "In Other (People's) Words: Plagiarism by University Students—Literature and Lessons." *Assessment & Evaluation in Higher Education* 28(5): 471–488.

12. Values Discussion. n.d. Orange County Department of Education. Retrieved from https://ocde.us/PAL/Pages/PAL-Activities-Ice-Breakers---Team-Building.aspx.

13. Source unknown. Adapted from sources such as Dweck, Carol S., Gregory M. Walton, and Geoffrey L. Cohen. 2014. "Academic Tenacity: Mindsets and Skills That Promote Long-Term Learning." Bill & Melinda Gates Foundation. Retrieved from https://ed.stanford.edu/sites/default/files/manual/dweck-walton-cohen-2014.pdf.

14. Taylor, Mary Lou. n.d. "How To Choose Your Major." Albright Experiential Learning & Career Development Center. Retrieved from https://www.albright.edu/wp-content/uploads/2018/02/How-to-Choose-Your-Major-Tip-Sheet.pdf.

15. Source unknown.

1. ***Be involved.*** On the one hand, recognize that you still have
   an important role to play in your adult son or daughter's
   college education, especially as they navigate college toward
   their career path. Some of the students who we see struggle
   the most are those whose parents seem to have a completely
   hands-off approach to their student's college experience.
   Of course, life can get in the way, and sometimes there are
   health, financial, or family issues that prevent parents from
   focusing on their student's experience as much as they wish
   they could. In other cases, parents may feel that the need
   to let their child figure things out completely on their own
   because that's part of "growing up." To the extent possible,
   we recommend carving out some time on a regular basis
   to connect with your student. Discuss what college is like,
   and see how you can help. The decisions they make during college obviously do not determine their whole lives,
   but they do have a significant influence on how prepared
   students will be for the labor market, and for life more generally. Parents can help emerging adults get the most out of
   college.

2. ***Don't be too involved.*** On the other hand, college provides the
   opportunity (and need) to transition your relationship with
   your adult(ish) student toward the eventual adult-to-adult
   relationship you will have going forward. That requires you to
   let go of the reins a bit, and let students decide for themselves.
   You will continue to guide them, but not direct them as much.
   It also means being open to their ideas, as half-baked as they
   may be. Perhaps their ideas need major refinement, but they are
   still attempts to choose for themselves who they are to be. That
   process of choosing and refining is important itself!

3. ***Counsel, but don't intervene.*** Most faculty and university
   administrators frown upon parents contacting them directly
   or emailing them on behalf of their students. We understand
   parents' desires to continue to express their love for children in
   similar ways as when they were in grade school and high school
   (the latter of which may have been just a few months ago!).
   However, most professors are taken aback when parents reach out
   to them directly, and despite parents' good intentions, this could
   have a negative effect on their children's experiences in college. It
   is important to realize that parental involvement in college is not
   encouraged, nor viewed positively, as it was at earlier schooling
   levels. While a parent can mean well in jumping to their student's
   rescue, such an encounter can cause professors to view their
   child as dependent on parental intervention, rather than seeing
   the student as an independent emerging adult. Instead, we
   recommend talking with your emerging adult about what kinds
   of contact *she or he* should have with people on campus, and
   advising emerging adults to make these connections *solo*.

4. ***Listen and interpret (do not tell and command).*** If your student
   hits some difficult financial circumstances, or squanders the
   resources you provided, it can be hard not to take over. What your
   children need right now, though, is to figure their finances out
   for themselves. During the reorientation that students undergo
   during college, they may have questions, concerns, even outright

conflict with you regarding the kind of upbringing they had, and their hopes and fears about the kind of life they want to build. We recognize that parents have different ideas about their roles in their children's lives (see the parent socialization styles discussed in chapter 3).

Nevertheless, college is a middle-class system, and thus it works best when students engage their professors and take an active role in shaping their education trajectory. This is something that parents should not take over for their kids, even though college students do not have it all figured out just yet. We recommend that you talk with your kids about their finances and budget. Have those—sometimes challenging— money talks. When you do, listen more than you tell. When you do talk, think of yourself as an interpreter, a sense-maker. Help them understand their situation and their options rather than command them to make certain choices. Again, easier said than done, but at least make efforts to shift your relationship with your student in this direction.

5. *Support and advise (do not cajole and fix).* Students encounter a variety of setbacks during college. It is helpful when parents support them as they overcome these issues, finding ways to be resilient despite challenges. However, unlike when children were young and directly in their parents' control, parents should not step in to fix problems for their emerging adult students. Understanding how students are passing through a key developmental life stage—when they are building skills to launch adulthood—means taking a step back. Parents are helpful as advisors from afar. Instead of hovering over your students, encourage them to connect with the many sources of support they have on campus.

6. *Try not to be an additional source of frustration.* Though you may sometimes feel frustrated by the experiences your student has on campus, we encourage you to think of yourselves as a relief valve for your students. Be a source where they can dump

their frustrations. Then, rather than venting back to the students, we think it is best to find other adults, your friends or perhaps colleagues, whom you can share these frustrations with. When we compare students who are really struggling in college with those who are weathering the storms that college brings, we notice that college can be especially hard on students who do not seem to have anyone helping to alleviate their frustrations and confusions, and, in many cases, they struggle more when their own issues are compounded with those of their parents.

For example, a call home may involve a student saying something like this: "I cannot believe it! I got a notice from the registrar's office that I can't enroll in any classes because there is a hold on my account from that parking ticket I got last year. I know I paid that!!" It would be completely understandable to respond by returning the frustration, saying something like this: "That is terrible! I can't believe how they are treating you. It's like they don't even know that you are there. Give me their phone number, and I'll call them up to give them an earful." But we recommend instead trying an approach along these lines: "Yeah, some of college can be like that. So frustrating! But lots of big systems are that way. Not everyone knows each other over there. Unlike in high school when your teachers may have eaten lunch with each other and been able to talk directly to the librarian if your library fine was preventing you from going on a field trip, you can't assume the people at the university talk with each other. So, pick up the phone and call the parking office, or better yet—stop by on your way to work, and let them know what an issue this has caused. Try to be calm, and ask them what they can do to help you, and quickly, so that you do not miss out on the classes you want to take. Then call back the registrar's office." In short, help your child by encouraging them to work through their issues with campus life without compounding the frustrations they will face in any large bureaucracy like a university.

7. *Encourage your emerging adult to connect with university faculty.* One of the most significant experiences that students can have during college is to bond with a caring adult outside their family. There are practical reasons for this: your student will almost certainly need a recommendation letter from at least one faculty member (if not many) in order to apply for awards and scholarships, study abroad programs, jobs, or graduate school. Incoming college students often do not realize how important these recommendation letters will be for them later on, and by the time they realize (often in their last year on campus), it may be too late. The problem is not that they do not reach out at all to faculty, but that they may end up asking people to write letters about them with very little substantive knowledge of who they are.

   A recommendation letter that says the faculty member has known the student from their first year on campus all the way through the last four or five years is stronger than one that says they have known them for a semester or a year. Especially strong is a letter that shows the professor knows the student not just inside but outside of the classroom, evidencing ways the student has been involved in the faculty's research or assumed leadership roles in student organizations, and the like. It takes time to build the relationships that produce those kinds of letters, so your student needs to begin working on being in touch with faculty, and faculty they truly enjoy and admire, as soon as they can. These same faculty relationships are also invaluable for other practical reasons, such as navigating the selection of a major, finding social connection across campus, and finding resources for academic success. We are no substitute for you, but we are integral to your student's success.

8. *Recommend that your burgeoning professional gain research experience.* Related to the last tip, research experience encompasses the most valuable set of skills your student can gain in college. Study abroad, participating in student organizations,

working—all those experiences can be valuable and necessary too. But with the rising emphasis in the US economy on analytical skills, research of any kind is sure to boost your student's marketability. Though many students take classes that involve research, it is really the research experiences outside of the classroom that give students deeper exposure to the hands-on research skills they will need after college. Encourage your student to approach professors whom they work well with to see if they have opportunities for students to contribute to their research in some way. Many faculty have research labs and projects that involve students, but many students never realize, or learn too late, just how many research opportunities college campuses offer. *Your student may have to do some searching around to find these opportunities.* If you guide them toward finding research experience, and they come back saying their professor said there were no openings in their lab, then encourage them to find someone else, even looking outside their major. We have written countless recommendation letters for medical school and law school applicants based on research experiences we had with students on a social science project. Sure, it helps if students have letters from faculty in their majors, but it makes application packets even stronger if they can demonstrate versatility and interest in research outside of their major as well. Nearly every career involves some aspect of people work, and social science research prepares students for that.

9. *Let your students explore a variety of career options.* We know that some parents have been telling their friends and family for years that their kid was going to be a doctor, or a lawyer. But the statistics on this do not add up. The majority of students change majors during college. Perhaps your child is among the minority of students who will wind up in the career they had in mind when they entered. Great! But if not, and even if so, they should explore other options while they are in the protective atmosphere of college.

10. ***Be open and flexible.*** Again, easier said than done! It can be
hard to let go of the deeply ingrained habit of responsibility
for everything from what your children ate to when they slept.
Sending your child off to college brings major changes. People
often talk in our society about the "empty nest," and that is a
big social status change. But underemphasized is how your
relationship with your child is also transformed once they head
off to college, even if they are still living at home with you. With
these challenges in mind, we encourage you to be open to the
ideas your evolving college student brings to you. Being flexible
to honor their changing sense of self, and their modifying
understanding of their careers, is healthy for their growing
ownership of learning. It is also key for your continued closeness
with them. Conflict with parents during emerging adulthood is
common, but some young people enter adulthood with loving
relationships with their parents, while others cut off all or
almost all ties to parents. Losing parents in the struggle to gain
independence is one of the heaviest burdens with which we see
emerging adults grapple. Being open to what your adulting child
wants to tell you is the best way to ensure they will continue to tell
you about their lives, and stay connected as they change.

In this appendix, we review the main content of the book for academics. This includes faculty, instructors, administrators, and professional staff working in universities and having some degree of contact with college students. To help academics navigate the topics of this book, we provide scholarly focused chapter titles below that correspond to the more accessibly written chapter titles geared toward our primary audience of incoming college students. These academic titles will enable academics map the primary table of contents to the scholarly topics and keywords included within the content of each chapter.

## TABLE OF CONTENTS FOR ACADEMICS

Each chapter features the following four sections: (1) student stories;
(2) summaries of scientific research; (3) advice on accessing campus
resources to gain social support; and (4) activities to promote reflection
on the topics of the chapter. The final chapters of the book have two additional sections: (5) togetherness social interactions among students and in
groups; and (6) tips for navigating college now and with an eye to launching successful, satisfying, and long-term careers. Together, these can
be remembered with the mnemonic S-S-A-A-T-T (like the SAT college
entrance exam): stories, science, advice, activities, togetherness, and tips.

## STORIES: AUTOETHNOGRAPHIES

One aspect of the book that we know academics may be curious about
is how we collected the student stories. We did so by applying a method
for autoethnography described by Ellis, Adams, and Bocher (2010).[1]
Importantly, we did not use a random sample of college students. The
autoethnographies were collected within a sociology course, which raises
the issue of self-selection (which students elected to enroll in the course).
That means the findings of this study need to be understood alongside
other and more generalizable forms of data, such as those garnered from
nationally representative and randomly selected samples. Nevertheless,
we think that any self-selection issues in these case studies would be com-
parable to those embedded in many psychology experiments, in which
students from a broader campus elect to sign up. Moreover, that these

case studies come from a large, public university should mean that they are more generalizable than the stories of students from small liberal arts universities, especially those that are highly selective. Since many existing generalizations about young people are drawn from psychological experiments using students at small liberal arts universities, we expect our case studies to be at least be as indicative of broader patterns as many other contemporary studies are. Moreover, the course from which we draw our autoethnographies is used across the entire student body as one option to satisfy the required social science electives. As such, our sample includes students from across a range of interest in sociology and who represent a diverse array of social and economic backgrounds, as well as academic and career goals.

Additionally, it is important to acknowledge that the student-written autoethnographies were greatly influenced by the text used in the course: Susan J. Ferguson's *Mapping the Social Landscape: Readings in Sociology* (2013). Students were encouraged to use the materials from class to analyze their own lived experiences. To the extent that the students used this text in terms of writing their autoethnographies, this text also greatly influenced this work. Scholars interested in studying the qualitative aspects of student college experiences may be interested in advancing this approach without the students reading that text, to explore autoethnographies in the absence of a text, or specifically a sociology text, to inform students' interpretation. Alternatively, scholars interested in engaging students further with text-based analysis may wish to have students complete alternate assignments that focus on the applications of this text alone, in the absence of the autoethnography assignment that our students completed.

To provide some social context to the student case studies, there were a total of 49 autoethnographies collected, and from these we selected 36 for inclusion in the student stories. Of these, six are non-white students (16%). In terms of gender, there were 18 females and 18 males reported in the case studies. However, in 15 of these cases, we switched the genders in the descriptions (13 were switches from female to male, and 2 were from male to female). We changed the genders intentionally in order to contribute to constructions of gender that do not reify preconceived notions of which majors, emotions, experiences, and decision-making processes are most associated with each gender. We think it is important that students learn from both genders. Additionally, all student names were changed to protect confidentiality. Also important to note is that we sought and obtained an IRB protocol to conduct and publish this research, and we provided students with informed consent forms to include with their autoethnographies in this book. More generally, we recommend treating these autoethnographies as worthy learning tools, and we appreciate the raw and real-life stories that our students shared. That said, there are many other approaches available to collect qualitative and in-depth data.

## SCIENCE: LITERATURE REVIEWS

In conducting the literature review that informs this book, we employed three social science frameworks: sociological, psychological/counseling, and higher educational. In the sociological framework, we focused particularly on social inequality, especially the way personal hardships and privileges are social issues. For this reason, this book could be adopted in many introductory sociology courses; it shows students how the sociological imagination relates to their own experiences in college. The psychological and counseling framework undergirds most of our approaches to student advising. The focus in integrating advice sections was to empathize with the existential predicaments and life course developmental tasks that confront most young people during college, and to give them some practical tips for responding well to these. That said, we did not focus as thoroughly on the laboratory experimental research in psychology. There are many existing resources that delve deeper into those topics, and this book is meant to add to, but not replace, those approaches. In the higher education framework, the focus was on describing the university as an ecosystem full of diverse social supports. In integrating these social science approaches, we drew most heavily from scholarship on emerging adulthood, as well as studies of social inequalities and higher education.

## ADVICE: QUALITATIVE INTERVIEWS

To collect the advice for students provided throughout this book, we conducted qualitative interviews with advising staff who are part of our co-authorship team, as well as with the expert on social inequalities on our team. We trained a graduate student in qualitative research in order to conduct these interviews and developed a semi-structured interview guide. The graduate student audio-recorded the interviews and later transcribed them. The transcripts of these interviews became the original draft of the advice sections, which were then extensively revised by the first and second co-authors to integrate the ideas across interviewees. These interviews used the following questions: (1) "[Read case study.] What do you think is understandable, normal, or endearing about [Name]'s story?" (2) "If [Name] approached you for advice, what would you say?" (3) "What are the 2 most important takeaways for [Name] to know about how to navigate college?" In conducting and analyzing these interviews, our graduate research assistant learned a great deal about navigating college and ultimately used this project to inform her master's thesis data. Nevertheless, producing the advice sections in this way may have integrated more repetition across student responses than would normally be found in real-world advisor sections. Recording the contents of actual advising sections would be a potential improvement for future projects of this kind.

## ACTIVITIES: CLASS, GROUPS, AND INDIVIDUALS

Included later in an online supplementary appendix are numerous classroom activities that correspond to each chapter of the book. We envision this book being adopted in a one-credit, eight-week, first-year seminar, in which one chapter can be assigned each week. Alternatively, in a 15- or 16-week semester, one chapter could be read across two weeks, perhaps supplemented with additional readings. This book could also accompany a textbook in an introductory sociology course, as a way to aid students in applying the sociological imagination to their personal experiences, and the experiences of other students, in college. Most of our activities have these two kinds of courses in mind. Additionally, we believe this book could be employed within student advising and other service activities, or orientation activities; the activities would only have to be altered from a classroom setting to small groups. Faculty and staff who have the opportunity to meet with students individually—for example, in office hours—may also advise students to complete various activities on their own, as they can provide personal reflections.

## TOGETHERNESS: SOCIAL INTERACTIONS

The togetherness sections take a novel, experimental approach. The youngest member of our co-authorship team suggested the idea, thinking that the "reality TV" style of interaction would be appealing to younger generations of entering college students. The sociologists on our team reveled in the opportunity to show some of the social interactions that are crucial to college experiences, rather than merely discussing them in the abstract. Needless to say, we cannot begin to cover the range of social interactions possible among the students who became our case studies. Plus, the interactions described here may skew more positively than real student interactions, and it would be interesting for future scholarship to creatively integrate some of the more negative and de-energizing aspects of peer-to-peer interactions as well. To address this limitation, we encourage instructors to ask students what other interactions they imagine.

## TIPS: INTERPRETATIONS

We think of the tips sections of each chapter as akin to the discussion section of articles: they are interpretations based on research, not all of which have been directly tested. Our primary goal in the tips section is to bring scholarship on college-related social experiences out of the jargon-filled world of journal articles, which are often over the heads of most college students. In the interest of accessibility, the academic emphasis on precision was necessarily lessened. We recognize that campus contexts are diverse, and the advice we offer presumes the administrative structure of our own campus, which is similar to many large public universities; most notably, our university moved several years ago to a system of professional advisors who are distinct from faculty mentors. Other university contexts may not have this division, in which case the tips and advice will need to be reinterpreted relative to other institutional structures. Nevertheless, the overarching approach of helping students figure out who is best to approach for what kind of assistance can apply broadly, as can the general urge for students to take ownership of their learning process. Yet, we still emphasize the need for academics to engage with students in ways that are authentically tailored to the specific circumstances of the student's experiences.

## ACTIVITIES: WHAT WE (CAN) TEACH

Despite the challenges and stresses they can present, classrooms can be places of exponential learning, and social science classes in particular expose students to ideas that enable them to reflect on themselves. Self-reflection is an essential tool in finding one's way through college, and so for each chapter we offer activities that can promote such reflection. To find these classroom activities, visit the book's page on the Oxford University Press website.

These activities can also be implemented in other group settings, and are even amenable to individual reflection. We draw upon our own best practices (in classrooms, advising, and as former participants in student groups) to suggest ways to address the changes we describe, within the context of contemporary higher education and an up-to-date sense of the economic prospects that students have. Thus, in linking the previous sections, our aim with the activities for each chapter is to engage students in the problem-naming and problem-solving processes that are most crucial for success in college. These activities reflect the experiences, roles, and diversity of our author team and work well in raising student awareness of the issues this book addresses.

## NOTE

1. Ellis, Carolyn, Tony E. Adams, and Arthur P. Bochner. 2010. "Autoethnography: An Overview." *Forum: Qualitative Social Research* 12(1): 1–18. Retrieved from http://www.qualitative-research.net/index.php/fqs/article/view/1589.

## AUTHOR CONTRIBUTIONS

**Patricia S. Herzog** primarily authored each chapter, including synthesizing the social science scholarship, applying this scholarship toward the interpretation of the 51 student case studies, and authoring the science sections; drafting and submitting the IRB protocol to collect student autobiographies, de-identifying student data, analyzing student autoethnographies, and authoring selected text into case study narratives; supervising a research assistant in collecting in-depth interviews with the student development practitioners (listed in the next section), analyzing these interviews, and drafting interview data into the advice sections; authoring compiled activity ideas into the text of the website supplements and student appendix; authoring further reading selections; researching common hashtags for keyword linking, and authoring the hashtags and news handles preceding each student case study; and revising all other author contributions. Herzog also authored the prospectus and author documents; led the co-author team, responded to external reviews; and served as corresponding author with editorial and production teams.

**Casey T. Harris** contributed to the conceptualization and design of the book, including assisting in substantially revising all the chapters in ways that integrated substantively important content and clarifications; revising and organizing the 51 paired student case study narratives within each chapter to more thoroughly integrate the cases with the social science research sections; collaborating in the revision and organization of the appendices; and assisting with administration and management of the co-author team.

**Shauna A. Morimoto** assisted in the conceptualization and design of the project, including organizing and writing initial chapter topics and scenarios; helping develop and write the theoretical framework of the manuscript; contributing to writing, particularly in chapters 1–4 and chapter 6; assisting with data collection and analysis for the advice and tips sections of chapters; and providing revisions to the organization and content of the book.

## STUDENT DEVELOPMENT AND STUDENT SUPPORT PRACTITIONERS

**Shane W. Barker** contributed to the discussions that led to the creation of the book; discussed ways to integrate the perspectives of student development practitioners in advice interviews; collaborated in the design of and served as the primary author for the nine prototypical student case studies, as well as contributing to ideas for the togetherness sections of chapters 5–8. Additionally, Barker contributed to Appendix D and the activity supplements, as well as provided leadership to the student development practitioners involved in this project.

**Jill G. Wheeler** contributed to the discussions that led to the creation of the book; assisted in ascertaining the market for books aimed for first-year students, their faculty, and parents. Along with Barker and Boyd, Wheeler co-authored and refined the nine prototypical student case studies and contributed ideas for the togetherness sections of chapters 5-8. As a student development practitioner, Wheeler edited case studies and hashtags to appeal to student readers and contributed to identifying many of the classroom activities in the supplemental website.

**A. Justin Barnum** contributed to the creation of autoethnographies by instructing students in writing their autoethnographies; guiding students through multiple revisions; and mentoring students in identifying their personal experiences and interpreting those experiences by applying the learnings of key sociological scholarship. These autoethnographies were integrated into the book by other authors as the primary basis of 42 of the student case studies.

**Terrance L. Boyd** contributed to the development and revision of the nine prototypical student case studies and their interactive hashtags. As an academic and student affairs practitioner, Boyd collaborated with Barker and Wheeler to create generalizable and relatable exemplars of the myriad undergraduate experiences in the togetherness sections of chapters 5–8, specifically focusing on the topics of identity development, diversity, and involvement in those exchanges.

Tables and figures are indicated by *t* and *f* following the page number

*For the benefit of digital users, indexed terms that span two pages (e.g., 52–53) may, on occasion, appear on only one of those pages.*

community service, 181–82, 187
concerted cultivation, 71–72, 136
conformity, 98, 133–34, 151, 161
confusion, 13–14, 42, 80, 81, 114, 138, 142
#connection, 179, 187
connections
    making, 52–53, 204–5, 215
    through technology, 179, 184, 187–88
Connor, xv, 124, 129, 141–42, 210
conscientiousness, 131–32
control, sense of, 8–9, 89–90, 96–97, 100–1
Cooper, xv, 60–61, 67, 70, 76
coping skills, 50–51
*Cosmopolitan Canopies* (Anderson), 163–64
counseling framework, 14
counseling services, 26, 27, 50–51, 140
critical thinking skills, 43–44, 213–14
cultural background, 73, 155–56, 169, 207
cultural capital, 7–8, 22, 59*b*, 59–60,
    74, 167
cultural competence, 22, 23–24, 138–39,
    169, 171
cultural values. *See* values
culture of college, 20–21, 93, 97
culture shock, 151

dating. *See* romantic relationships
#deadbeatparents, 64, 82
debt, 6–7, 74, 76–77, 82–83
decision-making, 89–90, 137–38, 212–13
Derrick, xv, 39, 48–51, 144–45
Desiree, xv, 21–22, 66, 68–69, 181–82, 189
Desmond, Matthew, 162
developmental stages, 3
Devon, xv, 18, 20–21, 22, 24–25,
    75–76, 192–94
digital footprints, 45
direction
    being lost, 106, 142
    lack of, 44, 95, 198, 204–5
    responsibility for choosing, 89–90
    self-direction and success, 139–40
    sorting mechanisms and, 102
disconnection, 137–38, 164–65, 167
#distracted, 61–62, 78

distractions
    family issues, 61–62, 78–79
    relationship problems, 39
diversity, 151. *See also* race
    advice on, 166–69, 171–72
    aspects of, 3, 161
    of college *versus* hometown, 144,
        151–54, 163
    identity and, 164
#diversity, 151–52, 154–55, 166, 168
dorms, 220
dreams
    the American dream, 40, 199–200, 207
    career choices and, 94, 110–12
    living the dream of college, 61, 77–78
#drivingwithoutdirection, 198, 204
#dutycalls, 61–62, 78
Dyer, Gwynne, 20–21

Eduardo, xv, 151, 155, 161, 162, 169
Ehrenreich, Barbara, 70
Ellie, xv, 44, 198, 204–5
emerging adulthood, 1*b*, 6, 19–20, 37*b*,
    141–42, 218–19
*Emerging Adulthood* (Arnett), 19–20
Emma, xv, 67–68, 90, 93–94, 109–10
emotional labor, 101
emotional stability, 48
#emotionalabuse, 128–29, 140
empathy, 153–54, 169, 207–8
entitlement, 72, 132–33
equality, 6–7
Erin, xv, 151, 159–60, 165, 170–71, 174
ethnicity, 6–7, 162, 164. *See also* diversity
everyday living, 18
exams, 44
exclusion, 67–68, 91, 93–94, 109–10, 150*b*
existential crises, 42
expectations of others, 84–85, 140–41
experiential learning, 213
exploration, 110, 111–12, 166, 211–12
externalizing behaviors, 132–33
extra-cognitive factors, 8, 96–97
extracurricular activities, 26, 67, 70, 73,
    139, 167, 205